PIMLICO

421

JOHN PREBBLE'S SCOTLAND

John Prebble was born in Middlesex in 1915 but spent his boyhood in Saskatchewan, Canada. He began his writing career as a journalist in 1934 and is now a novelist, historian, film-writer, and the author of many highly-praised plays and dramatised documentaries for television and radio. During the war he served for six years in the ranks with the Royal Artillery, from which experience he wrote his successful war novel, *The Edge of Darkness*. His other books include *Age Without Pity, The Mather Story, The High Girders*, an account of the Tay Bridge Disaster, *The Buffalo Soldiers*, which won an award in the United States for the best historical novel of the American West, and *Culloden*, a subject he became interested in when he was a boy in a predominantly Scottish township in Canada. *Culloden* was subsequently made into a successful television film. Its natural successor, *The Highland Clearances*, was published in 1963, and *Glencoe* in the spring of 1966. *The Darien Disaster* was published in 1968, *The Lion in the North* in 1971, *Mutiny: Highland Regiments in Revolt* in 1975, and *The King's Jaunt* in 1988.

JOHN PREBBLE'S
SCOTLAND

PIMLICO

Published by Pimlico 2000

2 4 6 8 10 9 7 5 3 1

Copyright © John Prebble 1984

First published in Great Britain by
Martin Secker & Warburg Ltd 1984
Pimlico edition 2000

Pimlico
Random House, 20 Vauxhall Bridge Road,
London SW1V 2SA

Random House Australia (Pty) Limited
20 Alfred Street, Milsons Point, Sydney,
New South Wales 2061, Australia

Random House New Zealand Limited
18 Poland Road, Glenfield,
Auckland 10, New Zealand

Random House (Pty) Limited
Endulini, 5A Jubilee Road, Parktown 2193, South Africa

The Random House Group Limited Reg. No. 954009
www.randomhouse.co.uk

A CIP catalogue record for this book
is available from the British Library

ISBN 0-7126-6684-2

Papers used by Random House are natural,
recyclable products made from wood grown in sustainable forests.
The manufacturing processes conform to the environmental
regulations of the country of origin

Printed and bound in Great Britain by
Biddles Ltd, Guildford

For
CASPAR CLARK
my grandson

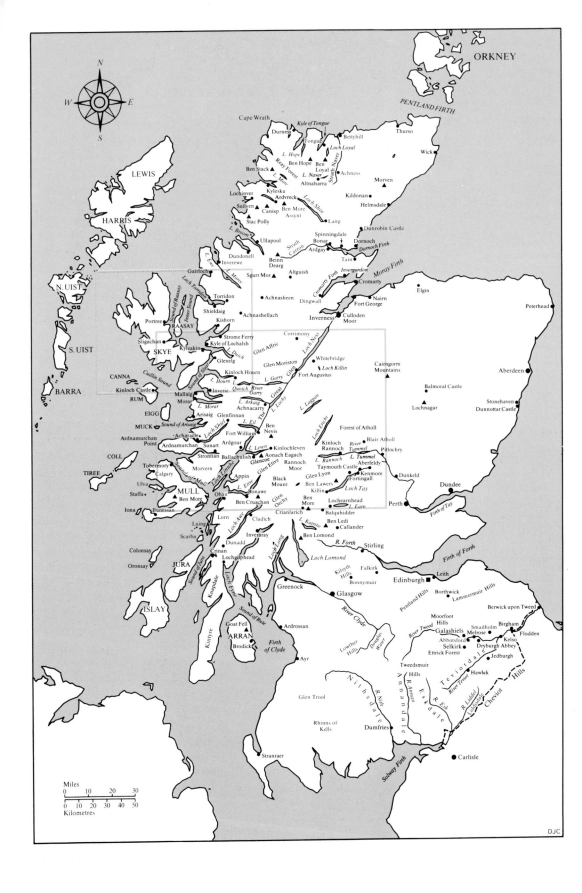

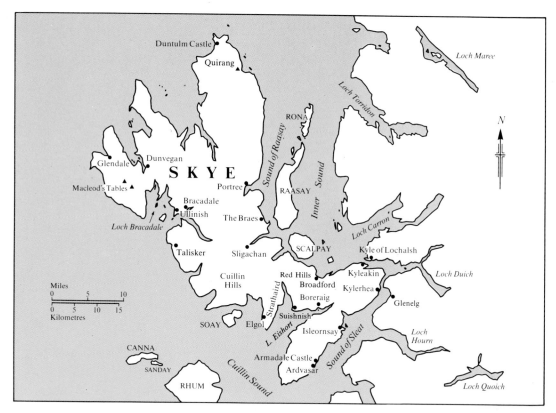

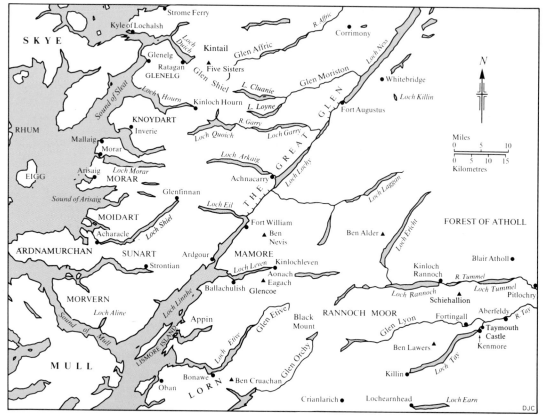

Scotland first touched my mind and my imagination more than fifty years ago, when I was an English boy in the short-grass country of Saskatchewan. That bleak and open land was blue-white in winter, briefly green when the warmth of a chinook melted the snows, then yellow sere in the summer days I best remember. A sunburnt plain where hidden scrub-trees crouched close to the slough-holes, and the highest points against a cloudless sky were the tall grain elevators by the railroad track. On endless afternoons, when school was out, I sat in the black shelter of their shadows, chewing the sweet kernels that dribbled from their timbers, and until the lonely whistle of the westbound freight recalled me to the prairie I dreamed of blue mountains, dark lochs, and gentle rain. Thus had my red-haired schoolteacher, Miss Campbell, so often described her homeland, but like others in the settlement she had never seen it. The picture was a sentimental memory, passed from generation to generation, and time had long since removed the bitter pain of remembrance once felt by those exiled Highlanders whom the coffin ships had brought from Thurso, Fort William, Greenock and Loch Boisdale.

As I think of it now, the township where I lived was predominantly Scots. At the beginning of this century a man called Sutherland gave his name to what was then a few clapboard shacks, a mail office, and a Canadian Pacific engine-house. He had come west from Winnipeg, my uncle once told me, and only later did I realise that his great-grandparents must have been among the first immigrants from the county of Sutherland, ninety-six young men and women whom the policy of Improvement had evicted from the parish of Kildonan and replaced with sheep. They settled in Manitoba in 1813, by the shore of Lake Winnipeg and along the banks of the Red River. They endured a Canadian winter for which even Highland snows had not prepared them, and in the spring they wrote despairingly to their parents, advising the old people to abandon all thought of joining them. They called their new home Kildonan. The land they broke with the plough and defended with muskets had been taken from the Assiniboin Indians, and if the evicted Highlanders were aware of that irony they left no record of their feelings. Some of their descendants, I believe, joined Mr Sutherland in Saskatchewan. By then the Gaelic tongue and culture which had solaced the homesickness of the first immigrants were forgotten. Although he was contemptuous of all emigrants, this would perhaps have pleased James Loch whose Policy of Improvement dispersed the people of Sutherland. He believed that the Highland sub-tenants of his noble English employer were ignorant and credulous, and that the changes he imposed upon their lives would deliver them from superstition and sloth. "In a few years," he wrote, "the children of all those who are removed from the hills will lose all recollection of the habits and customs of their fathers."

The third- and fourth-generation Scots-Canadians who lived in the township of my boyhood had no apparent recollection of their Gaelic roots, but their emotional attachment to Scotland was strong and persuasive. It coloured my day-dreaming and made that country more of a reality than an England I could scarcely remember. The feeling was encouraged by the common sight of tartan, flame-red or blue-green against the snow in winter. My father and my uncle, the men who worked with them on the railroad, farmers who came into town on the high seats of box-wagon sleighs, all wore tartan mackinaws. I knew, as did my friends, that this short winter coat had been so named for a Scot who had created it, a beaver-trapper who once lived with the Cree and the Assiniboin. We did not believe Miss Campbell when she told us that mackinaw was a corruption of Michilmackinac, an island on Lake Huron where British soldiers in the War of 1812 had tailored their blankets into coats. I know now that this is true, except that the blankets had not belonged to the soldiers but were intended for distribution among their Indian allies.

Mr Sutherland was still alive when I was a boy. He was the mayor, the fire-chief and the police-constable. He also delivered water to the houses of the township. In winter this came as ice, sawn in blocks from the Saskatchewan River three miles away. I cannot clearly recall his face but I remember the white icicles on his beard and eyebrows, on the mane and fetlocks of his horse. I think of him sometimes when I drive past the lonely kirk in Strath Kildonan where the young people of the parish, having marched in protest and retreated before the threat of artillery and bayonets, at last accepted their eviction and their bitter exile. The great herds of Cheviot sheep which then replaced them are now gone and the red deer moves higher into the hills above Borrobol and Suisgill, away from the black furrows of afforestation. Mountain sedge and yellow trefoil mask the scattered stones of vanished townships, but the grass still grows greenest where the people once tended their small potato-patches.

The thought of Scotland during my early boyhood was undoubtedly an escape for my longing spirit. I was not always happy in Canada. I still had not seen it when I first wrote about it. I was now a schoolboy in England and my romantic Jacobitism was a refuge, too, from the arid streets of West London. The short story

I wrote, for which I received the astonishing fee of nine guineas, more than thrice the weekly income of my parents, was partly inspired by the legend of Roderick Mackenzie. A fugitive from Culloden, he was skulking in Glen Moriston when one of Cumberland's patrols came upon him and concluded from his appearance that he was the Young Pretender. He encouraged their error and by defending himself forced them to shoot him. A cairn marks the spot where he died, recovered from natural decay and the sport of unnatural vandals, and when I pass it I not only acknowledge his self-sacrifice but also my own personal debt.

When I did visit Scotland for the first time I was twenty-one and determined to see as much of the Highlands as I could, on foot with a Swedish pack, a Grenfell jacket and a kapok sleeping-bag. I sailed from Wapping to Leith on a ship of the old Dundee, Perth and Edinburgh Line, thirty-six shillings for as many hours afloat and the support of an upper-deck stanchion for my back at night. The little vessel was the *Royal Scot* and I had known her black hull and red-barred funnel since my childhood, from a coloured print my father kept in a tin with his medals, his Naval record and discharge papers. As a Petty Officer Guns he had served aboard her in the Great War when her innocent appearance had tempted U-boats to the surface and their destruction by his marksmanship. Her crew were Hebrideans for the most part, and my father remembered their alarming habit of prising fuses from the shells with the points of their fishing-knives. But he always spoke of them with admiration and gratitude. When he was washed overboard to port in a North Sea gale one of them plucked him to safety from the return wave that was carrying him to starboard. A

Leith Harbour as it was
in the year of George
IV's visit. He was the
first British monarch seen
in Scotland since 1651,
and in honour of the
event he came ashore
here in an admiral's
uniform, with a sprig of
thistle and heather
in his hat.

generation and more later, northward to the Arctic Circle, my son
was saved in the same manner, and by a Hebridean.

At Leith harbour I walked to the tram-head along the crescent
curve of The Shore, not knowing then that here on its cobbles in
1779 Highland soldiers had resisted with musket and bayonet
rather than submit to a breach of the promises made to them on
enlistment. The bodies of those who died were taken to Lady
Yester's Church where young Walter Scott and his friends from
the High School next door paid the sexton a penny apiece to see
"the highlanders lying stiff and stark." Their bloody corpses,
wrapped in plaids, gave him nightmares for a week, and remembering them fifty years later his sympathies were still with his
kinsmen in the Border regiment which suppressed the revolt.

The novels of Scott and his distant cousin and imitator, James
Grant, had locked my mind in the past and unprepared it for the
Edinburgh I saw when I stepped from the Leith tram that August
morning, although the silhouette of Castle Rock, smoke-hazed and
glistening with fragmented sunlight, must have been as they had
often seen it. I had an hour or so before I left for the Highlands
and instead of using it to look at the hot and noisy city I spent most
of it reading on a bench in Waverley Station. I would like to think
that I was reading Scott, or *Kidnapped* which I carried with intent
in my pack, but it was a novel by Grant which I had found in a
second-hand shop on North Bridge. I had read it before, with an
uncritical hunger I had consumed all of his monumental output of
second-rate books. I cannot believe that this was entirely a waste
of time, for he opened doors through which I later passed to
make my own discoveries. He is now a forgotten writer, perhaps

The Laird of Abbotsford as his readers no doubt imagined him, "doing his day's darg" with no sign of strain at a tidy desk. The cat, however, is real enough. Its name was Hinse of Hinsfeldt.

charitably so, but he is also a link in the circling chain of coincidence that holds me to Scotland. He was the great-grandson of a Grant of Corrimony and an Ogilvy of Kempcairn. After Culloden a platoon of the 21st Foot came to burn Corrimony's house in Glen Urquhart but its commander, an Ogilvy it is said, saw the arms of his name quartered with those of Grant above the door and he turned away, leaving the house untouched. Seventeen years ago, by chance in Robbie's Bar at the Station Hotel in Inverness, I renewed an old friendship with Hamish Wallace whom I had not seen since a perverse decision by Lord Beaverbrook separated us in Fleet Street. We dined pleasantly that night in Corrimony House, which his family now owned and where that protective quartering is still set in stone above the door.

When I first went to the Highlands they were not the holiday-ground they have become, or the caravan speedway they sometimes seem to be. There were few cars on the narrow roads, but tall-funnelled steamers passed through the Caledonian Canal by Telford's twenty-eight locks, and black Hornby engines trailed smoke along cuttings and embankments now abandoned to the

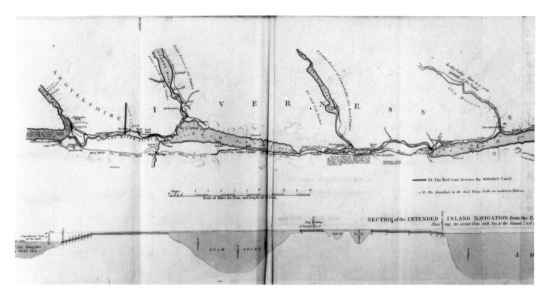

SECTION of the INTENDED INLAND NAVIGATION from the E.

Telford's plan for his greatest work, a "pleasure to every lover of national improvement". It has 28 locks, 22 miles of canal and 38 of natural waterway, joining the Atlantic to the North Sea. Begun in 1801, but not finally completed until 1847, it was arguably an economic failure.

eager growth of birch and rowan. From the station at Ballachulish I walked toward Glencoe. John Buchan's story of the Massacre had been published three years before and because I had read it and re-read it I was obliged to see the valley itself. I came to it through the indigo shadow of Meall Mor, by the water of Loch Leven where Prince Albert had studied the glen's dark gateway from the deck of the *Fairy* and concluded, so his wife recorded, that "it was fine, but not quite so much as he expected." It is hard to imagine what the man expected to see, but if it was a realisation of the preposterous Gothic engravings then popular, and not the simple honesty of a Daniell aquatint, his insensibility is explained. It was past sunset but still light when I came to Achnacone, where the glen is green with timber and grass before it turns towards the black escarpment of Aonach Eagach. I climbed to the south up the slope of Gleann-leac-na-muidhe and slept the night in the shallow ruin of the house where old MacIain spent his last summer before he was slaughtered by King William's command. There was no moon, I remember, but a sky scattered with stars. In the morning I awoke to a silent, bone-chilling mist, to such a Highland day as that which provoked Samuel Johnson to miserable complaint, "O, sir, a most dolorous country!"

But when I went down to Achnacone in search of breakfast columns of sunlight were already lifting the clouds above the nave of the valley, and the air was loud with the gossip of a hundred streams. I spent the day in the glen, walking to Rannoch and the sturdy isolation of the Kingshouse Inn where I took my breakfast at noon. The broad highway from the south had been built only recently but I followed the old track when I could, where black cattle from Ardnamurchan, Morvern and the Isles were once driven through the autumnal haze to market at the Falkirk Tryst. With John Brown on the box of her barouche, Queen Victoria had also travelled this stony way and felt a frisson of horror at the thought of how the MacDonalds had been betrayed and murdered.

"Let me hope," she said, "that William III knew nothing of it."
When she saw roadside heaps of stones that had once been homes
she thought they vividly illustrated "the bloody, fearful tale of
woe." Her emotions were admirable but her chronology was
inexact. The cottage-stones had been piled there when valley and
people were cleared for sheep, not long before her late husband
had viewed the glen from the *Fairy* and thought it less dramatic
than he had expected.

I slept a second night on MacIain's hearthstone, fitfully disturbed by a squall of rain and the melancholy cry of a night-bird.
In the morning, as best I could with *Kidnapped* and an Ordnance
map for guidance, I followed the flight taken by Alan Breck and
David Balfour after the murder of the Red Fox. No climber then
or since, I did not attempt to reach their high cave in a cleft of Sgur
na Ciche, the Pap of Glencoe which Stevenson called Corrynakiegh, but I walked with them above Loch Leven. I saw "thin,
pretty woods" of white birch as they did. I thought I heard the
bubbling call of a cushat-dove that fell so pleasantly on David's
ear, and with him I looked in wonder across the dark loch-water
to the thundrous mountains of Mamore. After a third night, how
passed I cannot remember, I went with the fugitives over the
Devil's Staircase and down to Glencoe again by Altnafeadh. Less
daunting than a map suggests, the path winds upward from
Kinlochleven along the track of a military road built more than
two centuries ago. From its high ground Stevenson's characters
saw only the small parties of dragoons in search of them and he
did not know, or rightly preferred to forget, that this was no place
to put his outlaws running. More than a thousand soldiers of the
road-gangs were deployed that year between Loch Leven and
Bridge of Orchy.

Another day and I went eastward by the military road below the
bare brown shoulder of Stob na Cruiache. To the south was
David's "low, broken, desert land", the wide emptiness of

Rannoch Moor, twenty square miles of black peat and sky-blue water, a bog that swallowed a primeval pine forest yet now supports a railway on floating mattresses of brushwood. That day I first saw a red stag, not far above me on the brae, motionless in the spiked grass and waiting for Mr Landseer to open his sketch-book. I have since seen or heard part of the great cull that takes place here and elsewhere, a necessary but numbing slaughter. I have seen a muddy Cortina speeding triumphantly southward on the A82 with the carcass of a ten-pointer on its bonnet, and before a hotel on Lochaweside I once watched a party of Scandinavians as they filled their estate-car with the freshly-mounted antlers of young stags. *Tri aois duine aois feidh*, says the Gaelic, thrice the age of man the age of a stag. It is not true, of course, and if it is then man has given the red deer no opportunity to prove it.

It was my intention after a night at a youth hostel by Rannoch Station to go northward to Loch Ericht, to Cluny's Cage below Ben Alder where Alan Breck and David at last took shelter with the Macpherson chief. I was dissuaded from this foolhardy attempt by time and exhaustion. And by something more, perhaps, a wish to be far gone from the brooding loneliness of Rannoch, the wide brown moor which diminishes even the granite hills that surround it.

I went to Glenfinnan on the Mallaig train. In my naive Jacobitism it was almost an act of pilgrimage to visit the marshy loch-shore where the Young Pretender raised his standard. At that age in that year I saw no unconscious irony in the monument that marks the spot, a stone Highlander on a tall pillar, looking at the empty hills with sightless eyes. A hundred yards from him, by a wooden pier on Loch Shiel, two men were sitting in the stern of a small boat, waiting to take passengers seventeen miles westward to Acharacle at the lochend. They accepted five shillings from me, their only fare, and I sat on a thwart facing the prow, my feet dry on a scattering of small branches, as the shoes of Johnson and Boswell were protected on the ferry from Mull to Oban. When the boatmen talked it was to each other. They spoke in Gaelic which I heard then for the first time, on dark water in a deep glen, deep as a sword-cut in the body of the mountains. Six miles from the pier and to the north was an opening, a gentle shelf rising between conical peaks, with a single house upon it like a white brooch on a green shawl. My map told me that it was Glen Alladale and I knew that the Pretender had slept here the night before his standard was raised. The thought of its solitude came to me often in the following years, and when I learned that the Laird of Glen Alladale had taken one hundred and fifty swordsmen to that useless Rebellion it inspired the last two sentences of *Culloden*.

Acharacle was a stronger Gaelic enclave in those days before the war than it is now, a cluster of small houses on the low ground between Moidart and Ardnamurchan, an Episcopalian community living in traditional amity with its Catholic neighbours. I saw old adults and children only, and was told that most of the young people had gone away to Glasgow for work. I was

welcomed to stay the night in a cottage, ate trout for breakfast, and can still remember the hurt in the cottager's face when I offered to pay. Now there are Bed-and-Breakfast signs in the windows, two hotels and room for caravans. To regret that is no intended slight upon those to whom such changes are a necessity.

I travelled southward to Loch Sunart on a cart, over low hills of birch and pine. There were butter-pat globe flowers by the roadside, water-lilies on tiny lochans, and where shelving rock broke through the thin earth there were ranks of that straight-stemmed, thornless and sweetly-named melancholy-thistle which is perhaps the true emblem of Scotland. As we came down the brae to Salen the sea-loch below was hidden by a dank mist that did not lift until I parted from the carter in Strontian. This was more than forty years ago and I did not know that here in the 18th century, not long after Culloden, Lowland miners discovered the metallic element which has become part of our enduring nightmare in the form of Strontium 90.

Perhaps I remember that distant August with too much hindsight. I had no reason then to ask why the mountains were empty, where the people had gone and why. In Edinburgh, waiting for the train home in the lingering light of a summer evening, I saw no absurdity in the tartan, velvet and calf-laced brogues that skipped over Princes Street on their way to a Highland Ball in the North British Hotel. Nor should I blame Scott entirely for falsely

The Jacobite monument at Glenfinnan. "At that age, in that year, I saw no unconscious irony in a stone Highlander looking at the empty hills with sightless eyes."

9

colouring my imagination. Two years before his death he became disenchanted with the chiefs and lairds whose company he had once enjoyed. Writing to Maria Edgeworth of the manner in which such men were now dispersing their people, he angrily declared "I would to God that gibbetting one of them would be a warning to the rest."

Although I did not visit Scotland again for fifteen years it continued to touch my imagination and my life. At an Army camp in North Wales some time in 1942, having secured the post of night orderly-corporal and the uninterrupted use of an office thereby, I at last had time to write *Where the Sea Breaks*. I set the story on a Hebridean island and believed it to be my own creation, but many years later when I saw the distant shape of Eigg from the deck of the Armadale ferry I immediately recognised it. The novel was published when I was in Europe, in a unit attached to the 15th Scottish Division. I remember the familiar star and saltire of Government tartan on khaki sleeves, Scots voices whispering in slit-trenches on the banks of the Maas, Highland and Lowland faces beneath the rims of steel helmets as we crossed the Rhine in the dawn of a bright March day. And there was a windmill by Venlo where we had briefly halted. The great beams that supported its shell-broken superstructure were caked with centuries of hardened flour. By the yellow glow of a Tilly lamp one night I chipped at the flour with my bayonet. On the wood beneath I found the carved names of soldiers who had fought on this ground three hundred years before with the Scots Brigade, men from the glens of Lord Reay's country where the wrinkled rock-face of Ben Hope looks northward to the Arctic. I cut my own name and the date beside theirs, moistened the flour with tea and pasted it over them all.

After the war a book on the fall of the Tay Bridge took me back to Scotland, and later still in 1959 when I went to Inverness I stood on the field of Culloden and decided to write of the men who are buried there, others who died on the gallows and prison hulks or were sent in bondage to the colonies, all those whose lives were brutally changed by the battle. I thought it would be the only book I would write on the Highlands and their people, but others came naturally from it. They have made this book inevitable and in that context I hope its title will not be thought immodest. It is selective and neglects much, perhaps, but it says something of what I think and feel, what I have learnt and seen of those parts of Scotland to which my writing and my love of the country have taken me.

In July, 1831, Mr Gilbert's "new and Superior Patent Safety Coaches" began their daily run from the Blossoms Inn by Cheapside in London to the Star Hotel in Edinburgh. For the first time a light post-vehicle made this long journey without pausing for the night at Carlisle, and by using more than a hundred horses, six drivers in relay and only one change of coach, it reached its destination in the astonishing time of forty-seven hours. Gilbert and his partners called it *Peveril of the Peak* in honour of the great novelist whose eccentric house at Abbotsford, gabled and turreted below the Eildon Hills, could be clearly seen from the four-in-hand as it turned northward by the Tweed into Galashiels. They promised to observe the same speed and punctuality as the Royal Mail, and because the fare they asked was one-third less than that charged by their competitors they were confident of loyal support from all the nobility and gentry, all merchants and travellers along the line of the North Road. Within a year faster coaches had cut the time by an hour, and by two a year later. This was the brave noontime of the stage-coach, its varnished panels, red-spoked wheels and braggart horn, but all would shortly come to twilight and final darkness. A sulphurous steam-kettle on wheels was already in motion and Mr Huskisson M.P. had inaugurated its arrival by becoming its first fatal victim.

The *Peveril* entered Scotland by Eskdale, Teviotdale and the Gala Water, by roads I take when the disciplines of my work do not oblige me to journey as did those early travellers who put their carriages on flat-cars behind the new locomotive engines. However expedient this may be, it does not compensate my loss, a lifting heart on a dew-bright morning when I drive northward from Langholm to Hawick. Here is the first gateway to my Scotland, to the distant Highlands, and once I have passed through it I know that I can be in Kintail by dusk, or on the summit of Struie, looking sadly across the water to the white house at Spinningdale.

There are three ranges of high ground between England and the carse-land of the Forth and Clyde. Once they were mountains,

Scott's home at Abbotsford was originally a modest farmhouse, Cartley Hole. He changed its name and rebuilt it into this Gothic wonder, filling it with antiquities. Time has since mellowed its pretentious grandeur.

some taller than any peak in Lochaber or Glen Avon until the timeless grinding of unimaginable pressures smoothed them into rolling hills. Fittingly for the part they have played in man's brief history they are ranked in battle order, three lines facing the sun from the north-east to the south-west. In the van and straddling the contentious Border are the Cheviots, whence came the sheep that emptied Highland glens and the district checks worn by the men who inherited them. Behind the Cheviots and beyond the Marches are the Lammermuir, Moorfoot and Lowther Hills. They climb in height southwestward to Cairnsmore of Carsphairn and to the blue spine of the Rhinns of Kells, to hill-fort and chapel overlooking the lovely tableland of Glen Trool where Bruce once hid from Edward's anger and our bureaucracy has thought of hiding its radioactive waste. Guarding Edinburgh and the Lowland plain, the Pentland Hills are the reserve of these formidable battle-lines. In the never silent winds that move across the Pentlands, from Cairn Muir to Scald Law and Rullion Green, it has sometimes pleased me to hear the God-obsessed voices of the Covenanters who marched here from Galloway, led by an old soldier with the felicitous name of Wallace. Sword in hand, they asked the King for a return to Presbyterian church and government, but were hanged instead, or sent to his colony on Barbados.

At one time, it is said, the bare hills of the Border counties were blanketed with trees, the valleys water-green with marsh and lake. Until the fierce coming of Saxon, Scot and Norseman they were inhabited by Brythonic Celts, the abandoned people of a Roman protectorate that stretched from the slopes of the Cheviots to the

Firth of Forth and the frontier of mountainous Pictland. They lived in palisaded manors and stone forts on high ground, in stilted villages on the lakes. Under beloved chieftains and kings, one of whom may have been Arthur, they rode to war in powerful divisions of cavalry, behind banners of many colours. They grew a little wheat, pastured stock, flew hawks, bred dogs for the chase, and worked simply in gold and silver. They passed at last into the darkness that obscures much of Scotland's early history, and little is left of them but the elegiac verse of the *Gododdin*, recording their loving cradle-songs and wasting conflicts. In the east they were overwhelmed by Northumbrian invaders, but the wild cattle of their hills survived them into the thirteenth century when abbey chroniclers marvelled at the wondrous beauty of the animals, their white hides, black muzzles, and flowing manes.

There is little ethnic justification for the erratic course of the Border, and when the kingdoms were united in 1603 its precise boundaries had still to be agreed. Its hatching on a modern map, along hill-ridge and valley floor, illustrates that indecision and old passions long-spent, greed, betrayal, and venal loyalties. It follows no natural division except for twenty miles or so where the Tweed flows sinuously seaward from Birgham. Before the river's mouth is reached it turns abruptly to the north, as if deflected still by English arrows from Halidon Hill, and the once fiercely disputed town of Berwick has not been Scots for five hundred years, to the satisfaction, no doubt, of the Great Plantagenet's spirit. There is nothing in the village of Birgham to-day to persuade a traveller's mind that it has been the pivot upon which history has turned. By

The Eildon Hills above the Tweed by Melrose were originally one, it is said, until the Devil cut them into three. He was challenged to do this by Michael Scott, a 13th-century wizard according to legend, but in fact a scholar of remarkable intellect.

a wooden bridge that gave it its English name a Saxon army was once destroyed. All Northumbrian ground between the Tweed and the Forth then became part of Scotland, and English speech and English customs began their dilution of that Celtic kingdom. In the twelfth century Birgham had become an agreeable trysting-place where delegates from each country met to resolve their present quarrels, or lay the foundation for others in the future. Here in the summer of 1290 it was agreed that the girl Queen of Scotland should marry the heir to England's throne, and had she done so their child would have ruled all Britain from Caithness to the Channel coast, and little of Scotland's history would have been the same. But Margaret died of sea-sickness on her betrothal voyage from Norway, in a ship laden with gifts from the English king – gingerbread, sugar-loaves, figs and raisins. From this sad accident came the harsh dispute over her successor, ambition, intrigue and sacrilegious murder, the bloody struggle of Scotland's War of Independence and the unquenched fire of its nationhood.

Southward from Birgham the frontier climbs to the brooding shoulder of The Cheviot, and onward then by wooded valleys, stark hill-tops and stone-white streams to its end on the Solway Firth. The empty uplands from Bowmont Water to Kershope Burn were once the contested ground of mindless blood-feuds, rape, robbery and revenge. Scots and English formed alliances against their own compatriots, then turned upon each other in disputes of complex duplicity. They defied the March Wardens from black peel towers that are now husks of stone choked with ivy, or fled with their families and stock into the safety of desolate bogs. The great, hewing battles between the two countries were not fought here, nor could be, but on the flat merse-land near the coast. Border spearmen who took part in these wars often did so from self-interest. In the darkening sunset at Flodden, when the best of Scotland was dying, some of them reined back and watched the slaughter from Branxton Hill. "He does well that does for himself," said their leader. "We have fought our vanguard, let others do as well." Centuries later, and in a whimsical moment, his descendant said that but for this instinct for self-preservation he would not have been born, and become Prime Minister of Great Britain.

The sinewy names of their valleys reflect the nervous spirit of the old Border reivers. *Eskdale and Annandale ... Liddisdale and Teviotdale ... Lauderdale and Tweeddale ...* The trotting music of the syllables, with grace-notes from bridle-chain and scabbard steel, was heard in the panelled study at Abbotsford where the verse it inspired cast the Blue Bonnets in a role that might have astonished some of them. It was in Scott's day that the Borderers – by then industriously concerned with wool, water and weaving – began to boast that no part of Scotland was more Scots than their hills, and the claim is perhaps proved by the disproportion of its suffering they endured. For more than a thousand years the first assault by invading torch and sword fell upon them. The thought of this is awesome, and there are times on the climbing road above Jed

Smailholm Tower near Kelso. Square and dour on its rocky outcrop, this stronghold of the Pringle family was built in the 16th century, and is a fine survivor of the old Border keeps. Scott played in its shadow as a boy, and later put it into *Marmion*.

Water when the pink sandstone surface ahead of me seems to glow blood-red in the rain. It could indeed be said that the iron of national pride was roughly forged in the Borders, to be tempered later on Stirling plain by the peasants who fought with William Wallace and the bonnet lairds who rode with Bruce. Border lords were among those magnates who attached their seals to the Declaration of Arbroath six long years after Bannockburn, maintaining that if but a hundred Scots were left alive they would not be brought under English rule. It has been cogently argued that although this bond was written at Arbroath in Angus it was sealed far to the south in Newbattle Abbey, behind the Moorfoot Hills and a morning's hard ride from the Border seat of war. Despite its justification by fanciful legend and questionable fact, the Declaration is the most important document in Scottish history, and the most inflammatory. Few who quote its heady words know or remember that it was not a defiant challenge thrown into the

The old bridge over the Tweed at Kelso. The present bridge, built by John Rennie in 1800, was used as a model for his Waterloo Bridge in London. That is now gone, but two of its lamps are on the bridge at Kelso today.

teeth of the English. It was a desperate appeal from war-weary men, asking the Pope to persuade the King of England "to leave us poor Scots in peace, who live in this poor little Scotland, beyond which there is no dwelling-place at all." The distinction is perhaps academic, if not churlish. The petition affirmed a people's right to independence with a nobility beyond nation and race.

> It is in truth not for glory, nor riches, nor honours that we are fighting, but for freedom, for that alone, which no honest man gives up, but with life itself.

The Pope did little to help the Scots, and Edward of England sent a great army northward to the Tweed. For another four hundred years the Borders continued to be the killing-ground of freedom. When Scotland's Parliament then surrendered its independence it did so without one reference to the Declaration of Arbroath, and English regiments waited below the Cheviots, ready to march should the Scottish people rise against the Treaty of Union

A resolute and sturdy nationalism, distilled into burghal pride, distinguishes the Border towns. Selkirk and Galashiels, Melrose, Jedburgh, Hawick and Kelso ... holding a loose knot of roads behind the north-eastern flank of the Cheviots. They were created by a need for walled protection, and by a Church which graced them with tall abbeys of red sandstone, rebuilding and rebuilding them whenever they were destroyed by an avenging English torch. The wars fought in the name of God were excessively hard on his houses, and might not have been had the wealthy vanity of the Church not made them a temptation to ill-paid armies on both sides, their commanders and their kings. When Lord Hertford came to the Borders, on the Rough Wooing that was intended to enforce another union between the heirs of the kingdoms, he sent Henry VIII a joyous account of his progress. *Seven monasteries burned, four abbeys, five market-towns, two hundred and forty-three villages*

The now gentle valley of the Tweed looking north-westward over Melrose to Galashiels. This was the bloody road taken by invading armies for a thousand years.

... He was not only reporting the robust nature of his marriage-broking but also that the campaign might well pay for itself. This was the last great destructive invasion by the English, and a terrible climax for the Roman Church before the curtain fell upon it. The open walls and broken vaulting at Melrose, Jedburgh or Dryburgh are not the result of England's frenzy alone, they show the contempt of Scotland's zealous Reformers who first desecrated the remaining grandeur of the abbeys and then abandoned them to decay and humbler architectural uses. Many of their absent stones now lie beneath Victorian buildings in the towns, in the arches of bridges, or the floors of hillside farms.

From their beginning the Border towns were always a refuge, welcoming incomers if they brought profitable crafts and skills, and tolerating them if they did not, always providing their religion was not offensive. In time all became one, Scots, Flemings, Balts, Dutch and French. And lastly the Irish, those whom famine and eviction did not drive further to America. By Ettrick Water one day in early spring I stopped for the pleasure of an idle hour. Above me in the sea-blue sky a regatta of white clouds waited for a starting wind. The crumpled hills through which the road curled toward Selkirk were my first sight of the Ettrick Forest, which has been treeless since James V drove out its deer four hundred years ago and turned it to pasture for ten thousand sheep. On the far side of the Water a tight flock of their descendants was moving before a circling dog, like mercury on sloping glass. As I watched them, a man came from the brae of Singlie Hill and paused to talk. When we had done with the weather and the lamentable lack of responsible government, we exchanged names. His was Irish, and I asked if he knew that another with the same, a captain under Montrose, had once brought Irish soldiers here from Antrim. That when their battle was lost, on a riverbend outside Selkirk, three hundred of their women and children were slaughtered. And that the regiments of the Covenant, at last sickened by the butchery

Melrose Abbey was last destroyed by the English in 1544. The local Douglas family then used some of its stones to build themselves a house, mindful no doubt of their ancestor's attachment to Robert Bruce, whose heart is said to lie under the Abbey ruin.

their Church demanded, cried out against its ministers, "Have you not once gotten your fill of blood?" He listened to me silently, as the polite always do when I bore them with an uninvited lecture, and then said that he knew this of course, but it was all langsyne, and he was not himself a Catholic, not Irish but a Scot and a Borderer.

In the same corrective way I was once rebuked by a guide at Holyrood. I had been spending long hours in Register House and the National Library, making notes on the turbulent history of the Glencoe Men, including their part in the battle of Killiecrankie and the assault on Dunkeld. My visit to the modest grey palace below Arthur's Seat was a valediction to the past before I went home to England and the present. In dark trews of Government tartan, black tunic and white spatter-dashes, the guide came from the shadows to the stairway where I was looking at David Morier's painting of Culloden. Or at a copy of it, perhaps, for the owner of Inveraray Castle had recently told me that his was the original, and that the canvas in Holyroodhouse (once hanging above the Duke of Edinburgh's bed, he said) was only an imitation. The guide's lifted eyebrow indicated that the proper behaviour for visitors was to move smartly with a conducted party, from one unlocked room to another. I explained that I had stopped to look at the painting because it particularly interested me, and I thought it ironic that a work by Cumberland's military artist, celebrating his terrible victory, was displayed on the wall of a Stuart palace.

Walter Scott is buried under the yawning arches of Dryburgh Abbey, on a horse-shoe bow of the Tweed. With him are his wife, other members of his family, and his son-in-law and biographer John Lockhart.

He considered this shortly behind empty blue eyes and then said, "We're no a' Jacobites here, ye ken."

The reproof was not only just but heartfelt, as my taste for serendipity was pleased to discover while he marched me in pursuit of the last conducted party. He had been a time-serving soldier with the Cameronians, the only regiment on the Scottish Establishment raised by Scotland's Parliament, by the people and not the Crown. Within a year of their mustering, its Presbyterian zealots from Galloway and the Borders were fighting their first action, driving the Jacobite clans from the burning streets of Dunkeld.

Time and place knit such small strands of coincidence into my professional life, and did so once in Liddisdale. It is not a valley I enter with a quiet mind. Much of it is bleak, hard and unlovable, a narrow pleat in the western Cheviots. The road is always in shadow, or so it seems to me, and wet from sudden squalls of rain. Its emptiness appears temporary, and the ear listens for the sound of returning hooves. I can feel the daily misery of the medieval monks who served a small abbey below Lamblair Hill, or the railway navvies who laid the line by Saughtree Fell. The black fall of Liddel Water, running rapidly down to the Solway plain, bleeds from the side of Hartshorn Pike where reivers gathered before riding northward into the Middle March or southward into England. No valley in Scotland has so brutal a history, and the competition is strong. Its people were the most headstrong, self-willed and defiant of all Border families, with allegiance to nothing but their own interest. Invading English armies wisely bought their support, or at least their neutrality before advancing further, and if this precaution was overlooked they could be confident that Liddisdale men would not put Scotland's adversity before their own greed. In 1541 the Armstrongs and the Elliotts, Croziers and Nixons, rode out by Liddelbank to rob and kill the terrified Scots who were running from defeat on Solway Moss. When King Henry's victorious commander was told of this, and that men from Eskdale and Annandale had joined in the murderous sport, he said it was pleasing news for good Englishmen to hear. It also gives Scott's jingling rhyme a mocking ambiguity.

> Stand to your arms then, and march in good order;
> England shall many a day
> Tell of the bloody fray
> When the Blue Bonnets came over the Border.

Something of Liddisdale's lingering malevolence was in an overcast sky one afternoon as I drove through it from Hobkirk. To escape this, or perhaps to face its tangible manifestation, I turned northeastward by the road that goes over the brae of Arnton. There the sun at last broke through, first shimmering on the crest of Roan Fell and then flooding in a lemon glow toward the roofless keep of Hermitage. Although a medieval anchorite had a cell nearby, the castle is grotesquely named. It is hostile and sinister, with sloping walls of massive thickness, crow-step gables, high window-slits, and an arched gateway like a screaming mouth. In one form or another it was built to subdue Liddisdale if it could, and its captains were often as base and brutal as the men they were meant to control. A thousand of the King's men and two hundred horses were once quartered within it or on the marshy ground outside, but at the height of their power the Armstrongs could muster three thousand riders, in quilted jacks of leather and bonnets of steel. It has survived them all, lonely and indifferent. That afternoon white cattle grazed in its shallow moat, but it was still monstrous, its rain-wet stones glistening like scales in the unexpected sunlight.

James Hepburn, fourth Earl of Bothwell, once held the castle as Lieutenant of the Marches, and lay there wounded after a vainglorious attempt to take an Elliott reiver on his own. Mary the Queen, from whose brief and somewhat irrelevant intervention in Scottish affairs romance has made too much, rode thirty miles from Jedburgh to succour his wounds and comfort his bruised pride. I thought less of her at that moment than I did of Bothwell. He was a tragic and bloody man, but if remembered for nothing else he should be acknowledged as the only Scotsman of his rank and time who did not take a bribe from the English. He was a prisoner for the last eleven years of his life and long before they were over he was abandoned by those who had hoped to profit from his success or misfortune. My daughter had been in Denmark that summer and had seen his mummified body in the white church at Faarvelje, nine miles from Dragsholm Castle

If this is not, as some think, a likeness of James Hepburn, Earl of Bothwell, then it should be. It is the face of a bold, bloody and tragic man.

where he died in lonely madness, chained to a wall. As I sat by Hermitage Water in the westering light I thought of this, and her curiosity about him, and I idly devised a television play that might recall his final days. Unlike many of the ideas that walk briskly and briefly through my mind it was ultimately written and played.

In the quiet solitude of the Border hills it is sometimes difficult to believe their troubled history, until it stirs in sudden images. A buzzard circling over Ettrickdale, turning on its back at last to strike at mobbing crows with its talons. The white head of The Cheviot, grieving against a November sky. A copse of leaning birch trees, winter-bare in a Roxburgh valley, that for a moment become the slanting spears of the Kers of Cessford. The bark of an alarmed dog on Branxton Hill at dusk, and the rallying horn of a diesel above Liddisdale at night. And there are the ballads, their sadness and joy, humour, savagery and love. No other part of Britain is so rich in the voice and verse of the people. John Leyden, James Hogg, and others devilling for Scott's collection of these songs, rescued much that was slipping from memory, and the vanity which persuaded Hogg and Scott to improve lines they thought imperfect, to include stanzas of their own composition, was no doubt well-intentioned. Scott published them as *The Minstrelsy of the Scottish Border*. The word was oddly chosen, as if to inspire a picture of harpists in the firelight of a castle hall, in Camelot not Hermitage or Smailholm. It is soft and silken. It is not Scots, it is Middle English and Old French in origin. So too is ballad, of course, but that falls well upon the ear and is appropriate in meaning – a narrative song, a dancing song heard in the peat-smoke of a cottage or the wind of an open heath. It reflects the exacting life Scott willingly endured when gathering the

There has been a defence-work on Hermitage Water for seven hundred years. The first was a fortified house built by the English in the English style. The present ruin dates from the late 14th century, an empty, echoing shell for the lost memories and cruel histories of those who once owned it – Dacres, Comyns, Grahams, Douglases and Hepburns.

verses, travelling weary miles by hill and moorland tracks, eating rough food and sharing beer from a wooden bowl, sleeping on straw beside his horse, and once in the same room with a corpse.

The ballads were printed in 1803, in the middle of a global war that was twelve years yet from its final battle. Gentle readers may perhaps have welcomed their bucolic simplicity and small brutalities as a relief from the thought of depersonalised armies in enormous collision, of plague, famine and unending slaughter. A romantic need for them continued after the war was over, when the strange alchemy of new industries was working unsettling magic, and common Scots of the Border and the Lowlands had become a menacing work-host mouthing demands for republican rights. Europeans like Mendelssohn and his friend Klingemann came to Scotland with imaginations fired by the *Minstrelsy* and *Marmion*, and not even a brief and dismissive meeting with Sir Walter at the gates of Abbotsford could depress their enthusiasm. Forty years later in America, young Lochinvars of the Union and the Confederacy took Scott's ballads with them when they rode to war, and may not have read them again after their first battle.

Printed and published, the ballad is interred in a literary sarcophagus, for it is not thought worthy of preservation until it has all but expired. Its vital existence is when it is still part of an oral culture, the natural voice of an unsophisticated society speaking from generation to generation, each adding to it and broadening its narrative to embrace their own experience. The historic and heroic characters of the epic ballads are stubborn, cross-grained men, steadfast in opposition to unjust authority and ignobly destroyed by it. In death they become immortal, and in folk-lore they are mourned more passionately than the martyred saints. Their retold story, however inexact, heartens the despairing and encourages the hope that there may yet be a sword-stroke solution to all misfortune and oppression. When that glorious simplicity no longer sustains belief, the ballad has become a museum artefact.

There are, in truth, no *national* ballads. Their stories are universal, race and place are circumstantial. In a wet ditch in Normandy I once sat with two soldiers, an Irishman and a Cockney, and listened as they sang to each other, reciprocal ballads they had known since childhood and which they were certain would get them court-martialled if heard by an officer. Music, rhythm and narrative differed as each took his turn to sing, but theme and spirit were constant.

Many songs of the American West reflect the ballads of Eskdale and Liddisdale. Jesse James, nobly brave and treacherously slain, was "born one day in the county of Clay and came of a solitary race", and it is not impossible to think of him as Johnie Armstrang in black broadcloth and a white duster. Johnie Armstrang, John Armstrong, Black Jock of Gilnockie, was a sair thorn in the flesh of Scotland's king but he should be fairly seen in the perspective of his own time, when a political Border had little meaning to a man with kinsmen on both sides. His lawless reiving, and the increasing anger of the English who suffered the worst of it, at last made it

J. M. W. Turner (*facing page*) responds to a romantic interest in Scotland – Johnie Armstrang's Border keep, a dark gorge, and a raging torrent. But also a splendid bridge and a stage-coach that could now make the journey from London to Edinburgh in forty-seven hours.

necessary for James V to put an end to him. Black Jock's error
– and here truth confirms a recurring cliché in balladry – was to
trust the Crown and believe it would treat with him as an equal.
When the King came to Teviotdale with ten thousand men, Arm-

strong rode to meet him with fifty riders only. All were hanged from a copse of trees by Carlinrigg Chapel, below the black wall of Tanlaw Naze. "I am but a fool," said Armstrong to his royal executioner. "Had I known that you would have taken my life this day, I should have lived on the Borders in spite of King Harry and you both, for I know King Harry would down-weigh my best horse with gold to know that I were condemned to die this day." The ballad echoes the spirit of that valediction.

> John murder'd was at Carlinrigg,
>   And all his gallant companie;
> But Scotland's heart was never sae wae,
>   To see sae mony brave men die.
>
> Because they saved their country deir
>   Frae Englishmen! Nane were sa bauld,
> Whyle Johnie lived on the Border syde
>   Nane of them durst cum neir his hauld.

There is little admiration in the brief contemporary records of his life, but most of them were written by or for his enemies. What Black Jock and his like truly were is perhaps less important than a finer truth, that the folk-verse they inspired ennobled the spirits of ordinary men. Andrew Fletcher of Saltoun, a greater patriot than any Border rider, once spoke in admiration of a friend who said that if he could compose a nation's ballads he would not care who wrote its history. Two and a half centuries later, when asked why his Western films were not more faithful to fact, John Ford said that wherever legend is in conflict with history we should print the legend. My heart responds to this, but my mind still lags behind conviction.

More worthy men than the old reivers, but inheriting their sturdy self-reliance, have since come from the Borders and the South-west. Toward the end of the 18th century, when Scotland exploded in a starburst of talent and invention, the sons of hill-shepherds, craftsmen, labourers, farmers and little lairds from Berwick to Galloway enriched the arts and sciences of the world. Allan Ramsay, poet father of a great portraitist, was born in a lead-miner's cottage on a bleak moorland in Dumfries. Thomas Telford, son of an Eskdale shepherd, began work as a mason's apprentice carving headstones, but went on to build twelve hundred bridges and a thousand miles of roads. Alexander Murray, the linguist, learnt his letters from his shepherd father in Dunkitterick, writing with charred stems of heather. He taught himself Latin, Greek, Hebrew, French and German, published an enduring work on comparative philology, and died a professor of Oriental languages at Edinburgh. David Hume, philosopher and historian, one of the most powerful minds Scotland has produced and among the most influential in Europe, was the son of a bonnet laird in Ninewells. John Broadwood, humbly born in the shadow of the Lammermuirs, walked to London where he became a cabinet-maker and the inventor of "a new constructed pianoforte". A Roxburgh farm-worker called Cook also crossed the Border in search of

Allan Ramsay, by himself; a great portraitist, son of the poet Allan Ramsay, and the grandson of a Dumfries miner.

David Hume, one of the finest intellects of his time in Europe, was born the son of a Berwickshire laird, and brought more honour to his Border name than did its more noble possessors.

Rising close to the source of the Clyde, and 97 miles in length, the Tweed is said to get its name from a Celtic word for a boundary, and to most people north and south of its pleasant water it is The Border. For only twenty miles, however, do the two converge, and for its last two miles the river is in England.

The greatest artists of the day came to Edinburgh to record the King's Visit in 1822, including Turner, Raeburn and Wilkie. This was Turner's view of the Gathering of the Clans, and although he had come to Scotland, it was said, to "cast a cloud of glory" over the event, the King was unimpressed by the result.

David I built the first religious house at Jedburgh, more than eight centuries ago. Sacked and burnt many times by the English it was as often rebuilt. The Earl of Surrey turned his cannon on the Abbey in 1523, but had the grace to commend the people of the town for their spirited defence of it.

The enduring myth should be true – that the emigrants who left
their home here on the white shore of Mull gave its name to a new
settlement in western Canada. But Calgary in Alberta was named by
a redcoat policeman in 1876, a compliment to his relation by
marriage, the laird of Calgary on Mull.

(*Previous page*) The now gentle Braes of Balquidder were the home of the MacGregors, the most famous or infamous of whom, Rob Roy, is buried in the churchyard here with his wife Mary and two of his five sons, Coll and Robin Og. The latter was the youngest of the family and was hanged in 1754 for kidnapping and marriage by force.

The shore of Arisaig looking westward to the isles of Eigg and Rhum. In the 18th century this beautiful coast was said to be "a nursery and sanctuary of priests", a barbarous place where the people were better acquainted with Rome and Paris than Edinburgh and London. The Rebellion of 1745 began when the Young Pretender landed on Arisaig, and ended a year later with his departure from almost the same spot.

work, and the English now honour his son as their great navigator. Mungo Park left his birthplace above the lovely Yarrow Water to explore the course of a mightier river. At twenty-six he came home to practice surgery in Peebles, wrote a rattling narrative of his travels, and was then drawn back to the Niger and his death.

John Leyden, born in a shepherd's house in Teviotdale, was a rough-mannered, noisy but amiable man who became a poet, physician, minister, linguist and Orientalist before he died in Java at the age of thirty-six. James Hogg, whose wayward talents as a poet and novelist are still neglected, was an Ettrick shepherd, a red-haired, hard-drinking womaniser who taught himself to read at eighteen. Scott was a noble and generous patron of such men, although he sometimes wavered in their support. Thinking of them, and others of the same earthy origin, he said that suddenly "poets began to chirp in every corner like grasshoppers in a sunshine day." Standing upon the great monument of his own work, he towers above them all. Although he hung the walls of Abbotsford with the arms of noble families with whom he had traced a slender kinship, he was also proud of his grandfather who kept a small farm at Sandyknowe, by the square keep of Smailholm. He spent his boyhood there and filled his mind with wild dreams of his reiving ancestors who had "murdered, stolen, and robbed like other Border gentlemen."

James Cook, the son of a Roxburgh farm-labourer who crossed the Border in search of work, is now honoured as England's greatest navigator.

At Ferniehill in Roxburgh, and fittingly close to the old treaty-ground of Birgham, an obelisk marks the birthplace of James Thomson. A prolific but indifferent poet, he wrote the verses of that crashing exhortation to a still uneasy Union, *Rule Britannia!* Its implication that by heaven's command there were no longer Scots or English has been happily ignored, and a majority of the latter now realise that the word Briton can be used as a natural synonym for themselves.

From the Lammermuirs to Galloway the past has become a bloodless entertainment for visitors, scripted by guide-books and road-maps, and illustrated by post-cards in which the sun always shines. Where it is celebrated by the Borderers it is with proper concern for present enjoyment. Young men in tweeds and jodhpurs, Braw Lads and Callants, annually enact a ritual remembrance of the moss-troopers who rode from their hills to Flodden, to Halidon Hill and Ancrum Moor, or on a deep foray into England. In the Common Ridings and the Border Games there is a robust desire to share a physical experience with the past, to assert a rugged identity as Border Scots. And there is no irony, only historical paradox, when the followers of the Hawick Riding, and the town's Rugby team, shout a battle-cry that invokes the Saxon gods Thor and Woden.

Good roads now take drivers where they wish, and where they wish is where good roads may take them. There are no highways, nor should there be, where the shaggy squadrons of Border horse once passed, and grass has covered the tracks of the cattle they drove home from England. But the high ground of their hills, like the Highlands, is already under assault by man-made erosion, and their valley woodlands are being felled, or choked by a black blanket of alien pine. The boundaries of our society contract within the roads we build, and their littered lay-bys demonstrate our indifference to the survival of what lies beyond them.

The Borders are my first gateway to Scotland, and nowadays I pass through them too quickly. There are no watchmen in Eskdale or Teviotdale to greet me with the old peel cry of "Who comes!", but its echo is always in my mind as I move on to the Lowlands and the North.

EAST TO WEST, EDINBURGH AND GLASGOW
hold Scotland by the throat. Or by the
loins, perhaps, if its outline on a map is seen to resemble the
rearing lion of its standard. The latter image is more appropriate,
for almost two-thirds of the nation now live in these cities, their
widening suburbs and parasitic towns. Separated by forty-four
miles of increasing ugliness they are islands of rival cultures, or
so they maintain, and the land between them is a bridge upon
which each pays a toll in the worn coin of hostile humour or
mutual forbearance. Economic and industrial need, eviction, persecution, poverty and greed have brought the people here, century
by century, but it sometimes seems as if Providence cupped its
hand in a moment of frustration, gathered them up and dropped
them into this Lowland basin where they might do the greatest
harm to themselves and the least to others. And the same, good
Scots may justly argue, could be said of south-east England.

Of the two, Glasgow has the right to think of itself as a Celtic
city in origin and history. It remained part of a Brythonic kingdom
when the east had fallen to Northumbria. For much of its existence
it was a frontier town, facing the north in fear. As late as the 18th
century it locked its gates against foraying clansmen from Breadalbane and Balquhidder, but within one man's lifetime its meaner
streets had become ghettos for homeless people from the Highlands. When that mountebank chieftain Alasdair Ranaldson
MacDonell offered to muster some of these unfortunates into a
regiment of Glasgow Highlanders, Lord Provost Dunlop warned
the Secretary of War that it would be a calamity if any of them were
entrusted with a musket, for they were all vile Democrats. Today
the city's telephone directories and electoral rolls contain more
Gaelic names, Highland and Irish, than any other region in
Scotland, and there may still be civic officers who have the same
nightmares as Mr Dunlop.

With little justification of this nature, but with a keen eye for
seasonal profit, Edinburgh is the city which perpetuates a tartan
mythology wherein every Scottish heart is Highland. It has done
so since 1822 when the royal yacht brought George IV to Leith
Harbour, the first British monarch to visit the northern kingdom

Perhaps the main interest of this early 19th century view of Edinburgh from Princes Street is that it was taken "from an original drawing by the marchioness of Stafford". When it was made her husband's factors were busily clearing her estates in Sutherland.

for almost two centuries. Sir Walter Scott went aboard to welcome him with an ornate gift made by the "loyal ladies of Scotland", a diamond saltire on a field of blue velvet, with the words *Riogh Albhain gu brath* embroidered in pearls. This, His Majesty was quickly told, meant "Hail to the King of Scotland!" He did not go to Glasgow, where his people had recently risen in revolt against his Government, but any unhappy thoughts he may have had about that were smothered by the enthusiastic reception he was given in Edinburgh. Like the Young Pretender, whom he sentimentally admired, he held court at Holyroodhouse. His royal and corsetted body was draped in scarlet tartan by Sir Walter, and Highland lairds honoured it with a gathering of those kilted followers of their name whom they had not yet evicted from their glens.

Edinburgh is a proper setting for such theatrical manifestations. The English traveller Thomas Pennant rarely surrendered to emotion, but when he first saw the city from a distance he admitted that he was struck with wonder. "It possesses a boldness and grandeur of situation beyond any that I have seen ... a look of magnificence not to be found in any other part of Great Britain." That is still true, despite the city's self-inflicted wounds. The first sight of its gabled rock and louring castle, hazed in summer mists or winter sleet, can stop the heart and choke the throat. Pennant was writing of the old city, but it had already broken from its medieval chrysalis and was sunning its wings to the north, beyond the drained bed of a marshy loch which the Victorians would fill

with a railway line and a garden of geraniums. The classical splendour of the New Town is perhaps the finest achievement of domestic architecture in Britain, and the vision of what it would become moved one of its designers to add a poetic prophecy at the foot of his plans.

> August, around, what PUBLIC WORKS I see!
> Lo, stately streets! Lo, squares that court the breeze!

Its conception and creation were inspired – ambitious crescents, streets and squares climbing into the sun, grey stones and wrought iron in joyous harmony, and the sky mirrored in a million panes of black glass. At first it awed the people, and few were willing to move from the hugger-mugger of tenements on the rock until the city council offered a haberdasher exemption from burghal taxes if he would become one of its first residents. And then the great flitting began. The rich, the noble and the powerful competed for elegant houses in an astonishing new world, paying £5,000 for the best of them. Mindful of God's directing hand in this grand enterprise, the city at first proposed to honour its principal thoroughfares with the names of Scottish saints, but when George III was told that the finest prospect was to be called Saint Giles he spluttered in disapproval, *"What ... what? Never do! Never do ...!"* It was renamed Princes Street in honour of his quarrelling sons, but there is no historical justification for any lingering indignation the Scots may feel. The tutelary saint of Edinburgh was a Greek abbot who came no closer to the Forth

A view across Princes Street Gardens a hundred years ago, to be compared with Lady Stafford's drawing earlier in the century. The gables of the Old Town are now almost obscured by Victorian Baronial.

29

Edinburgh's New Town in 1830, viewed from Ramsay Gardens above the Mound then being constructed, with the recently completed Royal Scottish Academy in the middle distance. A view of Princes Street from the same spot today is less agreeable.

than Languedoc, and the High Kirk of his name on the Royal Mile was once a Northumbrian parish church. Moreover, when a Reformation mob threw his image into the Nor' Loch the city magistrates appropriated the holy relique of his arm and transferred its silver case, weighing five pounds three ounces, to the funds of the corporation.

With the building of the New Town much of Edinburgh became orderly and well-proportioned, and thus acceptable to the eye of an 18th-century English gentleman. And also to his nose, for the stench of the old city and the foul habits of its people had once been more objectionable than London at its worst. Acceptance by the English, and acceptance of English modes and manners, had been Edinburgh's growing concern since the Union of the Crowns. From the day James VI left them, without regret – to become a greater king whom the English stubbornly call James I of England – its douce citizens had looked southward for fashionable precept and example. Seventy years after the Union of Parliaments, Edinburgh was already "The English City" derided by Glasgow, and Samuel Johnson was pleased to record that its people had accepted the first requirement of this title, the need to make themselves understood when they spoke to an Englishman.

> The conversation of the Scots grows every day less unpleasing to the English; their peculiarities wear fast away; their dialect is likely to become in half a century provincial and rustick, even to themselves. The great, the learned, the ambitious, and the vain, all cultivate the English phrase, and the English pronunciation, and in splendid companies Scotch is not much heard, except now and then from an old lady.

It is reassuring sometimes to discover that rustick dialect still in use, and not only in the modern verse which bravely employs

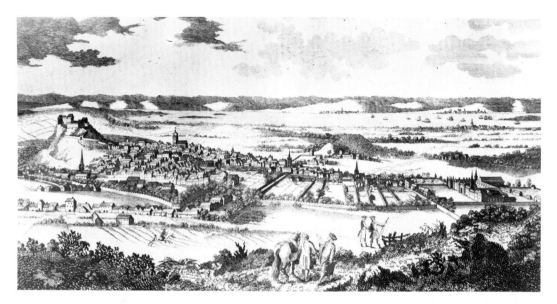

it. As a relief one day from the Darien Papers at the Royal Bank of Scotland I drove into the Pentlands, looking for Rullion Green where the Covenanters once sang the 74th Psalm and waited for the King's dragoons. Thunderhead clouds were walking on forked lightning from hill to hill, and having turned off the main road to watch this from higher ground I lost my way by Logan Burn. I asked for directions at a farmhouse, and understood but one word in five of the guidance I was given. We were perhaps ten miles only from the centre of Edinburgh, but here the Scotch despised by Johnson had survived the compression of time and distance. I did not hear its words and rhythm again until I first listened to Jock-upon-land and John-the-Common-Weal in a performance of Lindsay's *Thrie Estaitis*.

At the end of the 18th century, and perhaps with a copy of Johnson's *Journey* at his elbow, the journalist Robert Heron echoed its enthusiasm for the anglicisation of Edinburgh. Surprisingly, perhaps, for he was born the son of a weaver in Kirkcudbright.

> National prejudices are gradually losing ground on both sides; and the language, the dress, and the manners of the English begin to gain the ascendancy. In short, the happy era seems not very distant when the English and the Scots shall be, in every sense of the word, ONE NATION.

That one nation was meant to be British but was soon thought and spoken of as English, although for some decades ministerial clerks in Whitehall observed the spirit of the Treaty by referring to Scotland as North Britain. Only twice, I think, have I seen Government letters to Edinburgh which were addressed from "*London S.B.*" While the new United Kingdom prospered imperially Scotland had little objection to this insulting disparity. Its people had accepted the Union as an escape from famine and bankruptcy, and those who regretted the loss of their independence soothed their doubts with the truth that life was better now,

This mid-18th-century prospect of Edinburgh shows its modest size and its attachment, like a ship's wake, to the surging thrust of Castle Rock. Within two decades it was spreading to the north and south, beyond the Flodden Wall which was more of an abandoned ruin than the artist suggests.

and with the lie that they were joined in equality with a wiser and more experienced nation.

An incorporating union is inevitably disproportionate, for a country confident of survival on its own has no need of it. Once the marriage is made, the weaker and sometimes ingratiating partner is obliged to adopt the character and manners of the stronger, to walk in its shadow and wait upon its tolerance. English democracy was born in noble dissent but its application is too often an inflexible rule by majority, under which the rights of minorities can appear obstructive and heretical. When an English Member tells the Commons today – without objection from either side of the House – that excessive time is being spent on Scotland's affairs, he is speaking in a long and arrogant tradition. The forty-five Scottish Members who went to the first Union Parliament, to sit with twelve times as many Englishmen, incautiously protested that some of its proposed legislation was contrary to Scots law. They were told that "whatever are or may be the laws of Scotland, now she is subject to the sovereignty of England she must be governed by English laws and maxims." They accepted this, and over the next century their successors worked and intrigued to occupy the high offices of Government by which their fellow countrymen were made to obey those laws and maxims.

One such administrator was Henry Dundas, Viscount Melville, a tall and boldly handsome man whose family held the Edinburgh seat in its pocket for more than fifty years. As Home Secretary he was said to rule Scotland as if it were "a lodge at a great man's gate", and as Secretary of War he was the Government's most successful recruiting sergeant in the Highlands. His likeness in stone now stands upon a Trajan column in Saint Andrew Square, more enduring than the rag and straw effigy once burnt by an Edinburgh mob. Below him is a fine Augustan building where I spent many hours reading letters and reports sent long ago from the Scots colony in Darien. It was once the town-house of the Dundas family but is now owned by the Royal Bank, which keeps part of the archives of the Company of Scotland Trading to Africa and the Indies. Had this "noble undertaking" been wise enough to establish its mercantile colony elsewhere than the fever swamps and rain forests of Darien the Union might have been unnecessary, and Lord Melville's career less offensive to the common people in Scotland. There are times in the evening dusk of the old city when I wish I could hear King Joseph's drum, beating down the wide emptiness of the Royal Mile from the Lawnmarket to the gates of Holyroodhouse. A deformed cobbler from the Cowgate, he was the leader of the Edinburgh mob, and the sound of his rallying sticks could make authority tremble for a night, a day, and another night.

The slums of the Rock and the foul wet wynds I saw forty-six years ago are gone, but the pleasant restoration of some of its buildings, their transformation into flats for the professional classes, cannot replace the vigorous life that pulsed here for

The Canongate over a century ago. Not the Royal Mile of tourist Edinburgh, but the people shown here were the descendants of those who remained in the tenement houses when the rich and comfortable moved out to the New Town.

centuries. The Royal Mile is now a tourist highway – from Holyroodhouse where emotional crowds sing Jacobite songs in honour of a brief visit from Royalty, to the Castle Esplanade where every August their hearts throb with martial pride, and a lone piper on the floodlit battlements keeps alive that bitter myth. At night, for the rest of the year, there is silence where sixty thousand people once lived and brawled and prayed. Many of Scotland's martyrs have died here, Protestant and Catholic, King's man and the Crown's enemy, and sometimes a drover from Glenstrae whose only mistake was to call himself MacGregor. They died by rope, fire and axe, or by the Maiden, that falling blade used by Scotland long before Doctor Guillotine recommended it to the French. Every political and religious parrot-cry, clan and family slogan, has been shouted from its wynds, and so much blood flowed on the cobbles in one stabbing affray that the people called it Cleanse-the-Causeway. But among the stench, the filth, and the savage

One of Moses Griffith's best illustrations for Pennant's *Tour*, Edinburgh Castle from Greyfriar churchyard. Church and graves survive, famous for the Covenant signed in blood on the stones, for a fictional dog of impossible loyalty, and more factually for the graves of the Adam family of architects.

quarrels, gentle flowers also grew – haunting verse, good books, debate, argument, and the ennobling spirit of religious and political freedom.

Until the building of the New Town the people were fearful of moving beyond their encircling wall, and raised their houses higher and higher until some were a hundred feet and more above the back-lanes. Although little now remains of their last defence-work, its sorrowful name endures: the Flodden Wall. Erected quickly after the slaughter below Branxton Hill, it was no protection when the Rough Wooing brought Lord Hertford north to make "a jolly fire" of Edinburgh. Outwith the Wall he put a torch to the Abbey of Holyrood, and to the palace of Holyroodhouse which the dead king of Flodden had built beside it. Twenty-three years later, zealots of the Scottish Reformation plundered the restored Abbey and stripped it of its images and woodwork. In the next century another mob, this time inflamed by the Whig Revolution, tore down its stones and smashed its coffins. They then sacked the Chapel Royal of Holyroodhouse and destroyed its Jesuit printing-press. When the roof of the Abbey collapsed in the 18th century, the romantic fancies of Regency Scotland preferred it to remain a picturesque and filthy ruin. If the Scots have not always defeated England in the field, they may be sure they have sometimes outmatched it in the maniacal destruction of their property.

The vandalism of later centuries has been less violent, albeit motivated by egregious conceit. In 1829 the architect William Burn – who had successfully designed classical houses, hospitals and music-halls – refaced the Norman and Gothic fabric of Saint Giles with paving-stones believing he was making good the mistakes of medieval masons. Had the money available not been exhausted he would no doubt have improved the lantern crown of its splendid steeple, but it survived him and still stands nobly high above the Lawnmarket, mocking the prison-block ugliness of his insane botching. The Victorians and Edwardians erected

their own neo-Gothic follies, notably the great red-black pile of the North British Hotel which masks and diminishes the simple nobility of Robert Adam's Register House. They also built the Scott Monument, designed by a Pentland shepherd's talented son. At first it must have been a bizarre contrast to the remaining Georgian façade of Princes Street, but now that has been raped by commercial development, and only saved from wealthy squalor by the majestic Rock it faces, the monument has a solacing charm. Most people in Edinburgh are affectionately attached to it, and are offended if told that the Albert Memorial in Hyde Park, which it must have inspired, may be even taller and uglier. Nowhere in the world, however, is there so large a memorial to a writer, and for that reason alone I should speak of it with respect.

Contempt for the beauty of Edinburgh, and for their obligation to maintain it, has long been a characteristic of its purse-masters. Greed and profit, said the poet William Dunbar five hundred years ago, blinded rich merchants to the disgraceful state of their city.

> Think ye not shame,
> Before strangers of all estates,
> That sic dishonour hurt your name?

In the decades since the war no planning authority has felt shame or thought of dishonour, and Progress and Profit – synonymous terms for those who wish to make one toward the other – have subjected Edinburgh to abominable mutilation. The listing of buildings worthy of preservation has saved some that were under threat, but much more has gone. George Square to the south of the Castle was built in the 18th century and was a pleasure to the

It is possible to stand in the Lawnmarket today and see the architectural framework of this Edinburgh scene. But only through half-closed eyes, perhaps, for botching improvement robbed Saint Giles of the ethereal quality seen here.

eye and the spirit. When the University of Edinburgh bought it, three sides were "redeveloped" with towers of glass and concrete that stun the mind. Saint James Square behind Register House was thought expendable because although it was admittedly beautiful it was not the best of its kind in the New Town, an argument that could substantially deplete most museums and galleries. Thus its calm and simple Georgian houses were demolished, and in their place is a sprawling grey block that reminds me of the eyeless air-raid shelters that once dominated the ruins of German cities. Good sense befitting, much of its soulless interior is the administrative warren of a Government department. Another occupies Argyle House, a shoe-box of windows set thoughtlessly at the foot of the Castle and degrading its aloof grandeur. If such buildings have achieved anything beyond the provision of sterile capsules for computers, electronic and human, it is that they provoked an outraged public into forming associations to prevent further assaults upon its civic pride.

The golden age which created the restrained elegance or brooding dignity of Moray Place, Charlotte Square and Royal Terrace, was also erecting monuments to its self-esteem and material success, but it had the wisdom to entrust their design to men of aesthetic probity. They too were capable of absurdities, of course, but even these were sometimes precedents in good bad taste. Upon the crown of Calton Hill, looking westward to Princes Street and eastward to the sea, is a collection of meaningless masonry, time-blackened pillars and pediments. This, as much as Castle Rock, has encouraged men to think of the Parthenon and call Edinburgh the Athens of the North, as if a city so individual in character needs distinction by comparison. It was intended to be a great memorial to the Scottish soldiers of the Napoleonic wars, but lack of financial help stopped its completion. It was thirty years since Waterloo, and the people of Scotland had already contributed £7,000 for the Scott Monument. It is now a tragi-comic folly, and any man who has been a soldier may think that the best monument to his wasting trade. It was at Spinningdale in Sutherland, and from James Robertson-Justice, that I first heard the old story that public donations ceased when radical journalists wrote of the Clearances then taking place in Ross and Knoydart, and made it known that Highland soldiers had come home from Toulouse, New Orleans and Quâtre Bras to find their glens empty and their families replaced by Cheviot sheep. The story is untrue, I think, but once again we should perhaps print the legend.

If I am sometimes impatient with Edinburgh's self-satisfaction, it cannot irritate me for long. Like Glasgow, if to a lesser and more gentle degree, it is a human city. Its centre is becoming a residential area once more and is no longer empty and heartless at night. Moreover its classes can live cheek by jowl and not in cantonments in the English way. It is also a city of books, and has been since James IV gave Walter Chapman and Andrew Myllar permission to establish the first printing-house in Scotland. Although the press was originally intended to make books of law and ritual, it

was soon employed by the explosive intellects of the Reformation, and more enduringly by poets. They had always been attracted to Edinburgh, by royal patronage and by the rich inspiration of its people. They were the *Makaris*, the makers of songs whom Dunbar once mourned at a time of ailing despair. He was a satirist, ribald and bawdy, but in his *Lament for the Makaris* there is no scorn, only a morbid melancholy which, reflecting upon his own infirmity, puts the history of his country into one sad quatrain.

The Castle is a towering exaggeration, Arthur's Seat a caricature, and the bridge over Leith Water a conundrum. All combine to give Edinburgh that Attic nobility the citizens of the New Town believed it should have.

> The stait of man dois change and vary,
> Now sound, now seik, now blith, now sary,
> Now dansand mery, now like to dee;
> *Timor mortis conturbat me.*

In the best of Scottish verse, before and since his time, there is always sorrow and rage, an anguish beyond relief, and joy taken in pleasure is only a brief respite from the contemplation of mortality. I have read, but met too few of Edinburgh's poets who today honour and maintain the precedents set by Dunbar, Henryson, Beattie and Ramsay, by the boy Robert Fergusson whose vernacular verse inspired Burns, and who killed himself in an asylum before he was twenty-five. I remember Norman MacCaig speaking of him, and reading a tranquil but disturbing stanza of his own verse, sitting beneath a Daniell aquatint of Raasay, his mother's home he said. I cannot recall how I came to be in his tall, cool room in Edinburgh. It was in the company of others, Hamish Henderson among them, a man of eccentric wisdom who wrote some of the best soldier-verse of the war. He bought me a bad curry that day, I remember, but he always sends me a civil postcard of warning when he is about to write to the *Scotsman*, sternly exposing the errors in my work.

At best, contemporary Edinburgh only humours its *makaris*, and perhaps always did, for poetry challenges society to its face and will not, as prose often does, whisper dishonest encouragement in its ear. Church and Law, Medicine and Banking are the city's pride. In the past the Church directed its conscience, and by that the nation if it could, not always to its credit. Aged and dying, enraged by what he believed to be the rejection of his counsel, John Knox shouted a bitter valediction from the pulpit of Saint Giles, *"The ages to come will be compelled to bear witness to the truth!"* And so they have, but not his truth, perhaps. The Church he helped to build – now valiant and now craven, sometimes compassionate, but more often insanely cruel as its liberating ideology decayed into bigotry – this once revolutionary Church has too often been a blight upon the creative spirit of a remarkable people.

A probable likeness of John Knox. His menacing intellect and clanging polemics brought a Queen to tears, took Scotland into another age, and still influence the nation's mind and heart.

Not the least charge to be laid against it is that it strangled Scotland's nascent talent for drama. The promising light that suddenly burned with Lindsay's *Thrie Estaitis* was then extinguished for more than three centuries. Today, when Scotland seems to produce more actors in proportion to its population than any other part of Britain, I have sometimes thought that beneath their good fellowship and iconoclastic humour they suspect that one day they must answer for the irreligious frivolity of their profession. This may explain why many of them, unlike English actors, pretend they are not players and passionately involve themselves in other activities, not only because acting rarely pays a good man's living. Now and then the undertow of their country's history disturbs the surface of their thoughts. On the Black Mount where we were once filming, that fine character player Roddy McMillan sat beside me on a rock, dressed in Sabbath black for his part. For a while we silently contemplated the distant lochans of Rannoch, red with the dark stain of peat-moss. Then he plucked at his costume and smiled and said, "I've not looked like this, or felt like this since I went to my grannie's funeral in Ardnamurchan." The sectarian precepts taught in childhood sometimes bedevilled an adult tolerance, *bogle-wark* he called it. Two years or so before his death he took the part of Archbishop Spottiswoode in a short television play I wrote about the martyrdom of John Ogilvy. Although his performance was sensitive and perceptive, he said old prejudices had made it difficult to portray the inquisitor as the script required, a churchman who was as much the prisoner of doctrine and dogma as the Jesuit he was interrogating. "Not agreeing with him or his damn arguments. He was *wrong*, do you see?"

The admonitory spires of Edinburgh's Presbyterian conscience are the last to be seen of the city from Salisbury Crags before the street-lights stitch dusk to darkness, as they are the first to prick the mist at dawn. An Englishman's visit to Scotland should

The Grassmarket, Edinburgh, before the "improvements" of the early 19th century. It was the largest open space in the old city and thus "convenient" for public executions. The Flodden Wall, which closed the western end of the market, is seen on the slope.

properly begin and end here on Arthur's Seat, and not because stone from its escarpment was once sent to make pavements in London. Eight hundred feet and more above sea level the whole city may be encompassed, its historic and geographic setting dramatically realised. When I go there, I stand with my back to the firth and the sea. Inland I can see the three regions that make Scotland, the distant shadow of the Border Hills, the blue rise of the Highlands beyond the valley of the Forth, and westward the roads to Glasgow, crossing the Lowland plain between the Pentlands and the Campsie Fells.

The long brawl of Scotland's history began in the bloody cockpit of the Lowlands, eighteen hundred years ago when the Romans abandoned the Antonine Wall and left its forts burning against the night sky. The influential battles of its independence were fought here, and the cut-throat squabbles of Crown, Church and People. Except for the black stronghold of Stirling, like a hawk upon its basalt rock, it is impossible now to imagine the land as it once was. The trees which covered the high ground are long gone with the wolves and the knightly hunters of wolves. The earth is scarred by twisted roads, abandoned mines, urban sprawl and the straggling black towns of distressed or dying industries. On Bonnymuir, below the gentle Kilsyth Hills, new motorways are fittingly entwined in a hangman's noose. Here in the spring of 1820 radical weavers from Glasgow, Paisley, Rutherglen and Strathaven were bloodily dispersed by local yeomanry and English hussars. Their armed revolt may have been prematurely provoked by Government agents, although their demands for liberty, their uncertain Provisional Government, and the rioting strike of sixty thousand workers in Glasgow were proof that they were planning such a rising. Twenty thousand people watched the hanging of the rebel leaders and afterwards, on the walls of Scotland, protesting placards cried *Murder! Murder! Murder!* It was the bitter end of a revolutionary cause begun thirty years before, when one of its

Prince Albert, here laying the foundation stone of the National Gallery in Edinburgh, greatly admired the work of Sir Walter Scott. Therefore he may not have been upset by the artist who proudly exaggerated the height of the writer's monument and thus diminished that of everything and everybody else.

middle-class leaders – a Highland gentleman, no less – declared that the artisans, miners and peasants of Scotland were "marked by the finger of God to possess, sooner or later, the fullest share of liberty." But when such men began to talk of pikes and muskets, as the only argument authority might understand, he entreated them to "be not rash, be not impetuous". But his influence over them was now past. They were literate and well-read, and the weaver-poet Alexander Paisley had demonstrated that their radical fervour was no longer touched by the finger of God alone.

> *The Rights of Man* is now well kenned
> And read by mony a hunder;
> For Tammy Paine the buik has penned
> And lent the Court a lunder.

Two of the rebel weavers, Andrew Hardie and John Baird, were hanged at the gate of Stirling Gaol, and then brutally beheaded. They are buried beneath a corroded monument in Sighthill Cemetery, Glasgow, and it is not among the visits recommended by the Scottish Tourist Board.

I first heard of Bonnymuir during the war, and it is my shame that it struck no responsive chord in my mind, inspired as that was by the English Levellers and their brave stand in Burford Church-yard. An intake of conscripts from Glasgow came to the Welsh camp where I was a junior instructor, many of them aged thirty-five and thirty-eight. As I marched my section up the hill to their barrack-room I saw that some were breathing with difficulty, their lips an alarming blue. The Medical Officer was unimpressed by

this, and told them he knew the difference between a man with heart trouble and another who had been chewing cordite to simulate it. Remembering their fathers' experiences during and after the Great War, they had decided that this was not their struggle and were determined to avoid it if they could. Thirteen weeks later they went to North Africa without open complaint, although some may not have returned from embarkation leave. That first night in the barrack-room, as I introduced them to the military virtues of Brasso, boot-boning and blanco, they bragged of Red Clydeside, of John Maclean and Willie Gallacher, and talked of their rights. I said they would soon be told, and not gently, that the only rights a soldier could expect were twenty-four inches in the ranks and the right to breathe, anything more being a privilege. Upon which the oldest man spoke darkly of Bonnymuir, without explanation but using the word like a slogan, and one which all lance-bombardiers would do well to respect.

I remembered those men not long ago when a retiring Professor of History at Edinburgh University told a newspaper that my books, which he deplored, had "contributed a great deal to the state of mind of left-wing agitation" in Scotland. I thought it foolish of him to expose his own political bias so naively, and to believe that the memories of his countrymen are so short that they need such incitement. Since he added that he was 68 and had hardly heard of the Clearances until recently, an uncharitable mind may think that now and then there appears to be some truth in Johnson's harsh accusation that "men bred in the universities of Scotland obtain a mediocrity of knowledge between learning and ignorance."

The building of the Forth rail bridge in 1887. It is now said to have exhausted its usefulness, but it has lasted longer than it might had its first designer, Thomas Bouch, been allowed to proceed with his plans. His rail bridge over the Tay collapsed within eighteen months of completion.

41

Glasgow from the Low Green at the beginning of the 19th century, the growing suburb of the Gorbals on the left.

For all its turbulent history and the hard-faced, butting head it turns to the world, Glasgow began in simplicity and saintliness. Its name is Welsh or Gaelic in origin, meaning "green hollow" or "dear stream", and its vernacular pronunciation today is pleasingly close to those original tongues. It began as a chapel in the sixth century, built by Saint Kentigern, a Briton as his name suggests although he is familiarly known as Mungo. He came from the east, expelled by his grandfather Prince Loth of the Votadini, and thus the people of Edinburgh may claim that one of their Lothian predecessors founded the city of Glasgow. A miraculous team of white oxen led Kentigern to that dear stream which would later become the town's principal sewer. He preached from a mound which Providence had raised for that purpose, and in the 16th century the thought of this evangelical beginning gave the city its motto, taken from an exhortation on a church-bell, *Lord, let Glasgow flourish through the preaching of the Word and praising Thy name.* Later, when it stood on the threshold of its industrial greatness, it discarded all but the second, third and fourth words, these being most applicable to its pride and ambition. Saint Mungo's tomb, under superb fan vaulting, is now the heart of Glasgow's great, columned cathedral. Begun in the 13th century, inspired by English Gothic, it was two hundred years in building and was thus out of date in design when it was completed. That it still exists today is due to the forefathers of those men who ultimately inherited the city's soul. When the ministers of the Reformed Church gathered a mob to destroy it in 1578, it was defended and saved by merchants and tradesmen under arms.

Thomas Pennant was impressed by the cathedral, although in general he was disgusted by the "slovenly and indecent manner in which the houses of God in Scotland are kept." He thought the

streets of Glasgow were in good taste, but his praise was at best deflationary, "the best-built of any second-rate city I ever saw." It was already growing fat when he visited it. A town which had once lived by curing herrings and netting salmon in the Clyde was now importing forty thousand hogsheads of tobacco every year from the colony of Virginia, and selling it to Europe. When the American Revolution threatened this trade, Glasgow merchants raised volunteer regiments to subdue the colonists, and having failed to do that turned their active minds to cotton, coal and weaving, iron and shipbuilding, making the city one of the greatest in Britain, and ultimately second only to London in importance.

It is hard to love Glasgow unless one is born there, and perhaps not always then. It is easy to think it ugly if one sees only the filth on its face. Greed, indifference and poverty have neglected it. It is perhaps too large, and has spread itself thoughtlessly across the surrounding fields and green allotments where its hand-weavers once grew fine Savoy cabbages. As the rich and influential and uncaring moved outward in the last century, first to the pleasant suburb of the Gorbals across the Clyde, the "plain and unaffected" houses commended by Pennant became slums, and when they were replaced by tenements these too became slums, as did the inner suburbs once they were abandoned. Northward toward Lochlomondside and northwestward to Kelvindale, the new and ebullient middle-classes built themselves fine streets and mansions in emulation of Edinburgh's New Town. They razed the centre of the city with a freedom modern planners must envy, and in a euphoria of architectural abandon they erected great halls in which to place their fine libraries and galleries, red-stone kirks where they could thank God for rewarding their humility. Above all, they built grand public buildings which would properly honour the

Glasgow Cathedral in the 19th century. Built over the grave of the city's saintly founder, some of its stones date from 1197. Behind it is the sprawling Necropolis, now even more crowded. It was opened in 1832 as the Victorians' "hallowed depository of the ashes of our most distinguished citizens."

Glasgow's architectural abandon reached its apogee with the City Chambers, George Square. High on a pillar that was originally intended for a likeness of George III, Sir Walter Scott has turned his shoulder to this astonishing demonstration of municipal arrogance.

industries that brought them wealth and power – Renaissance, Flemish and Venetian palaces, baronial keeps, Gothic cathedrals, Greek and Egyptian temples. The only originality exercised was in the design of their central railway station, magnificently yawning in iron and glass. By this century the monumental orgasm had exhausted itself, and with bomb-clearance and slum-clearance there came tall, cloud-touching blocks of flats, standing like megaliths in peripheral wastelands, a terrible indictment of the men who designed and built them, and of authority's contempt for the people who must live in them.

It is the people who make Glasgow, not its arrogant, money-proud buildings. In Edinburgh it is possible to leave the National Portrait Gallery and see the same 17th- or 18th-century faces in a bus queue or across a shop counter, high cheekbones, wide-set eyes, pale skin and sand-brown hair. I have never had that experience in Glasgow, perhaps because its people are a more complex mixture, or have faces that were rarely painted in the past, either as the sitter or a servant in attendance. Their forebears came from Cork and Kildare, Lochaber and Morvern, the bitter fields and cities of Europe. They crowded into neglected tenements, believing they might one day earn or steal enough to buy their passage to America or Australia, but at last abandoned all hope of escape. They have made Glasgow a defiant city, a raw, bold and defiant city. They anaesthetise their despair with astringent and perceptive humour. They spit abusive contempt from broken windows, drink their grief away in night-dark streets, defend their perverse independence in folk-lore songs of obscene iconoclasm, and spray their aerosol irreverence across the purple grime of their city's sandstone walls.

Jamaica Street at the close of the last century. At the bottom, by Glasgow bridge, merchant ships once unloaded the West Indian sugar which gave the street its name and the city much of its early prosperity. Glasgow's tramway, "the caurs", lasted for ninety years, ending in 1962 with an emotional manifestation of public regret.

From the centre of the city to the grand Victorian terraces at Kelvingrove, Sauchiehall Street has been a cock-walk for Glasgow's pride, the home of the Empire Music Hall and Cranston's Willow Tea Room, a slogan for Saturday-night roisterers, and an essential part of the world-wide graffiti of the Scottish soldier.

45

In the mid-19th century a changing Trongate reflects Glasgow's belief that its merchant princes should have a Renaissance setting. Older citizens may have remembered less complacent times when the Trongate's inns were headquarters for the regiments called in to suppress riot and insurrection.

Building Glasgow's industrial empire, its middle classes have always feared the hostility of the work-force their prosperity required. A century and more ago its police were impotent when starving unemployed took to the streets in protest. Locked in their chambers, the members of the city council could only appeal to the people not to listen "to the bad advice of designing men, preaching to you about your rights." An old cry and a persistent cry. From the 18th century until this, each new generation, every arrival of bewildered incomers has created another stratum of distressed and deprived in Glasgow, pressing down upon those preceding. There was no escape from abysmal poverty but the sea and the Army. When the selective charity of emigration societies made the former difficult, there was only the latter, and long before the Great War the city had replaced the Highlands as Scotland's "nursery of soldiers". Some years ago John Baynes, an officer of the Cameronians, wrote a book* in which he sought a military and sociological explanation for the superb behaviour of his regiment in one particular battle. In March, 1915, it went into action at Neuve Chapelle and when it was withdrawn a week later only 150 men of the original 900 were left, commanded by a second-lieutenant. But their morale and discipline were still high. Baynes discovered that seventy percent of these riflemen, mostly from Glasgow, had come from a class so depressed, so far beneath any other in Britain that he could only describe it as "real lower-class". He did not, perhaps, find an easy explanation for their superlative courage and discipline, except that they were time-serving soldiers to whom the regiment had become family, friend and country.

* *Morale*, by John Baynes, Cassell, 1967.

Among the dead and the survivors were the fathers or brothers of some of those blue-lipped recruits I marched to their barrack-room at Bodelwyddan, forty years ago.

In grief and joy, Glasgow is still the prisoner of its past, and can still be corrupted by those who exploit it, but from its beginning on that providential mound it has been an inspiration to the religious and political conscience of Scotland. Its people could claim, if they wished, that but for their city there might have been no War of Independence and thus no Scottish nation. When Bruce murdered John Comyn before the high altar of the Minorite church in Dumfries he rode to Glasgow for sanctuary and absolution, and was given both by its pragmatic bishop who then sanctified his coronation at Scone. It was the people of Glasgow, not Edinburgh, who assembled under arms to resist the Treaty of Union, and again a century later in the cause of liberty which ended with the death of Baird and Hardie. The city has also been a seeding-bed for the cultural genius of Scotland, unpredictable and startling in its brief and sudden growth. For a while at the turn of this century Glasgow was the centre of that remarkable resurgence of talent now known as the Second Scottish Enlightenment, and the memory and influence of it have managed to survive that patronising description. Architects, designers, writers, painters and scholars brought originality, invention and excitement to a kingdom embalmed in Victorian mediocrity. Coincidental with this renaissance, a part of it and party to it, was a political awakening which, through men like John Burns and John Maclean, gave muscle and heart to the British socialist movement.

If Edinburgh rightly thinks of itself as the mind and intellect of

The Broomielaw has been Glasgow's quayside since the 17th century. It became an escape-hatch from the city, briefly or permanently. In its greatest years, which ended in 1914, forty steamers a day went down the water to the coast and to the Isles, and a trip aboard one of them was a Glaswegian's favourite outing.

View down the

Frth of Clyde.

Moses Griffith's engaging sea-plans of the Clyde and some of the Inner Isles drawn for Pennant's *Tour*. The gulls are not merely decorative.

Scotland, Glasgow is most certainly its generous heart. Its pride is not in fine streets, noble prospects, and in being a northern *pied-à-terre* for absent Royalty. Its brawling, questing people are its majesty. The tartan of their nationalism is not worn to Highland balls but irreverently on their heads as football bonnets, and the crowd that fills Hampden Park for an international roars a terrible truth from its ignorant defiance.

Driving slowly northward by Glen
Aray I paused at its highest point, where
the road twists down to Cladich and Loch Awe. I had seen a hare
moving toward me through the cotton-grass, and now, when I
stopped to watch it, a carrion crow dropped heavily to earth
beyond us, as if expecting the animal to be the victim of my
wheels. Rain was still falling on the lower glen behind me, from
slate-blue clouds above Loch Fyne. Four miles ahead another
squall was drawing a curtain across the Pass of Brander, but here
the sky was open, the sun strong, and the winter-dead land rising
eastward to Beinn Bhuidhe was as rich in glistening colour as the
best marmalade.

The brown hare of the Highlands has always reminded me of
the jack-rabbit of my boyhood, and this morning I remembered
a Saskatchewan summer when gophers were so troublesome that
farmers paid three cents for every tail we brought them. As we
flushed these appealing rodents from their holes, with water
poured from red lard-pails, two motionless jack-rabbits watched
us at a safe distance. The hare at the Glen Aray roadside studied
me as they did, by one black-wet eye in the elliptical profile of its
head, its body nervously tensed on powerful hind legs, and its fore-
feet lightly lifted like a pianist's hands above the keys. When it
moved it seemed to cross the road in one effortless leap, and the
crow took flight in rasping protest. I left the car and followed them
up the brae. It was early spring but already too late, I knew, to
witness a demented mating-tryst of brown hares. I had never seen
this leaping, whirling dance and I did not see it that day. When
I got to Neil Munro's cairn at the top of the rise the hare was long
gone into the russet heather.

The cairn is a lonely monument to a good writer whose homeland was here in Argyll. By its side one can look southward to the
steep slope of Scardon where the best of his Highland characters,
John Splendid and young Elrigmore, took refuge from the
Lochaber Men who came to burn the Campbell town of Inveraray.
It is not a cairn Munro would admire, I think. Like too many now,
its ugly rocks are cemented together, not assembled in the tradi-

The haunch of Ben Cruachan above Loch Awe. Near this spot on the Glen Aray Road I once saw three rainbows arcing over the length of the loch.

tional loose pile that invites all men to add their tribute. I put a stone at its foot, wishing I knew the Gaelic that should be said, and moved on to the outcrop of Craig nan Sassenach. I do not know why this is called the Rock of the Englishman, more exactly of the Saxon, but it was perhaps a fitting place to be, although my distant ancestors in the gentler valleys of Kent were Jutes not Saxons.

Below me, Loch Awe was black with the shadow of Brander's dark clouds, and the green isle of Inishail was misted with rain. A rainbow curved from the shell of Kilchurn Castle, south-westward to the loch-head in a perfect arc, clear and pure. As I looked at it in wonder another appeared above it, and then faintly and briefly a third. I watched until this sweet miracle faded beneath the widening bowl of blue sky. The clouds were gone from Brander, and beyond the now shining water was the high majesty of Cruachan, sunlit in a saffron plaid.

Loch Awe is the most consoling of Scotland's inland waters, and the longest – twenty-five and a half miles from the Glenorchy Campbells' old stronghold of Kilchurn to the pier-head below Sron Mhor. Before the Ice Age it was open to the sea, perhaps, making an island of what is now the Knapdale peninsula, but all that is left of this outlet is the tear-drop of Loch Ederline, tree-rimmed and reed-fringed below Beinn Bhan, a refuge for darting water-fowl and the winter visits of whooper swans. The loch now finds its seaward way to the north by the River Awe, through the

narrow defile of Brander. The deep surge of water here is powered less by nature than by machines inside the belly of Ben Cruachan, great hydro-electric turbines in a rock chamber three hundred feet long, one hundred and twenty wide and seventy-seven high. The triple-crowned mountain above and about this cavern gave the Campbells their battle-slogan and protected the loch and castle where they first set a possessive foot on Argyll, five hundred years ago. So secure and remote did it make them feel that they answered all threats with a defiant boast, "It's a far cry to Loch Awe!" Their confidence was never justified, and three times in one black century the northern clans came by Brander or the Strath of Orchy to burn the steadings of Argyll. The last of these terrible invasions was by Royal authority and with orders as merciless as those which sent Campbell soldiers against the people of Glencoe seven years later. *Destroy what you can ... all men who are not come off on your advertisement are to be killed or disabled ... burn all houses except honest men's ... let the women and children be transported to remote islands ...*

Lochaweside is now the tranquil heart of Argyll. It is also the dead heart of the old *Gaidhealtachd*, and of the Stone, Iron and Bronze Age settlements which were here before the coming of the Gaels in the fifth century, before the three sons of Erc, High King of Dalriada in Ireland, grounded their galleys on the coast of Knapdale and agreed to divide their new conquest equally. The tiny islands of the loch, fallen fragments of the green hills above, are set with the grey jewels of ruined keeps and empty chapels, but

Kilchurn Castle, Loch Awe, built by Black Colin Campbell of Glenorchy in 1440, and his clan's first firm foothold in Argyll. The terrible storm of 1879, which destroyed the Tay rail bridge across the country at Dundee, also ruined the remaining towers of Kilchurn.

beneath the monotonous plantations of Sitka spruce are the remains of burial-cairns and hill-forts built by those earlier and nameless tribes of pre-history. The narrow road which almost encircles Loch Awe is infrequently used, except by vehicles of the Forestry Commission which, to confound my dark dislike of what it has done and will do to the Highlands, has established an animal infirmary at Inverinan. Red deer and roe, squirrel and badger, hawk, raven and owl, all creatures that the foresters find sick or injured, are compassionately restored here and offered their freedom. It is some compensation for the changes which afforestation has brought to the Highlands, and not without irony. The night I first dined with Hamish at Corrimony, far from Argyll, he took me up the hill to the edge of a new plantation of spruce. In the moonlight, beyond the protective deer-fence, was a puzzled stag and its hinds. The old grazing-walk which they had taken for centuries, from the high braes of Guisachan to Loch Garbh, was now closed to them. In time they found another way, no doubt, but everywhere their freedom of movement is decreasing, and the mercy of the annual cull, by which man keeps a bloody balance between the deer and their available grazing, is made necessary by his encroachment upon the latter.

In twenty years I have seen much of Lochaweside changed by well-dressed ranks of alien trees, but unlike other parts of the Highlands more of its natural past still remains. There are red-columned groves of Caledonian pine like the empty nave of a Border abbey, white-stemmed birch woods rising from a froth of delicate fern, the twisted limbs of oak and ash in grey-green rags of moss. The wild white rose flowers on dark-leafed bushes, pink clusters of wood-vetch tremble in the roadside dusk, and fox-gloves bend in the wind that always blows down the narrow glen from Scammadale. There are flowercups of cloudberry on the high road by Loch Avich to Kilmelford, bog-bean and water lobelia in black lochans, lady's mantle and purple saxifrage where the igneous rock of a mountain's skeleton breaks through its thin skin of soil. The land is rich with their innocent colour, and because it is also too poor and unproductive for man's hungry needs he has not yet destroyed its vulnerable beauty with herbicide and pesticide.

Loch Awe is the centre of Argyll, and Argyll was the generative spirit of Scotland, the old Dalriadic kingdom of incoming Gaels who gave the nation its name. It has a majestic coast-line of long green peninsulas and smooth-flanked mountains stepping down to the tidal waters of its sea-lochs. Never more than thirty miles in breadth, it stretches one hundred and forty northward from the Mull of Kintyre, by the green walls of Knapdale and Lorn to the mouth of Loch Linnhe, the dark hills of Morvern and the storm-braving Point of Ardnamurchan. Open to sea and sky it shimmers with clean light on a blue day in summer, but in winter it wraps its white head in clouds and outfaces the driving winds that brought its founding warriors from the south-west. Its name maintains their claim to it, *earr a' Gaidheal* the boundary of the

The ruins of the Bonawe Ironworks at the narrows of Loch Etive as they were before their restoration. Built in the middle of the 18th century, they were perhaps the only successful effort to industrialise the Western Highlands after the last Jacobite Rebellion.

Gael, and one they held and lost, then took again in three warring centuries before Kenneth the Hardy, son of Alpin and the descendant of forty tribal princes, merged his people and the Picts into one kingdom of *Albainn*, the land of the Scots. Time and dynastic ambition moved its centre eastward from Dunadd to Scone, then southward to Edinburgh and Westminster. Now bureaucrats have reduced Argyll from a country to a meaningless District within an absurd Region that also embraces the city of Glasgow and the shires of Dunbarton, Renfrew, Lanark and Ayr. This they have called Strathclyde, perhaps remembering that much of it was once part of that Brythonic kingdom, but ignorant or unmindful of the fact that to include the mountains of the old *Gaidhealtachd* makes nonsense of their history and geography.

The sea was always the open highway of Argyll, the only safe and comfortable approach to it until the coming of the railway. Because of this its contact with the European continent was often closer and warmer than with the rest of Scotland, and when the MacDonalds peopled Kintyre, Jura, Islay and Ardnamurchan, maintaining their independence as Lords of the Isles, they defied the authority of the Scottish Crown and made treaties with the Kings of England and France. In the east Argyll has always been protected and sometimes imprisoned by the rolling wasteland of Rannoch, and by an aloof and magnificent barrier of mountains from Ben Arthur's black-stone cobbler above Loch Long to the granite knot of Orchy, across the Black Mount where MacIain's people summer-herded their cattle to the cliff-wall of Aonach Eagach and the sleeping mountains of Mamore. The roads that enter Argyll do so cautiously and circuitously – over the summit of Rest-and-be-Thankful down to the head of Loch Fyne, a moorland way past Crianlarich to the brown slopes of Glen Lochy, and thirdly north-about by Achallader and Glencoe to the old slate town of Ballachulish and the wide sea-water of Loch Linnhe.

Most of Argyll's probing sea-lochs – Leven, Etive, Creran and Fyne – end in the shadows of these eastern mountains, or in narrow straths that lead to hostile escarpments or the heart-stopping sight of yet more marching hills, high corries and snow lingering late into summer. Loch Etive in the glen of that name is perhaps the most beguiling, deep black water, bare walls rising steeply above a sentinel stand of Caledonian pine, and the pink-purple flowers of wild rhododendron bending to the water's edge. Beyond the loch-head is the corrugated cone of the Great Herdsman, a narrow track moving by its foot to Kingshouse and the eastern entrance to Glencoe. There is a belief that Deirdre of the Sorrows, in exile from Ireland and waiting for her lover to take her home, lived here at Invercharnan on a river bend, and the legend is maintained by some of the Gaelic names given long ago to falling streams and broken stones. One of the papers I found in the archives of Inveraray Castle was a treaty signed at Invercharnan in 1669 between MacIain of Glencoe and Archibald Campbell of Inverawe who held land at the bend of Loch Etive. They swore "to live in all good neighbourhood and to assist and succour one another in all our lawful affairs in so far as it lies in us both, in protection and defence of one another's person." This did not save MacIain when Campbell soldiers were sent to slaughter him and his clan, and no fugitive MacDonald came over the high snows of Benderloch to ask for the protection of Campbell of Inverawe.

It was at Dalness in Glen Etive that we filmed some sequences for *John Macnab*, and one morning all shooting stopped as we watched two golden eagles rising and falling above us, great leaves in the still air. When they were gone, wheeling suddenly into the darkness of the rock-face, a stalking-party appeared on the misted sky-line like the opening sequence of a Western film. They brought a stag we needed for the episode we were filming, its head roped back to keep its antlers from the feet of the pony that carried it, and its eyes wet with inanimate grief.

I first heard a fox bark in Glen Etive, twenty years ago at dusk when I was driving back to the Kingshouse Inn. I have heard its harsh, appealing cry many times since, sometimes across the garden shrubs of a London suburb, and it always recalls that evening, with a catch in my throat. There is no better place than Glen Etive to hear a fox for the first time, for Duncan Ban Macintyre, Yellow-haired Duncan of the Songs who worked here as a forester two hundred years ago, composed a fine poem in honour of it. He was possibly the best of the old bards, although I have no Gaelic to be a proper judge. He could neither read nor write and carried the six thousand lines he created in his head. Although he was High-land and passionately attached to his race and its past, he died in Edinburgh where he kept a little howff, selling whisky distilled by his wife, Mary MacNicol. He was buried in Greyfriars churchyard, far from Inveroran where he and Mary were born, where Roddy McMillan sat beside me that day in Sabbath black. The village is

long gone from the green shore of Loch Tulla, but when the Wordsworths visited it there were still men and women who remembered Duncan Ban. The sharp-nosed, prick-eared animal he admired is now hated by Highland shepherds, and for the same reason, but his song is more than a eulogy, it is a fierce protest against the coming of sheep, the burning of homes and the dispersal of men.

Dalness in Glen Etive below the Great Herdsman. Here there were two eagles in the mist, and a fox barking at dusk in the narrow pass to Glencoe.

> The foxes have my blessing
> because they hunt the sheep,
> the sheep with brindled faces
> that cause confusion throughout the world,
> laying in waste our land
> and increasing our rents.
> Now there is no place left for the farmer,
> his living is gone
> and he is forced to leave the home
> where his forebears lived.
> The townships and the shielings
> where there was warmth and welcome
> are now in ruins,
> and the fields are untilled.

When the 18th-century traveller John Knox came to Argyll he was excited by its promising future. New towns, well-placed and pleasantly designed, were being built at Inveraray and Lochgilphead, and the sea-lochs were white with the sails of square-rigged ships, moving out with the tide. He thought more yet could be done, that somewhere on this coast there should be "a Royal dock-yard where squadrons and transports could be secretly fitted out and from whence they could sail at all times of the year ... before the enemy could have the smallest intelligence of the design." He could interest no one in this imaginative proposal, but today he at least might be pleased to see the black tower of a Polaris submarine slipping down into the sea beyond Ardnamurchan Point.

A less unnerving guardian of Argyll's coast is a buckler of islands great and small, each with its conical or wedge-shaped hills, and with names like sharp fragments of granite – Islay, Coll and Tiree, Jura, Colonsay and Scarba, Luing, Mull and the Garvellachs. Remote and reassuring in a black swirl of storm-clouds, the Inner Hebrides break the force of the western weather, but sometimes when the sea is still and the sun is bright they lie upon the water like yellow flowers. The greatest of them is Mull, Mull of the Trees. On a map it is shaped like a frond of beech-fern, but

The Isle of Mull, a Victorian scene in a tranquil mist. "The land we loved lies under bracken and heather, every field untilled ..."

eastward from the sea, when its headlands and wide inlets are hidden by mist, it is a clansman's targe with the volcanic boss of Ben More at its centre. It was here that Johnson, wet and miserable, decided that the Highlands were a most dolorous country, and was put in a worse temper by a drunken ship-master who talked "great nonsense about Wilkes and Liberty." But he warmed to Mull before he left, and to his host, the chief of the Macleans. On Inchkenneth, the pleasant isle in Loch na Keal where Maclean had his house, the Doctor allowed Boswell to put a blue bonnet over his grey wig. He then strutted about the room with a broadsword in his hand. "However unfavourable to the Lowland Scots," said his companion, "he seemed much pleased to assume the appearance of an ancient Caledonian." Before they took the branch-strewn ferry from Lochbuie to the mainland, Johnson's heart was deeply moved by a visit to the holy soil of Iona, its low hills and yellow machair of wind-bent grass, cold abbey stones and the graves of sixty Celtic kings. "The man is little to be envied," he wrote in his account of the Tour, "whose patriotism would not gain force upon the plain of Marathon, or whose piety would not grow warmer among the ruins of Iona."

The restored Abbey of Iona, the spiritual womb of Celtic Scotland, gravel-pathed and sign-posted for tourists, and not too strenuous a stroll from the ferry-point. Kings of Scotland, Ireland and Norway are buried in its earth.

Fifty years later, Felix Mendelssohn's first sight of Mull was from the shell of Dunollie Castle above the town of Oban, and in a flush of responsive emotion he declaimed some appropriate stanzas from *The Lord of the Isles*. The first notes of his overture, however, were not inspired by the green surge of waves against Staffa's rocks but by the piston-throb of the little steamer *Highlander* as he lay below, sick in heart and stomach. He spent much

of that miserable voyage about the coast of Mull wrapped in a blanket and revolted by the smell of onions frying in the ship's galley. He did not go ashore on Staffa, unlike his healthful friend Klingemann who leapt onto its wet stones and shouted his elation against the basalt columns of Fingal's Cave.

Few things I write give me much pleasure at the time of composition, but I enjoyed writing a television documentary about the visit these idealistic young men made to Scotland. We filmed where they had happily and sometimes painfully travelled, by Dunkeld, Rannoch and the Pass of Glencoe. The greater part of their journey followed the old Road to the Isles which was traced for me on a map forty-five years ago by a monk from the Benedictine Abbey at Fort Augustus. He walked it once a month, he said, from one small congregation to another as priests had done in the years of persecution. He was a Kintail man, I think, a jovial monk, and before I went aboard the canal steamer he gave me a brisk blessing in Gaelic and an English-language tract published by the Catholic Truth Society.

The *Highlander* was recreated for our use from an old schooner in Campbeltown. She looked fine from the Ross of Mull, moving northward out of Loch Scridain, but for days low mist or rain made filming on Staffa impossible. At dusk one evening, her engine suddenly dead, she drifted seaward past the grey necklace of the Treshnish Isles and was approaching Tiree before she was taken under tow. When the production crew and the actors came ashore that night at Bunessan they were wet and cold, with no love

The Abbey of Iona from Pennant's *Tour*, as Johnson saw it two years later. He said it came up to his expectations and was deeply moved by the ruins and nameless graves. Boswell thought it was "far short of marble monuments like those in Westminster Abbey."

The lock at Fort Augustus when Telford's Canal was in its Victorian heyday. The Benedictine Abbey on the point was built on the site of the old fort, where Cumberland made his headquarters in 1746 and turned the country about into a desert.

for Mull or any part of the Highlands, and not even my flask of Lagavulin, dark Islay malt and the best of talking-whiskies, could change their mood. I left them with regret for their despair and drove thirty-five miles to my hotel on the eastern shore of the island, taking the high cliff road by Loch na Keal where every bend threw the beam of my headlamps across the water to Inchkenneth and the nippled hills of Ulva. I came late to the darkness of the hotel, where candles were lit. There had been a ceilidh that night, but all were now gone except a young islander and his wife. They had waited, they said, to sing a song for me, a Gaelic song she had composed about the Clearances.

The Clearances made it no longer possible to call the island Mull of the Trees. Most of its natural woods were long ago replaced by sheep-walks, but here and there in a hill cleft where the white-eyed whinchat flies, by a falling burn or quiet lochside, there is a reminder of their beauty – oak, ash and birch, white bark and scarlet berries, lemon and olive-green leaves against wet black

The snow-hills of Mull beyond the low green island of Kerrera. Cattle from Mull were once landed on the far side of this island and then swum across the bay to Oban in the foreground.

rock. The islanders were proud of their trees, and it was perhaps their vanity which provoked Johnson's ungenerous sarcasm. "Sir," he said, when Maclean invited him to admire a distant wood, seen from the boat that was taking them across the mouth of Loch Tuath, "I saw at Tobermory what they called a wood, which I unluckily took for heath. If you show me what I take for furze, it will be something." That something is there now, dark plantations of conifers above Salen and Loch Frisa, and the sweet curling road by Dervaig to Calgary Bay. Timber has replaced sheep, as sheep once removed men, and the lingering memory of the Clearances is further embittered by southern incomers who still buy, sell and mismanage the land, much as others did a century and a half ago when the bard Angus MacMhuirich lamented the burnings and the evictions they brought to his island.

> The jaws of sheep have made the land rich,
> but we were told by the prophecy
> that sheep would scatter the warriors
> and turn their homes into a wilderness.
> The land of our love lies under bracken and heather,
> every plain and fields is untilled,
> and soon there will be none in Mull of the Trees
> but Lowlanders and their white sheep.

In 1786, walking on the high braes of Ross of Mull "to view the appearance of the ocean in a storm", John Knox was invited into a cottage where he was given a pinch of snuff and told the great news. The Duke of Argyll himself, assisted by the King, was to cut a canal across the Knapdale peninsula from Loch Fyne to the Atlantic shore of Loch Crinan. It was built by more competent labourers within a decade, eight miles of winding waterway that shortened the sea-route from Glasgow to the Outer Isles by one hundred and thirty. It is still in occasional use, the slender masts of yachts and squat hulls of ring-net fishing boats moving miraculously overland above the Lochgilphead road. For me, the appeal

Dunadd, the rock-stack on the Great Moss of Crinan. Prehistoric man had a settlement on its summit long before the incoming Scots made it their capital. Columba ordained one of their Kings on a throne of stone.

of this small navigational marvel, which 18th-century Scots rightly regarded as evidence of their resurgent greatness, is that it enters the sea where their nation began, a green bay-shore that was the first landfall of some of its early Gaelic settlers. And two miles inland is Dunadd, the mystical and mysterious mound that was the political centre of their Dalriadic kingdom for three centuries, a thousand years before John Rennie designed the Crinan Canal.

Although it is less than two hundred feet in height this aloof and crumpled rock-stack dominates the grieving grass of Crinan Moss, *a' Mhòine Mhór* the Great Peat-bog of early history. It looks seaward to the brown headland of Jura and it guards the northern passes into the Kilmichael hills. Silent now, except for keening winds and the sad cry of the curlew, Dunadd was a noisy stronghold long before it was taken by the Gaels, and the rough-pasture of the Moss is encircled by the burial-cairns, forts and standing-stones of their predecessors. It was the incoming Scots, perhaps, who built what is left of Dunadd's defences – dry-stone walls and terraces, an earth platform upon which their timber halls once stood and where a bright spring now glitters in the grass. If this lonely mound was indeed the *caput regionis* recorded by Adamnan, Columba came here from Iona to preach and perhaps ordain one of Dalriada's kings, almost all of whom were inaugurated at Dunadd. The nature of that solemn ritual is now conjectural, as is the part played in it by the mystic designs cut into a rock-face

The carving of a boar on the summit of Dunadd. Its origin and meaning are unknown, but the boar had a totemic significance in Gaelic mythology, and was the crest of Clan Campbell chiefs.

below the summit – a footprint, a basin, a docile boar, and an unintelligible Ogam inscription. Who carved them and why is also unknown, but they have mutely survived the Pictish spearmen and Gaelic bowmen who disputed this land, the women who used the fine bone tooth-combs which an archaeologist's trowel sometimes turns from the black peat of Mhòine Mhór. There is now a quiet steading at the foot of the mound, and the River Add flows peacefully where Oengus, King of the Picts, almost changed history by driving the Scots back to their ships and drowning their king in a flowing tide.

When Campbell lords came to Argyll in the 15th century, southward from Glen Orchy to Loch Fyne, Cowal and Knapdale, their feudal crest was a boar, an animal of totemic significance in Gaelic mythology. The shennachies, the story-tellers of the clan, made much of the mythological belief that their chiefs were descended from Diarmid the Boar-slayer, Diarmid of the legendary Feinn who still sleep in the hills, awaiting Fingal's rousing horn. It is my fancy – relieved of a historian's disciplinary caution – to believe that the Campbells may have adopted that rock-symbol on Dunadd, or cunningly exploited its likeness to their crest, thus strengthening their claim to be leaders of the *Gaidhealtachd* and superior to the MacDonalds who had the same aggressive conceit. The boar, now equipped with fearsome tusks, was carried on Campbell banners at Flodden. It was trodden into the mud of Loch Linnhe when Clan Donald took a terrible revenge at Inverlochy. Half a century later the two companies of the Argyll Regiment who entered Glencoe to murder its people wore a boar's-head badge on their blue woollen bonnets.

These badges had been made in London by William de Remon, a Huguenot exile. I discovered that pleasing fragment of inconsequential information in the archives of Inveraray Castle when I was gathering material for *Glencoe*. I told my host about it, and that evening MacCailein Mor, the eleventh Duke of Argyll, not only wore a dinner-jacket of his tartan but also blue velvet slippers upon which the boar was embroidered in silver thread.

I spent more than a week reading the manuscripts of the archives, every day behind an iron fire-door in the vaulted cellars below the castle. The room was cold and cheerless, lit by a naked bulb hanging from the ceiling. If I plugged my tape-recorder into its socket I had no light to see, and if I used the light I was obliged to copy the papers by hand, an exercise which a lifetime using a typewriter has made unendurable after a few minutes. Until an adaptor was found in the town I read and made brief notes, listening to the singing and occasional brawling of the Mediterranean kitchen-staff along the stone-flagged corridor. The previous Duke, a retiring man with vain hopes of becoming an archivist, had attempted to transcribe many of the papers, and this might have been helpful had he paginated his transcriptions and restored the originals to their chronological order. Toward the end of the week there was still one wooden cupboard which could not be unlocked by any key brought to me. It was labelled *Lorne* on a yellowing card, and because Lord Lorne, heir to the first Duke, had been lieutenant-colonel of the Argyll Regiment I hoped it might contain more papers relating to his command. With permission, some effort and a small invocation, I was able to lift the door from its hinges. I was immediately overwhelmed by a clashing cascade of falling silver that silenced the startled kitchen-staff for half an hour. It took me longer to return the silver to the cupboard shelves – tea-pots and coffee-pots, jugs, bowls and vases, salvers, dishes and canteens of cutlery, albums of sepia photographs heavily encased in the same metal. Some of this tarnished treasure was engraved with the snarling head of the Campbell boar, and all of it had been loyal gifts from towns, burghs and cities, companies and corporations throughout the country when the House of Argyll reached its apogee, the marriage of the Marquess of Lorne to a daughter of the Queen in 1871.

In London that year the Campbell crest was also on a few pieces of silver tableware and some fine damask napkins treasured by Jenny von Westphalen. Through her Scottish grandmother she was a descendant of the Earls of Argyll, and when she was not obliged to pawn the silver she produced it for the special guests who came to sup with her husband, Karl Marx.

Inveraray is a small and pleasing town lying on the flat shore of Loch Fyne, on Bracken Point where it was once the custom to hang incorrigible Lochaber Men, and where their invading kinsmen consequently hanged fourteen young gentlemen of Clan Campbell. On a still summer-day, when the sun is high above the hills of Cowal, the grey and white houses of Inveraray appear to be supported by their own reflection in the blue glass of the loch. At sunset in December, with red snow in the westward sky above Knapdale, they are lost in dark and solemn shadow. The town was planned and built with simple taste in the 18th century, replacing the medieval castle and a muddle of filthy houses that had been Clan Campbell's capital for three hundred years. William Adam was first employed as Clerk of Works to produce something more appropriate to the climbing eminence of the Argyll family, and

The 18th century New Town of Inveraray on Loch Fyne. The hotel was once the Great Inn where Johnson first drank whisky and found it free from "empyreumatick taste or smell". The square tower, which many quickly passing take for a castle keep, is a church built in 1920, and a mistake I think.

when he died his son John, with Robert Mylne, created the only Highland town that completely delights the eye. The new castle they built within pistol-shot of the old was not a castle at all but an *opéra-bouffe* country house of blue slate-stone, round turrets and Gothic windows, outwardly theatrical but inwardly noble, enriched by Mylne's elegant and decorative talent. Despite its thick walls and Armada cannon, the Lochaber Men would have had no difficulty in storming and burning it, had they not been destroyed by grape and musketry at Culloden, or dispersed by the evictions that followed. But fire, that terrible Highland visitation, has twice attacked the castle, once in 1877 and again more disastrously a few years ago. On this second occasion, when a public fund was opened for its restoration, a Skye man wrote in response to the *West Highland Free Press*. All Highlanders, he said, must have sympathy with the Duke of Argyll at this time, for their ancestors had also seen their roof-trees burnt above their heads.

Johnson and Boswell came to the castle when it was still not completed, and with more deference than was justified by the Doctor's reputation or the fifth Duke's respect for it. They were driven about the parkland in "a low one-horse chair", and the grandeur of it all – tall trees and fine grass, slate-stone walls and lance-headed windows – greatly impressed Johnson. "What I admire here," he said, "is the total defiance of expense." He was also flattered thought Boswell, by an invitation to dine at the castle, and when he met the Duke he did not lecture him as he had the chief of Clan Donald on Skye, telling that anglicised baronet that he must be more Highland, that he should close the gates of his house and see that his arms did not rust. Boswell maliciously reminded the Doctor of this, and Johnson changed ground without shame. "Let us be glad we live in times when arms *may* rust. We can sit today at his Grace's table without any risk of being attacked, and

63

Moses Griffith's view of Inverarary Castle in 1771, before the old town was demolished and a new one built on the headland. Robert Mylne's beautiful arched bridge still takes traffic on the lochside road from Glasgow.

perhaps sitting down again wounded or maimed." Boswell's fear was that he himself might be snubbed by the Duchess, the beautiful and notorious Elizabeth Gunning, and although she did speak to him once, he may have wished she had not. Something he said implied a belief in second sight, whereupon she dismissed him and all such notions in seven words. "I fancy you will be a *Methodist*." Johnson was more successful, and spoke at length on the relative importance of wealth and food. "We have now," he said, introducing the subject, "a splendid dinner before us. Which of these dishes is unwholesome?"

Food indeed appears to have been a harmless topic when commoners dined with an ennobled chief of Clan Campbell. In 1803, James Hogg was also the guest of the fifth Duke, now a gentle, drowsing old man of eighty. After some initial embarrassment, having mistaken a footman for another guest, Hogg spiritedly defended his refusal to take gravy, mustard or spice with his beef, only a little salt, and he advised others to do the same if they wished to enjoy the true flavour of the meat. "By great good fortune," he wrote ponderously to Scott, "I was joined by several in this asseveration which my extremity suggested." By the end of dinner, the Duke was asleep and "the ladies were diverting themselves by throwing crumbs of cake at the gentlemen, and at one another." No one had warned Hogg to expect this, but before dining in the same room a century and a half later I was told not to be alarmed if another guest, having enjoyed his sherry, "soon drops off, with his head in his soup." He stayed awake, however, maintaining his bright Wodehouse chatter throughout the course. Catching my questioning eye, MacCailein Mor the eleventh Duke inclined his head in apology and said, "I'm sorry, but he always has before."

The Ettrick shepherd saw no tartan worn or arms carried at Inveraray. All the male guests came to dinner clothed in black like their host, and the servants were uniformed in southern livery. The somnolent old Duke may have considered Highland dress archaic, even distasteful perhaps, remembering the barbaric surge of Rebel tartan against his Campbell regiment at Culloden. And many of the yard-long, two-edged broadswords used in the last Jacobite Rising had long since been turned into railings for his house in London.

A generation later, when the yacht *Fairy* brought Victoria and her consort to Inveraray, they were met on the quayside by ribboned pipers and by local gentlemen of the Celtic Society, all dressed in belted plaid and bonnet. At the castle steps the Queen was welcomed by her future son-in-law, "just two years old, a dear, white, fat, fair little fellow with reddish hair" wearing a black velvet dress, scarf, sporran, and Highland bonnet. An honour-guard of the Celtic Society lined the room where the Queen and her husband took lunch, each gentleman with a halberd, she said, by which she no doubt meant a Lochaber axe, a limb-hewing weapon not usually associated with chilled hock and a light colla-tion. Her second visit to Inveraray, after the marriage of her daughter to Lorne, was a greater spectacle of tartan and steel. Her carriage brought her down the September gold of Glen Aray, and through the castle gates to a lime-tree avenue where she was delighted to see "halberdiers posted at intervals, dressed in Campbell tartan kilts, with brown coats turned back to red, and bonnets with a black-cock's tail and myrtle, the Campbell badge." Drawn up in welcome before the castle were the Duke's pipers, artillerymen, and members of the Argyll Volunteer Regiment in scarlet tunics and dark green tartan. On the third evening of her stay, in a great pavilion filled with tenants of the estate, Gaelic songs were sung, candle-light gleamed on silver dirks and the brass of basket-hilts, tartan swirled to the music of a Glagow band, and the Queen's daughters danced spirited reels with the Duke's foresters. Night and day throughout her visit, the kilted axe-men mounted guard in the deer-park and beneath the falling leaves of the limes.

Much of this theatrical trumpery was a loyal response to her love for what she believed to be true Highland dress and the tartans of the clans. Her faery castle home in the parkland of Deeside, across the Grampians to the east, was a picturesque temple for the ritual of her worship, and an insipid tartan designed by her husband was extravagantly displayed on its wall-furnishings, carpets and lino-leum. On a more modest scale than at Inveraray or Balmoral, the same rites and costume charades were performed in mock castles and Gothic shooting-lodges throughout the mountains where chiefs and lairds who had avoided bankruptcy, and southern incomers who owned the estates of those who had not, now dressed themselves in absurd caricatures of what had once been the simple clothing of the Gaelic people.

The wearing of tartan had become a romantic fashion shortly after the publication of *Waverley* in 1814, and to a great extent because of it. The hero of that novel, Fergus MacIvor, was based upon the preposterous and contentious chief of Glengarry, Alasdair Ranaldson MacDonell, whom Scott called his "treasure". A year after the appearance of *Waverley* this arrogant and obsessed man formed The Society of True Highlanders "in support of the Dress, Language, Music and Characteristics of our Illustrious and Ancient Race." Membership was limited to men of "birth and property", of whom ninety-six attended the inaugural meeting on a green field in Lochaber, where the Highlanders of Montrose's army had broken the power of Clan Campbell one hundred and seventy years before. Until Glengarry's death, the result of a fall from a steamer in the Caledonian Canal he had so long hated, the Society held annual gatherings to which its members came in gaudy waves of tartan, silver buttons, feathered bonnets, bright swords, dirks, powder-horns and pistols. They danced on the heather at moonlight, dined on roe-deer brought down from the hills, shouted toasts in Gaelic, and made a holy sacrament of the blood shed by their ancestors. The zenith of the Society was reached when George IV came to Edinburgh. Alasdair Ranaldson's gentlemen strutted about the city as the King's Celtic Guard of Honour, overwhelmed sceptical doubt and imposed the half-truths of a tartan mythology upon the hearts and minds of an imaginative people.

All this may now seem innocent and harmless, and the stubborn survival of that mythology today no more than a colourful expression of Scotland's pride in its past. But while these True Highlanders were play-acting their absurd dreams, the common people to whom the dress, language and music of the Gael had once been a solace and an inspiration were being driven from their mountains to exile in Upper Canada. The qualifications of birth and property which brought those ninety-six chiefs and lairds to Inverlochy would have excluded the same number of young men and women of Kildonan who took ship for Lord Selkirk's colony at that time, and the hundreds of sub-tenants already removed from Alasdair Ranaldson's own estates.

The fever of romantic emotion which tartan excited spread rapidly south of the Border, and England's affection for it increased as improved roads and a regular steamship service made the Highlands an accessible arena for the slaughter of its wild-life. Sportsmen who blazed away at almost anything that moved in the rock and heather above them, returned home with bolts of tartan cloth as well as the mounted trophies of their marksmanship. In 1834, after a shooting holiday with the Duke of Sutherland at Dunrobin, with Mr Edward Ellice M.P. in Glengarry, and with the Duchess of Bedford at Rothiemurchus, Lord Brougham called upon Mr McDougall, draper of Inverness. He ordered a great quantity of tartan in velvet and worsted for the tailoring of waistcoats, trousers, and women's dresses. Mr McDougall, said the *Inverness Courier*, "was delighted to find that his lordship knew the

A Royal lady and her servant at Balmoral, "a pretty little castle in the old Scottish style" she thought when Albert bought it for her. They turned it into something quite different, as real, perhaps, as the splendid sporran John Brown is wearing here.

various patterns of the clans." What the Lord Chancellor knew, or thought he knew, was only endearing nonsense. There is no historical evidence for a belief in clan tartans, and those bought by Lord Brougham, all that are sold and worn today, were designed a generation and more after a clan society had ceased to exist and while its bewildered people were being evicted and dispersed. In the days when it was a vibrant and sometimes terrifying reality, a clansman's familial loyalty was not demonstrated by the sett, the pattern, of his tartan but by the slogan he shouted in battle and by the plant badge he wore on his bonnet – heather for Clan Donald, bog-myrtle for the Campbells, a sprig of pine for MacGregors . . .

There were perhaps district tartans, sett and colour determined by preferential custom and by the availability of particular vegetable dyes, but the wearing of them crossed the frontiers of clan territories and clan loyalties. Highland gentlemen chose colours and patterns that pleased their vanity, no more, and early portraits show them wearing two or three setts in one costume, for plaid, jacket and hose. None of them resembles a professed clan tartan of today, and there is none to be recognised in David Morier's vivid and meticulous painting of Culloden, for which Jacobite prisoners were used as models. I am perhaps labouring the argument, but it need not end there. Separated from his command in the rain and powder-smoke of Falkirk in January, 1746, and finding himself alone among the Hanoverian army, Donald MacDonell of Tirnadris declared himself a member of its Campbell militia, a foolish pretence if he and they were wearing distinctive tartans. The same deception was attempted at Culloden by "a pretty young Highlander" who was pursued by James Ray, that brutal and unpleasant trooper of Kingston's Horse.

> (He) called out to me, Hold your hand, I'm a Campbell. On which I asked him, where's your Bonnet? He reply'd Somebody hath snatched it off my Head. I only mention this to show how we distinguished our loyal clans from the Rebels; they being dress'd and equipp'd all in one way, except the bonnet; ours having a Red or Yellow Cross of Cloth or Ribbon; theirs a White Cockade.

But fiction that serves a romantic yearning can easily replace a mundane truth. Even Neil Munro, who should perhaps have known better, believed the myth and used it dramatically. When John Splendid and young Elrigmore were fleeing from the defeat of their clan at Inverlochy they knocked at the door of a cottage in Glencoe, and asked a blind woman to shelter them for the night. They thought it wise to encourage her belief that they were friendly Appin Stewarts, but she discovered her mistake when she passed a corner of John Splendid's plaid through her fingers.

> Her face dyed crimson; she drew back her stool a little, and cried out – "That's not off a Stewart web, it was never waulked in Appin."

The Highlanders' love of tartan, the "princely cloth" extolled by Duncan Ban, was nonetheless deep and intense, as was their bitterness when the Proscription Act of 1746 forced them to darken its rich colours in vats of mud, and make breeches of their plaids. That love sustained the pride of the young men who volunteered or were pressed into the King's Highland regiments. They mutinied, and sometimes died, rather than be transferred to a Lowland battalion where they would no longer wear kilt and plaid. When the Act was repealed in 1782, Duncan Ban composed a song of praise. *"Now we are free to dress as we please ... a belted kilt in pleats ... checked and red-hued ..."* But few of the common people returned to their old costume. The clan system, of which it had once been a proud manifestation, was now broken. Old skills were lost in death, and new generations had become accustomed since boyhood to what Duncan Ban called *an droch fhasan*, the evil fashion of the Lowlander. Perhaps there was also a prideful hurt, a dignified refusal to put on their ancient dress now that an insulting mockery of it was being worn by chiefs who had abandoned them for *a'chaorach mhor*, the great, white-face from the Cheviot Hills.

On the Stirling plain and in the Border towns, weaving firms did well during the long Napoleonic wars, making uniform cloth and plaiding for tens of thousands of Highland soldiers. Peace ended these profitable contracts, but when Alasdair Ranaldson's parti-coloured harlequins came to Edinburgh, wearing tartan they said was exclusive to their name, the weavers quickly responded to the interest it excited throughout Britain and Europe, and in the Americas where plantation-owners wanted a durable and colourful cloth for their slaves. During the first decade of the 19th century the weavers' pattern-books had contained eight or a dozen setts only, identified by a predominant colour or by the name of a Highland district. Twenty years later the number had increased tenfold, and almost all were now presented as tartans of the clans.

Not surprisingly, many of them had an inspirational origin in the tartans worn by the sixty-five marching and fencible regiments raised in the Highlands during the French wars, and these were largely based upon the dark blue and green sett of the Government Tartan, first worn in 1740 by the 43rd Regiment, Black Watch. Other regiments adapted this by the addition of white, yellow or scarlet threads, and from these and other variations in colour and sett have come many of the clan patterns of today. When the 74th Argyll Highlanders were raised in 1778 they wore the Government sett crossed with yellow and white stripes, and Clan Campbell thus acquired its principal tartan. The Mackenzie tartan is also the Black Watch sett, with red and white stripes, and first worn by the 78th Seaforth Highlanders in 1778. In 1793, a manufacturer in Huntly was asked to supply plaiding for a regiment of Fencibles then being raised by the Duke of Gordon. He submitted three patterns, and the Duke chose the Government's black sett with a yellow stripe, giving future generations of his name something they could believe was the ancient tartan of their clan. Some patterns are more fortuitous in their military origin. When the fourth Duke of Atholl, chief of Clan Murray, raised a marching-regiment in 1778 its uniform clothing became the responsibility of its first-major, Hew Dalrymple. Rummaging through the Duke's closets at Blair Castle in search of a tartan that might be worn by the battalion drummers, he found one he thought was "very pretty, it has no black in it, but is composed of red, green and dark blue." No one told the Major, not the Duke and not the Duke's uncle who was lieutenant-colonel of the regiment, that what he had found was of course the ancient tartan of *Clann Mhoraidh*, but that is what it has since become.

By the year of the King's visit this order of precedence had been reversed, and it was now believed that the chiefs who raised these regiments had naturally clothed them in their own ancient tartans. The Black Watch is the only popular sett which pre-dates Culloden, and there is no contemporary evidence of its origin beyond an instruction from the Commander-in-Chief in Scotland, the road-building Anglo-Irishman George Wade, that "the plaid of each company to be as near as they can be of the same sort and colour." By 1822, however, Campbells believed it to be their tartan because many of the companies had been captained by men of their name, and the Munros maintained it was theirs because the regiment's first lieutenant-colonel was Sir Robert Munro of Foulis.

When James Logan published his *Scottish Gael* in 1831 a belief in clan tartans was so well established that he felt no obligation to justify it. His book included a pattern-table of fifty-three setts, "as many specimens as I could procure and authenticate." Despite his wide travels in the Highlands in search of information, most of these tartans were perhaps procured from Lowland weavers, and as for authentication, at least one of his advisers had been a member of the Society of True Highlanders. After the Queen made her first visit to the Highlands, Logan wrote another book, in collaboration with Robert McIan, a talented artist who shared his taste for whisky if not for quarrelsome dispute. Their *Clans of the Scottish Highlands* was dedicated "to Her Excellent Majesty who has graciously deigned to visit the country of the Clans and patronised their manufactures and costume." Although its introduction said that "accurate data will be furnished on the clan tartans" there was none in Logan's text, but McIan illustrated it with seventy-four splendidly coloured plates of Highlanders, each representative of a clan and each wearing tartan of a distinctive sett. Many of these plates may now be seen on the walls of Highland hotels, notably and perhaps properly at Lairg where the northern wasteland of Sutherland begins, and when they are still bound in their original form they may be bought from antiquarian booksellers for two thousand pounds.

Logan's preface obliquely acknowledged his indebtedness to "the recent splendid work" of another partnership, two charismatic brothers who called themselves Charles Edward and John Sobieski Stolberg Stuart. They were in fact the sons of a naval lieutenant, Thomas Allen, but appearing in Scottish society a few years after Waterloo, where they said they had fought for Napoleon, they persuaded some of its more susceptible members that their father was the legitimate son of the Young Pretender. Why that drunken and embittered exile had not acknowledged the existence of his heir was never satisfactorily explained, except by the brothers' magnanimous refusal to press their claim to the throne of Britain. Until their fashionable patrons tired of them they lived under the protection of the chief of Clan Fraser, on a timbered island in a gorge of the River Beauly where they were known as "the Princes" and where, they said, "the sun of our life rose to its meridian." Their prolific writings on the dress, arms, and traditions of the Highlands showed wide scholarship and sympathetic understanding. They wisely saw that the national costume of a dispersed people could not be restored by the "sumptuary vanity and personal caprice" of charlatans like Alasdair Ranaldson, although they never referred to him as such, being frequently his honoured guests. On the matter of clan tartans, however, they were either the victims or the originators of a forgery as bold as their claim to be descended from the most disastrous of Scotland's romantic heroes.

Their *Vestiarium Scoticum*, in which this deception was lavishly

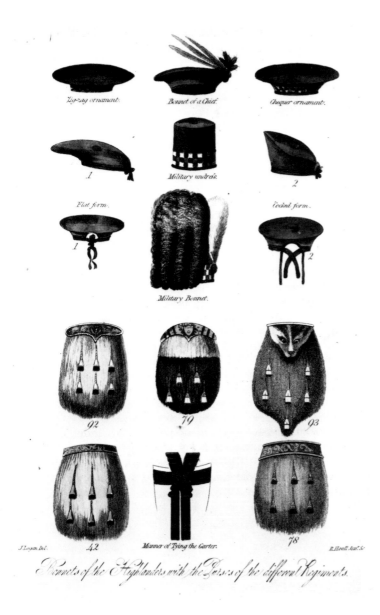

J. Logan Del.   42   Manner of Tying the Garter.   78   R. Heath. Sculpt. Se.

Bonnets of the Highlanders with the Forms of the different Regiments.

"Highland fever" and "Tartan mania" were already raging when James Logan published his *Scottish Gael* in 1831. It included this illustration of the monstrous caricatures that could be made of the Highlander's simple dress.

presented, was published in 1842, a limited edition in imperial quarto, impressively bound in red leather. The substance of it was already known in Scottish literary and historical circles, for the brothers had been writing and talking about it for more than a decade, and Scott had dismissed its evidence for the validity of clan tartans as spurious and absurd. It was allegedly drawn from a 16th-century manuscript "formerly in the Library of the Scots College at Douay" and later in the possession of the Young Pretender, from whom it had passed to the brothers as his inheritors. John Telfer Dunbar has convincingly argued* that belief in the authenticity of this manuscript and its inheritance was essential to the Sobieski Stuarts' romantic pretensions. If it did not exist they

* *History of Highland Dress*, by John Telfer Dunbar. Oliver & Boyd, 1962.

could not have inherited it, and knowledge of that deceit would have aroused doubt about the honesty of their claim to royal descent. But if one were accepted on trust, so might be the other. For this reason, perhaps, no one was allowed to see the manuscript, although John described the appearance of its vellum pages in persuasive detail. He did produce what he said was an early 18th-century version of it, and based upon this, the original, or upon patterns obtained from Lowland weavers, the *Vestiarium* contained seventy-five plates of "the terteinis apperteinand unto ye chieff Hieland clannes." No one appears to have asked why, if clan tartans were once an important part of Highland life, and almost within living memory, the only documentary evidence of them was a 18th-century copy of a manuscript written two centuries earlier.

The Douay manuscript was never produced or found, but at the end of the 19th century, after the brothers were dead, the transcript was re-discovered. It was subjected to critical examination and declared to be suspect at best, and at worst an inexpert forgery. By this time, however, the use which Logan, McIan and many others had made of the *Vestiarium*, helped by the enterprising energy of the weaving trade, had long since turned fiction into stubborn truth.

When I see red, green and blue folds of tartan moving in the wind outside a clothier's shop in Inveraray, I am as susceptible as others to its barbaric charm. It would be pleasing to remember John Ford's advice and print the legend, if only it correctly reflected the spirit of history. But I cannot forget what was truly happening in the Highlands when the chiefs and lairds, their inheritors and their shooting-guests, were placing orders with Mr McDougall in Inverness or Messrs Wilson in Bannockburn. And I know that I have been right when I have said that instead of being an enduring legacy of the old Gaelic society of the mountains, clan tartans are its shroud.

The braeside way through Ardnamurchan to Strontian, a good road
to walk when one is young. Even better to travel on an ambling
cart, in the sun of an August day.

(*Overleaf*) The Meeting of the Waters in Glencoe where Victoria took
lunch, and John Brown pursued inquisitive reporters. On the left are
the heads of The Three Sisters – Beinn Fhada, Gearr Aonach, and
Aonach Dubh. The MacDonalds hid their cattle in the high corries
between these peaks, and found bleak shelter there themselves one
February night.

The Black Mount, on the western border of Rannoch Moor, is a
horseshoe of seven majestic peaks, most of them over 3000 feet. The
names given long ago to some of its high corries, swift streams and
small lochans recall that the Glencoe people summer-herded their
stock on its gentle braes.

Glen Garry looking westward to the high ground of Knoydart. Alasdair Ranaldson leased the land on the right to the Lowland grazier Thomas Gillespie. James Hogg spent two days here with Gillespie, in a shepherd's hut and sleeping "together in a small stooped bed." The grazier became one of the richest and most successful sheepmen in the Highlands, his advice sought by impoverished or improvident lairds.

(*Overleaf*) Liathach, "the grey-headed", is the noblest of the Torridonian peaks in Wester Ross, a terraced ridge six miles in length. When the snow has melted, and the sun is high, these splendid mountains wear capes of white quartzite.

The mouth of Glencoe from Carness, seen by William Daniell in 1815. The loch is busy but the glen itself has already been converted into two large sheep-farms. Its population, according to Sarah Murray in 1803, was less than thirty. By 1840 most of these were gone, and a valley that had once been the home of five hundred of MacIain's people was now empty.

Daniell saw four ocean-going vessels anchored in the narrow trench of Loch Hourn, a magnificent entrance to the Rough Bounds, to Glen Garry and Glen Moriston. From here MacDonell gentry went by water round the Knoydart peninsula to their summer house at Inverie.

On THE NORTHERN SHORE OF LOCH
Leven in Lochaber, one hundred and
sixty-nine years ago, William Daniell drew the preliminary
sketches for his Engraving No. 104, a view of *Glen-coe taken near
Ballachulish*. He always worked quickly, for the task upon which
he was engaged was monumental, and he was perhaps long gone
before the evening shadow of Sgorr Dearg darkened the bright
grass of the MacDonalds' burial isle. The aquatint he published
five years later is a scene that comes often to my mind when I speak
of Glencoe. I have sometimes stood where he made his drawings,
on the flat peninsula of Carness and looking south-east by east to
the mouth of the glen. This green spit of land was the old ferry-
point and here on the first Monday of February, 1692, two companies of the Earl of Argyll's regiment crossed the narrows of the
loch and marched upon MacIain's people. In red coats and yellow
hose, their uplifted pikes like a moving hedge of thorn, they were
closer in time to William Daniell than we are to him. Thus may
our thoughts leap-frog through history and make the past seem
yesterday.

Unlike others who have put this valley on paper or canvas,
Daniell did not feel obliged to convey the horror of the winter
night that made it the best known of all Highland glens. It was
late summer when he came to Carness, on a tranquil afternoon of
rain-washed sunlight, I am sure. The broken cone of Stob Coire
is clean and clear against an egg-shell sky, and the low braes are
warm with the cinnamon hue of rock and heather. This was a time
before the Clearances emptied Loch Levenside, and the aquatint
is busy with commonplace life. A southerly wind unravels a tangle
of smoke where seaweed is burning. Four fishing-boats, high at
stem and stern, are drawn up ashore, and three more are pulling
across the choppy water. Six sea-going ships move through the
loch on a flood tide, making for the distant walls of the slate-quarry
which Daniell may have wished us to believe are the grey turrets
of a ruined castle. From Carness today, looking across the now
deserted loch, only the towering upthrust of mountains remains
unchanged, the scarred flank of Aonach Dubh and the skirt of

Meall Mor. But when herring-gulls wheel above the water on black-tipped wings, writing Daniell's unmistakable signature, I can also see what he saw – the red plaids of two men beside the boats, an inshore oarsman bending before his passenger, the bare masts of ships moored beyond the point, and the sun-pink sails of a heeling ketch, tacking toward the pier at Laroch.

Daniell was unique among the artists who painted the Highlands in the last century, and despite the contrived composition of some of his scenes they remain unequalled in honesty and charm. He was the son and grandson of Surrey innkeepers, and learnt his craft from his uncle Thomas who took him to India as his young assistant in 1785. The skills he acquired then were brilliantly exercised in his aquatints of the Highlands, faithful detail, evocative perspectives, the telling contrast of light and shadow. Unlike the work he did in Bengal and Oudh, their colours are delicately muted, brushed on the paper by girls who worked to his direction and were paid a few pence only for each enduring print. Daniell was forty-five when he began the eight volumes of his *Voyage round Great Britain*, and the physical strain he put upon himself would have exhausted a much younger man. At the same age, with all the comfortable advantages of modern transport and accommodation, I began my own travelling researches in the Highlands and was often tired by them. Two-thirds of the 308 illustrations in Daniell's work are of the islands and mountain coastline of western Scotland, and the sketches for most of them were drawn between May and October of one year, 1815. It was, however, an unnatural summer of continuing fine weather. Nowhere in his work are smoking mists or sheeting rain, and only occasionally the shafts of cloud-breaking sunlight that give the Highlands their moods of introspective despair. If I regret this it is because my sometimes melancholy nature is most content in such weather.

It was Daniell's original intention to observe the title of his work and travel by sea only. This became impossible in the time he set himself and he covered many painful miles by rough hill-tracks and lochside roads. With only a few exceptions, however, all of his aquatints include the grey-water waves of sea-loch and ocean. Like McIan's plates, many of them are now displayed in Highland hotels, properly enclosed in the black and gilded border designed by Daniell's friend, the London frame-maker Hogarth. At Sligachan on Skye, below the jagged teeth of Sgurr nan Gillean, there was once and may still be the largest collection I have ever seen, on the walls of the hotel lounge and best studied in idle leisure above the rim of a glass of Talisker.

There is no longer a ferry at Ballachulish, not at Carness nor half a mile westward at *Caolas Mhic Phadruig*, its more recent point and so named for the young Hebridean raider who was drowned here before the MacDonalds came to Glencoe five hundred years ago. Since 1975, Loch Leven has been crossed by an iron bridge of angular girders that was at first an affront to my eye. Time has made it familiar and from a distance, from Invercoe or Onich when it is pearl-grey or sea-green according to the light, it is only a neat

The first car to cross the narrows of Loch Leven at Ballachulish, almost seventy years ago, was lashed to the thwarts of an oared boat. Now an iron bridge has replaced the ferry, its southern span touching the hill above the road. Mature trees now mask the white stone from James Stewart's farm, marking the spot where he was hanged.

stitch across the water. No more offensive, perhaps, than the wide-beamed car-ferry which once rode the tide on a crescent of foam, clanging its successful arrival against the high rock of Sgorr Dearg. The roads from Oban, Glasgow and Fort William meet here at the narrows, and waiting for the ferry was sometimes a strain upon impatient natures. The time was best employed in computation – the number of assembled vehicles divided by each ferry-load and multiplied by the minutes needed for every crossing. The decision to be made was whether or not it would be quicker to take the land route to Appin, sixteen circling miles about Loch Leven. The bridge, now crossed in seconds, has made such arithmetic unnecessary, and the Regional highway board, as if conscious that it has been remiss – or perhaps at the prompting of tradesmen in Kinlochleven – signposts the lochside road as "the scenic route".

It is indeed a pleasant journey on a summer's day, eastward below the soaring slopes of Mamore, then westward over the shoulder of Garbh Bheinn where David Balfour and Alan Breck sheltered in a trembling hide of birch leaves. On a harsh winter night, when there is no moon and mountain mists thicken the dark, the road can be hazardous. Coming south through the Great Glen because the A9 was closed by snow on Drumochter, Raeburn Mackie arrived at North Ballachulish too late for the last ferry of the evening. He travelled by Lochlevenside, and on a sharp bend above Caolasnacoan his life ended as he drove into the back of a lorry. By that cruel accident I lost a young and pleasant friend, and Scotland a good writer from whom much was expected.

The iron of the Ballachulish bridge touches a timbered hill on the Appin shore, by a monument that marks the spot where James Stewart was hanged in 1752. And three miles westward above the Oban road, in a dark glade of pine that has replaced the old rowan Wood of Lettermore, there is a slate cairn where he was said to have shot Colin Campbell of Glenure, the Government factor whom Stevenson called the Red Fox. James Stewart's skeleton, picked clean by crows and bleached by the sun, swung on a gibbet above the narrows for more than two years until a January storm tore it from its chains. It was secretly buried by his kinsmen, but when attempts were made to throw the gallows timber into Loch Linnhe this was twice returned by the tide, first to a sandy bay on the Appin shore and then to another across the loch in Morvern, both of them named in memory of the Holy Cross. This coincidence was thought to be an awesome warning and the wood lay untouched for many months until a farmer, indifferent to superstition or Providence, removed it to build a bridge across a burn.

The Appin Murder is the most intriguing mystery in Highland history, but might have been unknown to the outside world had not Stevenson made it an essential part of one of the best novels written in English. James Stewart of the Glen, an industrious farmer of Appin and an unrepentant Jacobite, was undoubtedly a wretched sacrifice to Campbell vengeance, as much for the Appin Stewarts' involvement in the recent Rebellion as for the crime he did not commit. When he was told of the murder he himself said, "Whoever be the culprit, I'll be the victim." He was tried at an assize court in the old church of Inveraray, in the hostile environment of Campbell country and at a moment when there were fears of another Jacobite Rising. The Duke of Argyll sat on the bench as his principal judge, and eleven of the fifteen jurors were Campbell gentlemen. Innocent too, I think, was a second man named in the indictment but never caught and tried – Stewart's onetime ward, Alan Breck, a far less agreeable fellow than the swaggering blade in *Kidnapped*.

Who truly fired that murdering shot from a long Spanish gun in the Wood of Lettermore has never been determined. For a hundred years few people cared, but since Stevenson wrote his novel (*"The one I'm proud of and that I delight in"*) there has been a century of debate and conjecture. It is my belief, admittedly difficult to prove, that Red Colin was probably killed by one of two Camerons, Donald Roy and Dugald Roy MacOllonie, father and son.* Clan Cameron's hatred of Campbell of Glenure was strong,

---

* The name is spelt variously – MacOloney, MacIllonie, MacOnie and MacGillonie, from the Gaelic *Mac-Ghill-onfaidh*, the son of the servant of the storm. People of this name held land on Loch Arkaigside long before the Camerons of Lochiel became their masters.

despite the fact that his mother was a daughter of their greatest chief. They believed that he intended to remove many of them and replace them with others sympathetic to the Government. Evidence taken in Lochaber at the time of Stewart's arrest stated that there had been a Cameron plot to kill the factor, and that Dugald Roy had agreed to be its instrument. Glenure had certainly not felt at ease when riding through his cousin's land. Coming ashore from the Ballachulish ferry, and within an hour of his death, he turned in relief to his companions. "I am safe," he said, "now that I am out of my mother's country." More than this – during the bloody harrying of the glens after Culloden, Donald Roy MacOllonie had been accused of a murder that was oddly similar to the killing of Red Colin six years later. An officer of the Hanoverian militia, Munro of Culcairn, was shot from his horse in the Wood of Muick on Loch Arkaigside, in revenge, it was said, for the death of one of Donald Roy's sons. The MacOllonie was ruthlessly hunted in the mountains but never taken, although his fugitive chief, Cameron of Lochiel, appealed to him to surrender and save his clan from reprisals.

The similarities in these murders may be coincidental, but I think they can be significant. Both men were killed from a protective screen of woodland, and a braeside that made vigorous pursuit of the assassin exceedingly difficult. They were also shot at a moment when they made themselves easy targets. Munro was stationary, and Glenure had reined back his horse on the narrow path. Whether or not the MacOllonies repeated the pattern of Culcairn's murder, this time in the Wood of Lettermore where Appin Stewarts might take the blame, I am sure Stevenson used the manner of Munro's death for his fictional account of Glenure's killing. Munro was shot when he stopped his horse to speak to a woman at the roadside. In *Kidnapped*, Glenure is hit when he is halted by the sudden appearance of David Balfour. Stevenson heard many Highland tales in his boyhood at Bridge of Allan, and as a young man when he visited the western coast with his father. Stories of the Appin Murder and Culcairn's death were among those commonly told at cottage firesides, and I would like to think that when he heard them he too suspected that both killings were perhaps committed by the same man, Donald Roy MacOllonie *alias* Cameron.

As I cross the narrows and see James Stewart's monument above me, a gnarled white stone from his farm in Appin, I occasionally think of the unconscious irony in Glenure's words that day he stepped ashore from the ferry. And the irony, too, in the Camerons' continuing association with this spot. Until the bridge was built, the present Cameron of Lochiel was said to be a member of the board that operated the car-ferry, and it was the gentle custom of some habitual travellers to grumble at him when the fares rose yet again. On a grey spring morning, with rain strung like fine wire from sky to loch, the ticket-seller tapped at my car window, a white face bending in an oilskin cap. I paid the fare and added a blessing upon Lochiel. "Aye," said she in understanding, "if he had charged like this at Culloden he would have won." Good sense, I hope, prevented me from telling Lochiel this story when I met him later. He had asked Hamish to bring me to tea at Achnacarry, there was a small error in *Culloden* which he hoped I would permit him to set right. We arrived late from Corrimony, a puncture having delayed us near Fort Augustus, and the residual grease on my right hand was transferred to that of Mac-Dhomnuill-Duibh as he welcomed us in his doorway. It was an English occasion, English voices at an English tea-table, and the gentle sound of gossiping water beyond the open window. We discussed the great history of the Camerons then being written by Lochiel's brother-in-law. We examined the Jacobite relics in the old house – weapons, miniatures and faded tartan. We spoke of the Young Pretender's lost treasure, the 30,000 *louis-d'or* buried somewhere along the Loch Arkaig shore, and the men who visit Achnacarry with metal detectors, hoping to find it. We talked of the cormorant seen that week, coming inland from Knoydart to take the brown trout of the loch, and the once familiar osprey which might never come again. Throughout that languid and pleasant afternoon the grievous error in my book was courteously ignored.

I have regretted the passing of the Ballachulish ferry, and others elsewhere in the Highlands, as men may once have been saddened by the loss of the old oared boats they replaced. A rocking passage across a sea-loch, enclosed in the capsule of a car, added much to the pleasures of travel, the wide sweep against the pull of the tide, the throb and smell of complaining engines, the ring of falling platforms echoing against the hills. Few of them now remain. To Skye from Lochalsh, of course, but there is always talk of the bridge to be built there, spanning the tidal race where Haakon the Norse king sailed southward to defeat at Largs, and where Daniell drew the sketches for a spirited aquatint. There is still a crossing at Corran, over Loch Linnhe to Ardgour, an exhilarating experience when the wind is stiff and the tide flows strongly. But a bridge has now replaced the Kessock ferry over the Beauly Firth to the Black Isle, and in Wester Ross, twelve years ago, a fine new road was cut along the eastern shore of Loch Carron, bringing an end to the crossing at Strome.

This was always a beautiful journey, dark water in the shadow of the twin hills that guard the narrows, a solacing climax to the long drive from Inverness. In the 18th century the loch-shore was thickly-populated, black with dry-stone cottages, green and yellow with good fields of grain. The water was famous for its shoals of herring, so plentiful, said John Knox, that they "tumbled upon the surface, and others leaped fairly out to the distance of two or three yards." His companion fired at them with lug-shot, "but we knew not with what effect." James Hogg came to Strome in 1803, on a Sunday morning in June, having travelled eleven miles over the high pass from Kintail before breakfast. He stood angrily on the southern shore, shouting and waving his hat until the ferryman came over and agreed to take him for sixpence and a dram of whisky. Sixteen years later, when Thomas Telford finished his

James Hogg's reputation as a writer still suffers from the sometimes diminishing nickname "The Ettrick Shepherd", but he was himself not above encouraging the condescension of those who thought themselves his betters. He made three tours of the Highlands, during which he wrote vivid letters to his friend Scott. At the end he swore "never more to take another journey, of such a nature, at my own expense."

highway along the western shore, the ferry became the busiest in the western Highlands, linking Inverness and Dingwall with Lochalsh and the Isles. Telford's friend, Robert Southey, travelled along this new road within a few days of its completion and was delighted to discover that his carriage was the first to reach the ferry at Strome. It was my hope to put my car on the last boat to make the crossing, but when I arrived, coming through the pass at Achnashellach to a wondrous sunset, I found the eastern road already open and the ferry-boat moored and idle. Later that year, when I came again, the boat was gone and the only movement offshore was a lone shag, straight-necked and black above the water, direct in flight and hurrying seaward to its evening rest on a rock-island beyond the narrows.

I stayed at the Ballachulish Hotel in the last days before the bridge was opened. We were filming in Glen Etive, the final location sequences for *John Macnab*. Every evening in the residents' lounge the director played traditional jazz, and the assistant floor-manager danced in bare feet. The public bar was full, a noisy wake for the dying car-ferry, and the centre of it was an aged boat-master in peaked cap and reefer jacket. He had spent a lifetime on *Caolas Mhic Phàdruig*, backward and forward, to and fro in all weathers, countless voyages of five minutes duration. But as the hour became later, noisier and more maudlin, it was easy to believe, with help from The Glenlivet, that a great deep-water sailor had come home from the sea.

Until the building of the railway, Telford's road to the northern shore of the ferry at Strome was a vital link between Inverness, the West and the Isles. Now a new road on south Loch Carronside has closed this car-ferry.

A crewman of the Ballachulish ferry once helped me with my researches for *Glencoe*. He lived at Laroch, in a cottage by the abandoned slate quarry and below the tall cones of debris which cover the dead of a great battle fought long ago between invading Norsemen and the Gaels. The blue slate of Ballachulish was used for Argyll's mock castle at Inveraray, and its tiles still cover the roofs of Edinburgh's New Town. It was cut into smooth slabs to make headstones for the walled grave-yards of the Highlands, and because it resists moss, does not corrode or crumble, the inscriptions on them are sometimes as clean and deep as the day they were carved. Because of this they have often supplemented or added another dimension to information I have found in the manuscript archives of Register House or the National Library. There is a Clan Fraser burial-ground on the eastern shore of Loch Ness, not far from the high ground where patient men sometimes encamp with orange fly-tents, tape recorders, telescopes and trip-cameras. They wait for the appearance of a monster which surely could not have the impudence to show itself, not since Saint Columba drove it back into the loch fourteen hundred years ago, with the Sign of the Cross and a stentorian warning, *"Think not to go further ...!"* Within a decaying vault of the burial-ground lies a man who died early in the last century, advanced in age, graced with honours and greatly esteemed. A week before I found his neglected grave, at that time almost hidden by a loving growth of birch and rowan, I had been reading about him in a memoir of the last Jacobite Rebellion. On April 16, 1746, he and his friends played truant from their tutor at Petty. They climbed to the spine of Culloden Moor, hid themselves in the wet heather and watched as their fathers and the men of their clans charged into the smoke of cannon and musketry.

I had been told that the ferryman of Ballachulish had a small boat and would willingly row me out to Eilean Mhunna. This is the largest of a cluster of green islands in Loch Leven, a burial-ground once shared by the MacDonalds of Glencoe and the Camerons of Callart. Some of the stones of an oratory built by Saint Mundus in the 7th century are still there, and also the broken walls of the MacDonald grave-yard where the slaughtered MacIain and his wife were buried by their sons. The ferryman was at his mid-day meal when I called, and he agreed to row me out to the isle if I would first help him to bale out his boat. We did so in the cold sunshine of the spring afternoon, with sea-pie foraging in the shallows a few yards away, high-stepping on long pink legs. The ferryman was a Gaelic-speaker. His family had lived on Lochlevenside for generations and he was much attached to it and its past, although he cared little for the Massacre, believing its importance exaggerated by people living outwith the district. It was he who first directed my attention to Carness as the site of the old ferry. He said it was still used "not long ago", in the Highland way of meaning yester-year or a century since. And perhaps it was, but a map in my 18th-century copy of *The Trial of James Stewart* indicates that by 1752 boats were already crossing the narrows at

Caolas Mhic Phàdruig. We were joined at the baling by the ferry-man's daughter, a child of twelve or less. As we talked of the past – fishing, farming, and stalking, and kinsmen lost in two terrible wars – she sang Beatle songs and cupped the water in white hands studded with scarlet nail-varnish. No doubt she is long gone from her ancestors' land. The seductive appeal of southern society draws young people from the Highlands, and although it is said that they come back in wistful middle-age, I doubt if it is often true.

Of the many visits I paid to Glencoe, the longest was for three weeks. I spent some of the time walking on the braes above the old road, and I went again to the ruins of MacIain's summer house in Gleann-leac-na-muidhe. But often I sat for hours watching the valley's changing moods, the sunlight that breaks through the cloud and floods the wall of Aonach Eagach with shimmering gold, the grey plaids of moving mist on the shoulders of the Three Sisters, the blue and silent dusk that joins day to night. I ate cheese and bread on a rock by the Meeting of the Waters, peat-brown foam and waves of black metal. Victoria had lunched here ninety years before and been much put out to discover that "impudently inquisitive reporters" were watching her through telescopes. John Brown was sent to disperse them, which he did with strong words and a willingness to use his fists, but their presence quite spoilt the Queen's day. "Such conduct," she told her diary, "ought to be made known." She had the customary feeling of horror Glencoe is supposed to inspire, but I have never found it oppressive, perhaps because I became its familiar friend and felt some of the love it once inspired in its vanished people. In winter, it is true, it can become a roaring funnel for cruel winds and driving snow.

Early morning on Loch Leven, and the unmistakable hill that guards the entrance to Glencoe – the Pap of Glencoe, Sgur na Ciche, the Corrynakiegh of *Kidnapped*.

It once pleased the Picture Editor of the Scottish *Daily Express* to have me photographed there, toward dusk in February and on the anniversary of the Massacre. Nature obliged with a sudden squall of snow and sleet, and neither I nor the cameraman (a Glasgow man with a Highland name, of course) could endure more than three minutes outside the warmth of the car. But in summer I can understand the 17th-century traveller who said the valley was "a garden enclosed", and another who discovered that it was "fertile, plenteous of corn, milk and butter." I have tried to ignore the broad road that brings traffic from the south, and imagine the years when Loch Leven was white with the silver scales of herring, when there were abundant trout in the little loch by Achtriachtan, red deer coming down from the high braes, and wild flowers where caravans are now parked at Achnacone.

I was told at the Kingshouse Inn that Mr MacDonald in Glen Orchy was a descendant of MacIain's people, and that he possessed an ancient account of the Massacre, as well as knowing much folklore as yet unpublished. My informant was not certain where he lived, but it was in Glen Orchy to be sure, and a patient man like myself would have no difficulty in finding him, if not today then tomorrow, or the day after, perhaps.

I drove by Rannoch to Bridge of Orchy and south-westward through the glen, on a winding single-track that idles for fourteen miles over and about the hummocked earth, or beside the oak and ash that shadow its white-stoned river. I called at farm by farm and at each I was told that Mr MacDonald lived in the glen, but not there. Two hundred years before, Thomas Pennant had travelled along this same road, looking for a blacksmith called MacNab whose family had lived in Glen Orchy since 1440, when they wrought much of the iron used to build the Campbell castle on Loch Awe. Pennant found MacNab, as I at last found Mr MacDonald, a short, sharp-eyed man in shirt sleeves. He invited me in to take a dram with him and promised that when we had finished it, and perhaps another, and any conversation we might have while passing the time so agreeably, he would show me the desired account of the Massacre. And so, at last, he did, a pamphlet published by the National Trust for Scotland and prepared by my lamented friend Iain Cameron Taylor. I think Mr MacDonald may now be dead, but if he is not I hope he continues to commemorate the anniversary of the Massacre in his individual way. It is the custom for the Episcopalian minister of the parish to hold a morning service at Invercoe on the thirteenth day of February, after which there is a laying of wreaths below the cross that inaccurately marks "the site of the Massacre". Mr MacDonald and a few close friends, however, were usually there long before this, at midnight with a hand's-clasp of fresh flowers and a bottle of whisky. They stayed until the whisky was gone and then made their several ways homeward, in the dark and in the cold.

Loch Leven and the entrance to Glencoe are at the southern end of Glen Mor, the Great Glen sometimes called Glen Albyn, a long trench from sea to sea, dividing the northern Highlands historic-

Glen Orchy's swift torrent on a dour day. Here Thomas Pennant came looking for a family of ironworkers and two centuries later I searched for "a direct descendant of the MacDonalds of Glencoe."

ally as well as geologically. Looking at a map, it can be seen how the land-mass to the north-west shifted in some timeless moment, like the palm of one hand drawn across another. The Great Glen is thus a fault, a curious term when taken literally, as if geologists believe that the earth should have a proper balance and symmetry, and where it does not Providence has faltered. The countless millennia during which the Great Glen was formed, the terrible noise, burning colour and boiling rock, are incomprehensible, but there are times in the stillness of a storm above the mountains of the Monadhliath, or the blue peaks of Kintail, when it is possible to believe that the great convulsion of Creation has only paused, and will shortly continue its meaningless frenzy. Until the beginning of the last century the high ground of Knoydart and Morvern to the north-west of the glen was still known as *Garbhchriochan*, the Rough Bounds, a wild, inaccessible and sometimes inhospitable land. Those few travellers who entered it cursed it for breaking the wheels of their carriages or the legs of their saddle-horses. Even when its Gaelic people were gone to the slums of Glasgow or the emigrant ships at Isle Ornsay its new owners – brewers, drapers, lordlings and gentry from the south – visited their playgrounds by water, by side-wheel steamers to Loch Aline, Sunart and Loch Hourn. The stones and slate, bricks and sand, furnishings, furniture and food for the grand houses they built also came by sea, and in the high glens of the Rough Bounds the sheep which made all this possible now grazed above the deserted townships and the abandoned drove road through Glen Geal to Strontian.

Glen Mor, the Great Glen, a natural fault dividing the Highlands historically as well as geographically. From Laggan Locks in the foreground, Telford's Canal moves over the flat ground to the Laggan Swingbridge and Loch Oich. Here Glengarry fought his long battle with the canal-builders, claiming he alone had the navigation rights on Loch Oich.

Thomas Telford, the engineer whose mind and energies were challenged by the remote Highlands and the need to open them to the South. "If the Government will only grant me £1,000,000 to improve Scotland, or rather promote the general prosperity and welfare of the Empire, all will be quite well." And all was, although it cost a good deal more.

Thos. Telford

I am glad I was able to see the Great Glen when it was still a busy waterway, when white-decked steamers from Oban and black trawlers from Peterhead passed lock by loch along Telford's canal. He began this engineering marvel in 1804 but the original inspiration was not his. Thirty years earlier, James Watt had surveyed the glen and made the first proposals for a system of canals that would link its four lochs and join the North Sea to the Atlantic. By such a highway, it was said, sailing-ships would avoid the storm-hazards of the long north-about voyage by Cape Wrath, but before the canal was finished the coming of steam had eased many of the dangers of that passage. Even so the venture prospered, and was the greatest engineering achievement in Scotland until Thomas Bouch built his calamitous railway bridge across the Firth of Tay.

Telford's malicious incubus during the building of the canal, and one he prayed God and the Government to remove from his

shoulder, was Alasdair Ranaldson MacDonell of Glengarry. Perhaps I write too much about this anachronistic clown, and I know that there are members of the Clan Donald Society who would agree. When I wished to reproduce Dighton's vivid pencil sketch of Glengarry, as an illustration in *Mutiny*, the Society's representative in Edinburgh refused me permission to use the original it holds on loan, informing me that I had denigrated him enough. It would be hard to improve upon the theatrical caricature he himself created, particularly when he posed for Henry Raeburn's superb portrait. He was a handsome but mock warrior obsessed with dreams of glory, although his regimental career was a comic disaster and it was his agreeable brother who became a hero at Waterloo. Had his wish to have been born two generations earlier been granted, his contemporaries would still have thought him insufferably bizarre. He lived as he believed they had lived, dressed in a fanciful elaboration of their costume, strapped about with fearsome arms, and always accompanied by a tail of body-servants in equally absurd dress. Although he evicted his clansmen to find the money to support his melodramatic way of life, he was angered when they emigrated. He tried to stop them, and was denounced by Burns who called him a tyrant for preventing their escape from slavery. He made a misery of Telford's hard-working days, raiding the Canal Company's saw-pits and brick-stores, threatening the workmen with his terrible anger. When the Commissioners rightly accused him of stealing their timber, he told them that a Highland-man had different notions of property (meaning theirs, not his), and when brought to court in expensive actions that further ruined him he defended himself by saying that not only was a Highlander naturally generous and brave, he was an enemy to all oppression. It was such braggadocio, perhaps, that persuaded Scott to think of him as a treasure. Bitter and angry, Telford saw MacDonell and his ilk in a different light. Highland landlords, he said, were the most rapacious in Europe.

Thomas Bouch's rail bridge over the Tay was a brief triumph of engineering until its high girders, a train and 75 passengers fell into the river during the Great Storm of 1879. Bouch was declared culpable and he shortly died. In 1955 his grandson told me that when he was a child his parents would not speak of his grandfather or the Tay Bridge Disaster.

All that is left of Alasdair Ranaldson now, beyond the Clan Donald Society's jealous concern for his memory and my repeated denigration of it, is the ridiculous Glengarry bonnet he designed. When he was buried, fittingly in a Wagnerian thunderstorm, his wake was renowned. One hundred and fifty members of his True Society came to Invergarry for the funeral meats, shouting his slogan as they raised their glasses to his yellow standard, below candles stuck in the white skulls of the stags he had killed, sometimes with his dirk. Outside in the rain, bread and cheese and whisky were given to fifteen hundred people of his clan, most of whom would be evicted within two decades. "Many of his faults," said the *Inverness Courier* in a generous obituary, "were traceable to he having been left, like Byron, without a strong guiding hand in youth." The blind bard of Glengarry, Ailean Dall MacDougall, spoke a more grieving valediction in the storm, *"Blessed the corpse the rain falls on ..."* It is impossible not to see some irony in that, for Ailean Dall had earlier composed a bitter threnody for those whom his chief and others were driving from their homes.

> A cross has been placed upon us in Scotland.
> Poor men are naked beneath it.
> Without food, without money, without pasture,
> the North is utterly destroyed.

Alasdair Ranaldson's profligacy had squandered his inheritance, and to pay his debts his son Aeneas kept the lands of Knoydart in his possession but divided the rest of his estate, more than 100,000 acres, into three parcels and sold them for £198,150. The grazing was offered on lease to Border sheepmen, and while all these arrangements were being concluded by Aeneas MacDonell's agents they were also issuing Writs of Eviction against the encumbering people of his clan. That same year, he too became an emigrant, but not crowded into a coffin brig in the Sound of Sleat, with three square feet on a lower deck for himself and each of his family, and already in debt to the master for food and water. He left for New South Wales in style, with his wife and child, his piper and his servants, clothing, bedding and bolts of tartan, furniture, agricultural tools and a number of prefabricated timber houses. "We cannot regard this expatriation of the head of an old Highland family," said the *Inverness Courier*, "without some regret and emotion."

The new owners of the Glengarry estates were Edward Ellice, M.P., Lord Abinger, an aged opponent of the Reform Bill, and Lord Ward, a young man so affected by his novel lairdship that he dressed himself in kilt, plaid and feathered bonnet when he visited it. Between them, for their pleasure and expected profit, they had acquired a sad and beautiful land, sadder still for the departing of a people who had lived here for a thousand years. Although afforestation and a hydro-electric scheme have altered its appearance, it still moves the heart. The new road to Kintail and Skye now passes through it from Invergarry in the Great Glen,

"That hot-headed, weak young man ... composed of vanity and folly." A contemporary's opinion of Alasdair Ranaldson MacDonell of Glengarry, here dressed for the King's visit in 1822 and vividly caught by Denis Dighton's pencil.

climbing above its lochs to the brown head of Meall-leac-ulaidh where I once watched a party of English visitors toasting the majesty of the view with gin-and-tonic. Nine hundred feet below the summit of the road, in the benevolent sunlight of a clear day, the green valley stretches westward from the Great Glen, by Loch Garry's timbered banks to Loch Quoich in its blue bowl of mountains, over the high pass to Glen Barrisdale and the Knoydart shore. The lower valley, where a river thread joins the sapphires of the lochs, was once rich with oak trees, so plentiful that they were known as "the weed of the country". Most of them are now gone, but in spring, when the green powder of their leaves lightly dusts the sombre face of the forestry plantations, there is a brief and wondrous reminder of their lost greatness.

Edward Ellice paid twenty-one shillings and fourpence for each of the 30,000 acres of his Glen Quoich parcel. Within three years of the day he took possession of the Lodge at the foot of Gleoulaich, his guests had slaughtered four thousand game birds, a thousand hares and more than two hundred deer. The Game Book at the Lodge also recorded the "vermin" it had been thought necessary to destroy before a buyer would take the estate – fifteen golden eagles, forty-eight otters, one hundred and ninety-eight wildcats and more than a thousand hawks, as well as ravens, badgers, martens and foxes. The chiefs of Glengarry had worn an eagle feather in their bonnets, and *Creagan-an-Fhithich!*, the Raven's Rock, was the war-cry shouted by their clan. All these creatures now regarded as vermin had once been part of the subtle and colourful mythology of the Gaelic people, but they too had become incompatible with the grazing of sheep and the sporting pursuit of game.

In his Visitors' Book, Mr Ellice's distinguished guests recorded their reason for accepting his hospitality and their reactions to the country about them. Although Richard Cobden called it "a dreary glen, into which gas or other modern improvements have failed to penetrate", and the Marquis of Dalhousie wrote in horror of "hills white, loch black, wind howling like a whole legion of demons", most of the visitors were euphoric in approval. They had come *"for pleasure . . . for peace and quietness . . . idleness and good company . . . to find the heart of the Highlands . . . the key of the Highlands . . . to see Glengarrie her nain-sel . . ."* When they left, they wrote valedictions in execrable verse, or mocked themselves with heavy jocularity. For no understandable reason now, John Delane the great editor of *The Times* described himself as "a physician extraordinary", and in the column reserved for *Complaints* he laboured through a remarkably bad pun.

> That my Hart is in the Highlands (Mr Delane
> was very unfortunate with the stags, on three
> occasions he always left his Hart on the Hills)*

None of the guests who stayed in the mountain cup of Glen Quoich, and at other estates of the new proprietors, can have been unaware that the peace and quietness they so much enjoyed had been made possible by the removal of the native peoples. It cannot be thought that John Delane, agreeably housed at the Lodge or pursuing his hart below the fluted escarpment of Gairich, did not once remind himself that the recent clearances in Glengarry had been as bitter as the evictions in Easter Ross ten years earlier, during which *The Times* had intervened as the champion of justice and humanity. Delane sent a special correspondent to report them, and published the dispatch which that angry journalist wrote from the inn at Ardgay. After a long and harrowing account of the eviction of the Glencalvie people, and a declaration that the destitution which followed all such removals was the result of "a cold, calculating heartlessness which is almost as incredible as it is disgusting", the correspondent quoted a letter he had received from a minister of the Free Kirk.

* This and other quotations from the Visitors' Book and Game Book are taken from *Place-names of Glengarry and Glenquoich*, a rare and illuminating book by Edward C. Ellice, published fifty years ago.

Nothing short of a visit to this quarter and conversation with the poor creatures themselves could give an idea of the misery and wretchedness to which the people of this parish are reduced by the heartless and cruel tyranny of their oppressors. Here there is a kind of slavery ten times worse than that which for so long disgraced Britain.

I once found a more agreeable Visitors' Book in a small fishing hotel near Whitebridge, where the meandering military road climbs up from Foyers. It stood by a river bend and several small lochs, above the pleated wilderness of the Glendoe Forest and the brown, immobile waves of the Monadhliath. This was more than twenty years ago, and the hotel is undoubtedly changed now, but when I stopped there for an hour it was held in a curious limbo between present and past. The leather on its old chairs was worn and split, and the yellowing curtains at its windows buzzed with trapped flies. A stuffed wildcat snarled in a dusty corner, and varnished fish of prodigious size hung in glass boxes that lined a corridor leading to the source of a pervasive smell of boiled cabbage. As I waited for my coffee I read the Visitors' Book. It lay open on a table near the door, by an oriental vase filled with horned walking-sticks and green umbrellas. The entries began in the last century, a seasonal record of the kills made in loch and stream, each with date and place meticulously recorded, and some-times with the sportsmen's laconic comments on the weather, their good or bad fortune that day. On August 4, 1914, two words only were written, perhaps by the landlord or by a hurriedly departing guest – *War declared*. There was no further entry until 1919.

The road outside the hotel is one of the earliest built in the Highlands, thirty miles from Inverness to Fort Augustus. It was cut by General Wade two and a half centuries ago and it is perhaps his monument, and a memorial, too, for the hundreds of soldiers and drafted Highlandmen who laboured on it. They worked from April to October in the rain and heat, tormented by midges, drinking and fighting, cursing God and their petty masters. For much of its length, one fork of the road is direct and straight like a sergeant's halberd, along the shore of the loch from Dores to Foyers, where it then climbs into the hills, to the whispering brown grass of Stratherrick. Here it ripples over the uneasy earth for eight miles until it curls by Loch Tarff and comes down through the narrow green decline of Glen Doe to Fort Augustus. If there is no need for haste, as there should never be in the Highlands, it is the best road to take by Loch Ness, with a thought for Wade's men who built it in the dust and mud, and sometimes roasted oxen whole to honour their general when he visited them in his old brown coach.

But for this military road the pacification of the Highlands after Culloden might have been more difficult and thus, perhaps, less terrible. Four weeks after the battle, the advance guard of Cumber-land's Army, three battalions of infantry and eight companies of Campbell levies, left Inverness and reached Fort Augustus in two days. A week later they were followed by the rest of the Army, eight more battalions in faded scarlet and white pipe-clay, marching briskly along Wade's road by tap of drum and the thin fluting of fifes. At Fort Augustus, an uninhabitable ruin since the Rebels destroyed it, they entered a strange and threatening land. At first there was little to cheer them when they set up their tented lines beside the River Oich, on a flat meadow that later became a golf course. "The mountains," wrote Private Michael Hughes of the Buffs, "are as high and frightful as the Alps in Spain, so we had nothing pleasant to behold but the sky. 'Tis rainy, cold and sharp weather." He and his companions watched as the Campbells "made a pretty place for the Duke to reside in, with handsome green walls, a fine hut with doors and glass windows, covered at the top with green sods or boughs, so that His Royal Highness resembled a Shepherd's life more than that of a courtier." Flushed with the glory of his decisive victory, and the ease with which he had entered the heart of the Highlands, Cumberland called Fort Augustus "this diamond in the midst of hell." The hell was of his creation. The Army stayed there for six weeks, and in that time the whole of Lochaber and much of Badenoch was laid waste, and the back of the clan system was broken for ever. "For the space of fifty miles," said Hughes, "neither house, man, nor beast was to be seen." And a junior officer told a friend in Northumbria that "We hang or shoot everyone that is known to conceal [the Pretender], burn their houses and take their cattle, of which we have got 8,000 within these few days."

It is easy to see the British soldier as an inhuman beast in the sad story of Culloden, and there are witnesses enough to his savagery in the dusk of that afternoon. But it is not always realised that he was as much brutalised by his superiors as he was brutal in the execution of the orders they gave him, and the Age of Reason that employed him was not an age of compassion. There was none the less a human being inside his red coat, and often a thinking mind beneath his black three-cornered hat. Men like Michael Hughes, Alexander Taylor of the 21st, Enoch Bradshaw of Cobham's Horse, and other common soldiers who put their halting thoughts on paper, helped me, I hope, to see and write of the battle with sympathy and concern for the ordinary men of both sides. I have been a private soldier in the ranks of a victorious and occupying army, among a defeated and demoralised people. I think I understand something of the elation, self-pride and arrogance of Cumberland's men at Fort Augustus. And more – the weariness, shame and disgust that can disturb a soldier's sleep after his war is won.

South-westward from Loch Ness to Fort William, George Wade's road is now covered by a modern highway, twenty-two miles by the water of Loch Lochy and a brooding council of seven mountains dominated by Ben Nevis. Now that Ballachulish is becoming more pleasing to the eye, its slate cones planted with trees and grass, Fort William is the ugliest town in the Highlands, and grows worse as a dribble of Teasmade hotels moves down the shore of Loch Linnhe. Its car-park, built out into the loch, threatens to become as large as the town itself. On its central street,

its only true thoroughfare, there is a small sloping square and a museum where relics of Jacobite hagiolatry are preserved in the amber of lingering regret. The rest of the town, in summer at least, is a crowded lodging-house and depressing bazaar for the tourists upon whom it must increasingly depend. It was its misfortune that at the close of the 18th century no ducal overlord or Fishery Board thought it as worthy of Improvement as Inveraray, Loch-gilphead or Ullapool, and the industrial transfusions of recent years have given it neither spirit nor dignity, whatever they have or have not done to staunch the bleeding of Highland economy. As I remember it forty-six years ago, it was then a more pleasant place, but perhaps I am wrong. When Victoria drove through it in 1873, to go aboard the smart little steamer placed at her disposal by Donald Cameron of Lochiel, she thought it "very dirty, with a very poor population". But she was in a romantic mood, inspired by the beauty and history of Lochaber, "which I am proud to call my own ... for Stewart blood is in my veins, and I am *now* their representative." She was right, of course, but it is a pity her words make Cumberland's dragonnade seem like a civilised Deed of Conveyance.

The town was once called Maryburgh, a mud and timber, fever-soaked village on the western approach to the 17th-century fort. When the Government sold this decayed stronghold to the West Highland Railway in the last century it was dismantled to make way for the waterside line to the station and pier. The gateway, however, was rebuilt at the entrance to the town cemetery where

General Wade's road-making soldiers built forty bridges like this one at Whitebridge above Loch Ness. They were paid six pence a day extra, and the money was brought on horseback from the Royal Bank in Edinburgh.

it still stands. The choice of the new site was perhaps no more than sensible economy on the part of the town council, but it was also peculiarly appropriate. The star-shaped fort of stone and timber at the mouth of the River Nevis was once a miserable pit of sickness and death. Fever, flux and despair winnowed its successive garrisons, and every week in winter, in the mist-rotting days of spring, burial parties slow-marched from the gateway of the fort, by muffled drum to the old grave-yard now covered by much of that expansive car-park.

The continuous wasting of his command greatly distressed Colonel John Hill, the English Governor of Lochaber during the last decade of the 17th century, even though he thought his soldiers were mostly an undisciplined mob of rogues. He came here first in 1654, a major of a Cromwellian regiment, with instructions to build a fort and keep the clans at peace. He did so with firmness, fairness and understanding, and was respected by the Highlanders. Six years later, at the Restoration, he surrendered his keys to Ewen Cameron of Lochiel, and when he was gone from Lochaber the Highlanders razed his fort stone by stone and burnt its timber. Had that been the end of his association with the Highlands he would have been no more than a footnote to their history, but after the Revolution of 1688, when he was living at the door of poverty in Ulster, he was given a commission to rebuild the garrison fort of Inverlochy and become Lochaber's governor once more. He accepted the post with enthusiasm, believing that the Revolution had affirmed the libertarian principles for which he had fought in his youth. His masters in Edinburgh and London neglected and betrayed him. They ignored his good advice and rarely sent him the recruits, supplies and medicines he urgently needed. In his green-painted room at the fort, the panels of which are preserved in the town's museum, he strove to serve his conscience as much as Crown and Government. This is an enduring and labyrinthine problem for honest public servants, as it sometimes is for the private citizens they are presumed to serve. In the end, John Hill's conscience surrendered to what he believed to be a soldier's inexorable duty, obedience to orders given him. After a week of evasion and inaction, he at last accepted the terrible instructions he had received by the King's command. He signed the order which sent Argyll soldiers to murder his friend MacIain and the people of Glencoe.

It has been the belief of some writers that Hill was as much the villain of the Massacre as Sir John Dalrymple, the Secretary of State for Scotland who planned the extirpation of the MacDonalds. At one time I would have agreed, but piecing his life and character together from letters scattered through a dozen manuscript sources I came to understand him, and see him as the truly tragic figure of the story.

In most of the books I have written on Scotland there has been one man, and sometimes two, to whom I have responded in the same way. They were victims of circumstance and duty, and of their own natures as much as the events which briefly controlled them. Like John Hill, William Paterson was a shadowy figure for much of his life. His dream of a Scots colony on Darien, a great entrepôt that would be "the door of the seas, the key of the Universe" ended in a shattering disaster for his country, forcing it to accept the Treaty of Union. It robbed him of public respect for many years, but more than this – it took from him his wife and children, whose graves are somewhere on the mangrove shore of Caledonia Bay in Panama. Sir James Oughton, the commander-in-chief in Scotland in 1778, was a rare man, if not unique, an English officer with respect and affection for the clans whom he had faced at Culloden. So great was his willingness to understand and help them, albeit influenced by the persuasive fiction of *Ossian*, that he diligently studied Gaelic. But the four mutinies of Highland regiments in his command brought upon him the successive strokes that killed him, and before he died he rationalised his disillusion by concluding that the Highlanders were intractable, ungrateful, and beyond the tolerance of civilised men. In a more eccentric frame there was also Thomas Mulock, an obsessed Irish journalist and besotted father of Mrs Craik, the author of *John Halifax, Gentleman*, "a very celebrated writer, kind and obedient to me, and worthy of every respect and honour." Mulock came to the Highlands in 1849, and with the cry of "Justice to Scotland!" he edited the little *Inverness Advertiser* in defence of the victims of the Clearances, and against the landed establishment. The great magnates he attacked, principally the second Duke of Sutherland, eventually broke him, and brought him to his knees in abject apology. He was not well-served by life, or by his temperament, and was sometimes foolish in his response to misfortune, but he did not deserve the valediction he was given by Donald MacLeod, the stone-mason of Strathnaver. MacLeod was also a tragic figure whose fight to expose the iniquities of the Clearances brought him grief, poverty and bitter exile. He said Mulock had been bought by the Duke of Sutherland. It was possibly true, but that should not diminish the courage of Mulock's brief but honest fight against injustice.

There is no memorial to John Hill in Fort William, and the town today is a poor place in which to remember him. I tried hard in many months to find some personal details that would widen my knowledge of him – his birthplace, the life he left when he went to fight for Parliament against the Crown, an English grave-yard where he is buried. But beyond the fact that he had two dependent daughters, whose welfare troubled him during his last years, I found nothing. It was his daily custom at Fort William to stand upon its battlements, looking down the wide stretch of Loch Linnhe between the dark walls of Ardgour and Mamore, waiting for the supply ships that so rarely came in answer to his appeals. The loch is now summer-white with other sails, the pleasure yachts of an age that would astonish and perhaps sadden him. A wide highway curls from a roundabout across his parade-ground, and the windows of a police-station look over the vanished grave-yard of his forgotten soldiers.

On Tuesday, the ninth day of November, 1948, seven men of Knoydart boldly challenged the property rights of their absentee landlord, Arthur Ronald Nall Nall-Cain – second Baron Brocket of Brocket Hall in Hertfordshire and other estates in England and Ireland, a Knight of Justice of the Order of Saint John and the patron of six livings, past-president of the National Sheep Breeders' Association, chairman or director of several companies including breweries, one time host to Joachim von Ribbentrop in the Glen of the Dark Pool, and an honoured guest at Adolf Hitler's birthday celebrations in the year of Munich.

The desperate action of these men was a human response to the realisation that Lord Brocket was determined upon further reduction of the stock and crofters' holdings on his sporting estate, one of the finest for salmon and deer in the Western Highlands. Its population, already diminished a year before by the reluctant departure of fifteen families, was now little more than fifty men, women and children, most of them dependent upon Brocket for employment and housing. In 1810, fifteen hundred of Alasdair Ranaldson's tenants had lived on this beautiful peninsula of the Rough Bounds, between the mountain-dark waters of Loch Nevis and Loch Hourn. His lordship was seemingly ignorant of this, for when coming events brought him unwelcome publicity he told reporters that the frequency of rain made it an unsuitable place for too many people. With that considerate thought in mind, perhaps, he had successfully opposed a development plan for the idle acres of his estate, by which there could have been an increase in its population and in the production of foodstuffs essential to a struggling nation. The Knoydart people's consequent petition to the Secretary of State for Scotland had also been ineffectual, and now they decided to make their misfortune known beyond the Great Glen and the Borders. That Tuesday morning each man marked out sixty acres of the estate for his own use, and as they scythed these chosen plots they planned the seizure of more land for hill-grazing on the higher braes of Choineachain.

Their little raid followed a pattern set by the Land League

The Knoydart land-raiders reading the interdicts. Three are wearing battledress, tunic or trousers, and one a 14th Army bush-hat. "We would have been far better to do as the old boys in the olden days did, stick on the ground until they put you to gaol."

Father Colin MacPherson spoke for the raiders, publicly and at a Court of Enquiry. Knoydart has been fortunate in its Catholic priests. Twice in the last century they defended their parishioners, and one went with them into Canadian exile.

seventy years before when brave and successful efforts were made to secure some legal protection for crofters, and thereby stem the continuing haemorrhage of eviction and emigration. It was also inspired by the living memory of similar land-raids at the end of the Great War, on Raasay and the Long Isle, when returned soldiers drew public attention to the misuse and mismanagement of land, the cynical neglect of its native people. According to those who knew the Knoydart raiders, they were "very sound, solid, good Scotsmen, well-seasoned Scotsmen." Some had expended their young manhood in defence of the country, and all believed they were entitled to a just share of its potential wealth. In the changed political climate of the post-war years they were confident that public opinion would support them, as indeed it did.

For a brief while during that harsh winter they became widely-known as "The Seven Men of Knoydart", a sub-editor's catch-line but more than an indication of numbers and place. In euphony and rhyme it recalled The Seven Men of Moidart, the band of aging Jacobites who landed with the Young Pretender in 1745 to challenge an entrenched Hanoverian establishment. Whatever the men of the Rough Bounds thought of this irrelevant comparison, it did excite the imagination of good people throughout Scotland. And also, less emotionally, the interest of Fleet Street where my renowned Scottish editor, having listened silently to my proposals for a deeper examination of the land-raid and its historical background, then said it was of no great interest to English readers, but could I explain why I thought he would send me to cover it.

The process of law is rarely influenced by the public's view of social justice until that is embodied by statute. Lord Brocket quickly secured interim interdicts against the raiders, on Wednesday while they were still breaking the earth at Kilchoan. Encouraged by the response of the Scottish Press whom they had invited to watch and photograph their raid, and by many letters and telegrams of sympathy, the seven men agreed to recognise the interdicts and engage lawyers to continue their fight. Long before spring melted the snow on the long black claw of Ladhar Bheinn, that struggle was lost. The Labour Secretary of State, son of a Lowland brassfounder, came to Loch Nevis by ship, examined the white hills and seaweed rocks through his field-glasses, and departed without going ashore. The raiders' case was heard and rejected by a Court of Inquiry, called by a government which the soldiers of my generation had elected three years before, believing it would bring an end to privilege by rank and power by wealth. When The Seven Men of Knoydart sent an appeal to the voyaging Secretary of State, this too was rejected. The sad dispersal of the people continued, from Scottas, Inverie and the green Glen of the Dark Pool. But at least Lord Brocket soon thought it prudent to sell the estate, and children were no longer forbidden to pass along the loch-shore before the windows of Inverie House lest they disturb her ladyship's view as she sat at the keyboard of her white piano.

Remembering that winter, the high hopes raised by public meetings in Glasgow and the encouragement of distant sympathisers, one of the raiders has sadly admitted that he and his companions had perhaps been wrong to entrust their defence to lawyers and politicians.

> We would have been far better to have done what the old boys in the olden days did, stick on the ground until they put you to gaol. We all thought it was a very good idea, that it was going to be legal, but afterwards when we saw the whole thing, and you look back on it, you realise it didn't pay to be doing it the modern way.*

* Quoted in "The Seven Men of Knoydart" by Iain Fraser Grigor, published in *Odyssey – Voices from Scotland's Recent Past*, Polygon Books, 1980. Drawn from the Odyssey series broadcast by B.B.C. Scotland, and produced by Billy Kay, this is a remarkable and invaluable record of oral history.

There is a great melancholy in the beauty of Knoydart, and it is easy to think of the failure of this land-raid as its last cry of despair, an echo of its grief during the wide clearance of the estate almost a century before. Longboats from the emigrant ship *Sillery* were then beached below the mountains at Sandaig, Doune and Airor, and on the shelving shore where a hastening river twists down to the ford at Inverie. The little vessel itself, avoiding the shoals and tides of Loch Nevis, was anchored across the Sound of Sleat in the lee of Skye, its lower decks cleared and scrubbed with vinegar and water, ready to take the last of Glengarry's unwanted tenants into exile. There were six hundred of them, and some of the older men, like Allan MacDonell in the township of Airor, had once accompanied Alasdair Ranaldson to Edinburgh for the Royal Visit, standing guard at the door of his lodgings in belted plaids and Glengarry bonnets. But now they were all a burden upon the purse and the patience of his inheritors.

Aeneas MacDonell, the sixth Chief of Glengarry, had made no permanent home in Australia, returning to Scotland with his health and spirit broken. When he died, at Inverie in the summer of 1852, he was buried beside his flamboyant father in the gaunt family mausoleum at Kilfinnan. To his credit he had always been reluctant to press the Knoydart people for their rents, amounting to £2,774 10s 8d *per annum*, but his widow Josephine, like all Glengarry wives, was more realistic and less compassionate. Acting as the principal guardian for her son, the new Chief and a minor, she put the estate on the market in the spring of 1853, and before its sale to a Lowland ironmaster was completed she made arrangements for the disposal of its people with the committee of the Highland Emigration Society, the Board of Supervision of the Poor Law, and the government's Colonial Land and Emigration Department. She then served writs of eviction upon the Knoydart tenants, and told them what was required of them with a firmness Lord Brocket might have envied, had he known of it.

> As the minds of the guardians are perfectly made up on the subject it will be better for the people to acquiesce *quietly* in these arrangements for their removal. If they emigrate without trouble or annoyance they will be allowed to remain where they are until the *committee are ready to take them*; but I must tell you that those who may imagine they will be allowed to remain after this are indulging in a vain hope, as the most stringent measures will be taken to effect their removal. They will best consult their own interest by being ready to move when the committee are ready to take them. Sir John MacNeill* has promised they shall ALL be removed in *one* ship to Australia.

* Chairman of the Board of Supervision for thirty years. A conscientious, fatherly old man, he was none the less an example of how good intentions may be corrupted by power and responsiblity. After a visit to the Highlands he told the Home Secretary that there should be no increase in Poor Relief, and that emigration was the only solution to destitution. He accused the Highlanders of laziness, and of expecting relief as a right. "People who some years ago carefully concealed their poverty have learned to parade and of course exaggerate it." The Highlands and Islands Emigration Society was a direct result of his report, and was welcomed by those proprietors who were finding it increasingly difficult to sell estates encumbered by a pauper population.

The evictions were carried out in August, under the direction of the Glengarry factor. Although no longer young, he was tireless in his duty, organising parties of men to destroy the cottages with axes, crow-bars, hammers and levers. Women who refused to leave their homes were dragged from them to the beach, and at least one was beaten with sticks as she clung screaming to her door-post. Families who fled into the high glens above the loch were hunted and brought back. There was no mercy, no delay, said that indefatigable journalist and advocate, Donald Ross. When the last boat had left for the *Sillery*

> ... as far as the eye could see the face of the strath had its black spots where the houses of the crofters were either levelled or burnt, the blackened rafters lying scattered on the grass, the couple-trees cut through the middle and thrown far away, the walls broken down, the thatch and cabers mixed together, but the voice of man was gone.

Thirty-eight of the people still remained, however, avoiding the evictors or rejected as worthless material for the colonies. There were two or three families with middle-aged parents, but most were widows or spinsters. Twenty-four of them were more than seventy years of age, three were in their ninth decade, five over ninety, and one was a centenarian. All were paupers in receipt of the Poor Law allowance. For the most fortunate, that is to say the most infirm, this was eighteenpence a week, but the majority received a shilling, and some less than sevenpence. The allowance was paid quarterly by the Inspector of the Poor Law, but that winter following the evictions he did not visit Knoydart. The old people kept themselves alive as best they could in the ruins of their cottages, in ditches and the wind-break of rocks along the shore. Many were without warm clothing and shoes, and some used their stockings to patch their blankets. They had no meat, and they lived on diseased potatoes which they boiled with dulse, gathered from the cold sea at low tide. They were all that remained of a people whom a Clan Donald bard had once described as "the young saplings of Knoydart ... strong and proud."

When he heard of their condition, Donald Ross went to Inverie by a small boat and in the company of the people's selfless priest, Father Coll MacDonald. Appalled by what they found, he wrote an angry pamphlet in protest, and then a report for the *Northern Ensign*. He called this *Aunt Katy's Cabin*, telling his readers that if their interest and indignation had been aroused by the recent publication of Mrs Beecher Stowe's "popular creation of female fancy" they would find his "simple narrative of fact" much more strange.* The strength of his public attacks upon Highland proprietors, and upon the Emigration Society which enabled such men to be rid of their tenants so easily, forced the Lord Advocate

---

* His sceptical opinion of *Uncle Tom's Cabin* was remarkably perceptive. Harriet Beecher Stowe had undoubtedly produced the most influential novel ever written, and Abraham Lincoln was said to have greeted her as "the little woman

to order an investigation into the condition of the paupers in Knoydart. Thus the Sheriff-Substitute, the Sheriff Clerk Depute, the Procurator Fiscal and the senior medical practitioner of Lochaber set out from Fort William on the first day of February. They travelled forty miles by road to the white coast of Arisaig, and eighteen by boat to Loch Nevis where they gratefully accepted the warmth and shelter of Father MacDonald's little house at Sandaig. The neglected misery of the paupers, as reported by the Sheriff, was now worse than it had been when Ross visited them before Christmas. The local Inspector of the Poor was held to be responsible, but in an addendum to the report the Fiscal doubted whether legal action could or should be taken against the man. "A conviction to some extent might perhaps be obtained," he told the Lord Advocate, "but it is morely likely that the inspector would be acquitted, while the Parochial Board might be blamed." The latter was no doubt grateful, for it was irregular in constitution and incompetent in practice. It chose its own representatives from the ratepayers, instead of accepting them by election. Twenty-three of the ailing paupers of Knoydart had not once been visited by its medical officer in the two and a half years since his appointment. The four land-owners of the parish were obliged to be members of the Board, but none of them, or their mandataries, ever attended its meetings.

The Sheriff's report contained no criticism of Josephine MacDonell, and only a passing reference to her as one of the four proprietors. It was sympathetic but impatient with Catherine MacKinnon, whom Ross had called Aunt Katy, and whose cabin was made from canvas sacks, branches and ropes. She was "an obstinate, perverse person," said the Sheriff, "declining to remove from a wretched hovel at Inverie." He ordered her to be carried to a farmhouse at Scottas, "but the tenant objected to her, and the poor woman lay that night and the succeeding one at the roadside, and for aught I know is still without house or shelter." Surprisingly there was one death only, the widow Mary MacDonald who died at Nigart in the first week of spring and in her ninety-fourth year. A month later, the *Inverness Courier* reported that "proceedings have been taken to remove those crofters and families who were allowed to remain at the time of the evictions last year." And when they were gone, James Baird the ironmaster took possession of Inverie House and put his sheep on the hills.

whose book started this great war." But all her first-hand knowledge of slavery had been acquired during a brief weekend visit across the Ohio River to Kentucky, and as a true picture of that iniquity it was closer to comedy. Perhaps it was as well, however, that she had no intimate association with Southern plantation-owners. When she came to the Highlands in 1856, as the guest of the Duke and Duchess of Sutherland, she wrote an ecstatic defence of her hosts and of James Loch's Policy of Improvement, "an almost sublime instance of the benevolent employment of superior wealth and power in shortening the struggles of advancing civilisation."

To a greater or lesser degree, the harsh treatment of the Knoy-dart people was common to most evictions, as was the self-interest of many chiefs, each by tradition the *ceann-cinnidh*, the head of the clan and father of the children he was now deserting. It has been impossible to write of such events without feeling, and my emotions admittedly influenced the style and language of *The Highland Clearances*. As a result, the book has sometimes been dismissed as politically inspired, but the implication that it was written to the direction of an *agit-prop* committee has never distressed me. And when I am called a barrack-room lawyer by my most amiable Scots critic – a distinguished product of Stowe, Oxford, Edinburgh and the Third Guards – I can perhaps accept it as a compliment. The term is rarely heard in a barrack-room, but is often used by some warrant and commissioned officers who believe they know best what a private soldier should think, and are uneasy when he makes up his own mind.

I can understand those academics who maintain that the science – not the art – of historical writing requires dispassionate detachment, and I think such coolness of intellect must explain their silence when the inhumanities of the past continue into the present. I cannot agree, however, that it is unrealistic to make moral judgements in the context of the Clearances, or incorrect to suggest that there could have been a humane alternative to the Diaspora of the Gaelic people. It is true that no such alternative was considered by the few who profited from the misery of the many, but this was not because their age did not or could not supply one, or that the spiritual teaching of the time did not oblige them to seek it. Apart from Christian precepts, to which lip-service was paid by 19th-century proprietors and their placemen in the Church of Scotland, there were men of intelligence and compassion among their contemporaries – like the agriculturalist Sir John Sinclair of Ulbster, the Swiss social scientist Sismondi, and Delane's reporter at Ardgay – who not only shared Walter Scott's anger at the removal of a native population in favour of sheep but also suggested means by which both might be profitably sustained upon the land.

The chiefs were the first instrumental party to the great changes which began in the decades following Culloden, and because academic study of these events is not concerned with moral responsibility it has too often ignored their obligations within an obsolescent clan society which still thought of them as protectors and providers. Their property rights, based upon tenure-at-will, made eviction easy, and the lack of violent resistance to it – the manner in which Highland men, if not always Highland women, walked into exile with the docility of the sheep which replaced them – can be explained in part by the fact that the people acknowledged the power of the *ceann-cinnidh* to act as he thought best for them and the land.

In 1794, the seventy-two men of his clan whom Alasdair Ranaldson summoned into a company of the Strathspey Fencibles did not challenge his right to demand this military service as a condition of their tenancy. Their minds and hearts were still close to a recent past when another MacDonell chief had boasted that his rent-roll consisted of five hundred swordsmen. These young men, however, were uneasy in a changing world and while agreeing to follow Glengarry where he wished, they asked for an assurance that their families would not be evicted during their absence. In a petition to him they said they expected "to enjoy those possessions which our ancestors so long enjoyed under your ancestors." Furthermore, "as we do not wish that you should lose by us we shall give as high rents as any of your Lowland shepherds ever give, and we shall all become bound for any one whose circumstances may afford you room to mistrust." Their faith in his continuing protection was nobly naive. They could never have competed with the rents Border graziers were willing to pay, and soon after their discharge in 1802 many of them were gone to the Canadian woodlands between the Ottawa and Saint Lawrence rivers. When it was too late, in Lochaber and elsewhere, the bards who had once praised the chiefs in resonant and clanging verse now denounced them for their betrayal of the Gaelic people.

> Their land and they themselves
> will die together,
> since they have become hard monsters,
> stiff-necked, cruel,
> with no mercy of remorse ...

It is absurd and indecent, I think, to pretend that the familial interdependence between clansmen and chiefs, which many of the latter so easily abandoned, can be maintained or resurrected today. My use of that word *indecent*, and the subsequent addition of *obscene* under questioning, inflated a small bubble of outrage some years ago during an International Clan Gathering in Edinburgh. Whatever the sincere intentions of many involved in its organisation, this was fundamentally a theatrical exercise on behalf of the tourist industry, and most people in Scotland seemed content to accept or ignore it as such. That same week I was invited to give an extramural lecture in the University. I had prepared some notes but I was given no lectern, only a low table eighteen inches from the floor, and I was thus unable to read them, despite the flourishing use of three pairs of glasses. Having failed to hold the papers successfully in my hand, I eventually discarded them and spoke of what I felt about the Gathering and the men and women of Scots descent who had come to it from overseas. I regretted that many of them knew little, and were being told nothing during their visit, of the manner in which their ancestors had been driven from the Highlands by chiefs whose descendants were now splendidly arrayed in George Street to greet them. I said there was something indecent in a tartan charade which pretended there had been no sadness and betrayal, and that at best it was "as if the undertakers who long ago buried the corpse of the clan society were now holding its wake."

The natural indignation this aroused charged the emotions of some Highland gentlemen at a press conference the next day, called to refute a growing belief that the Gathering was a failure. Having denied this, and dealt with an American reporter who wished to know if Highlanders still ate their porridge while standing, the convenors and their supporters reluctantly answered questions about the Clearances. The Countess of Sutherland admitted she disapproved of much of her family's responsibility for them, but added that she did not care to live with them for the rest of her life. When she was asked what she thought of my intemperate criticism, an island chief intervened on her behalf. "You get experts on everything. John Prebble is one of these experts, an English expert." Agreeing with this, another said, "It grieves me that my clansmen from abroad should see these attacks. John Prebble does not know the least thing about what it feels like to have Scottish blood." Taken literally this was meaningless, but metaphorically it was not without irony. Because of his ancestors' marriages he is almost as English as myself, and only marginally less well-favoured in that respect than others of his obsolete rank. The search for wives in England was common among Highland chiefs in the 18th and 19th centuries, and after seven generations of this amiable preference one of the greatest today, in name if not in property, has no more than one per cent of "Scottish blood."

The incident was of course trivial, and might have been less acrimonious had I been provided with a lectern or better eyesight. Beneath its lightsome ripples, however, there were darker undertows. More had been challenged than the masquerade of that urban Gathering, which profited the tourist trade of Edinburgh but did little for the Highlands where it could have been more properly placed. The fabric of the private ownership of land in the mountains today was woven during the years of Improvement. The threads run taut from Josephine MacDonell to the late Lord Brocket and his living ilk, and censure of the past arouses unwelcome criticism of the present. The strongest apologists for the evictors are to be found among a tenacious property class, and in maintaining that the Clearances can now be forgotten they argue that a man should not be called to account for the behaviour of his ancestors, or of those who once possessed the land he now owns. In general this is obviously true, but where he has inherited the residual comfort, station, profit and influence secured by the Clearances he may not dismiss the enduring memory of the suffering they imposed upon a helpless people. Of that, too, he is a legatee.

Knoydart today is an empty echo-chamber for such angry thoughts. Still unapproachable by road, it is isolated in its sorrow. The yellow hawkweed and violet campion which grow in the northern pass above Inverie are no longer crushed by the hooves of the black cattle its people once drove to Loch Hourn, joining the herds that came from Glenelg and the Outer Hebrides. There are still footpaths over the ascending mountains to the east, wild tracks that twist by dark escarpments and drumming streams to a braeside above the drowned township of Kinlochquoich. It was

on this wind-tortured massif of Barrisdale that Edward Ellice's guests, having reached the western march of his estate, abandoned their pursuit of his deer and were then rowed down the loch by singing boatmen, coming at night to the spartan comfort of iron bedsteads and cane chairs at Glen Quoich Lodge. Not having the spirit or strength now to enter Knoydart from the east, I have persuaded myself that its cloud-touched splendour is best observed from Skye, at Isleornsay where the *Sillery* was anchored, or on the coastal road from Kilmore to Armadale Bay. In the morning its peaked shadows darken the Sound of Sleat, and the indigo mask that hides its face may not be lifted until an hour before noon, or later still if there are black storms above Caillich and Ladhar Bheinn. But sometimes at the end of a kindly day, when it is seen on the port beam of the Mallaig ferry, the glory of a departing sun can ennoble the slopes of its corrugated hills and fill their watered ravines with falling gold.

The five peninsulas of Glenelg, Knoydart, Morar, Ardnamurchan and Morvern are the extended hand of the Rough Bounds, forever grasping at the Isles of Mull and Skye. Above the Sound of Sleat the blue mountains are arthritic knuckles on the thumb and forefinger of Glenelg and Knoydart, but southward there are more gentle hills, rolling inland to the higher ground of Lochaber. The narrow trenches of the sea-lochs, where a sudden fall of sunlight can change the water from dark jade to beaten silver, were once an anchorage for merchantmen from France and Holland, a safe landing for Jacobite letter-carriers and the agents who came

Glen Barrisdale on Loch Hourn, the heart of the Rough Bounds. Here there was once a MacDonell township and a great house "with eighteen fire rooms, besides many more without chimneys." All was burnt by Cumberland's militia in 1746, and a century later the people were replaced with sheep.

The bend of Loch Hourn from the Glenelg shore. To the east is the high ground of Glen Quoich and the deer forest where Delane of the *Times* lost his hart.

to collect the rents which maintained an absent chief in exile. Until the beginning of this century side-wheel and screw-driven steamers from Oban and the Clyde regularly visited their wooden piers, and within my own memory Aberdeen trawlers sheltered in the lee of Loch Hourn before leaving for the North Minch and the Icelandic seas. Ironically, now that their native people are largely gone and there are no townships in their small glens, the Rough Bounds are penetrated by three principal roads, the ribs of a leaf branching from the spine of the Great Glen and touching the coastline of all but the remote loneliness of Knoydart. The northern way goes over the timbered pass of Mam Ratagan to Glenelg Bay and the waiting majesty of Skye across the water. In the centre, another follows the shore of Loch Eil to Glenfinnan and thence to Morar and the raucous herring-gulls at Mallaig. The third comes down the western shore of Loch Linnhe from Corran, where Alasdair Ranaldson was fatally injured as he leapt ashore from the wreck of the *Stirling Castle*. This road forks at the entrance to Glen Tarbet. One tine thrusts through Morvern to the pier of Lochaline on the Sound of Mull, and the other bends by Sunart to Salen where it divides again, northward to Acharacle, Moidart, Arisaig and Mallaig, and westward through Ardnamurchan to the lone lighthouse on its Point.

There are few Highland roads so beguiling as these. In Moidart and Arisaig the track wanders leisurely above the green fiords that gave both districts their Norse names, past gaunt survivors of a great forest of oak and through a corridor of pine where I once saw a pair of red cross-bills, far north of their customary ground

From the head of Glen Pean looking westward down Loch Morar to the sea and the Isle of Rum. The water below is a thousand feet deep, but the glacier that was once here was four times as great.

and spinning like sparks in the evening shade. Hawk and raven quarrel above purple outcrops on the upper slopes of Ardnamurchan, and at the shoreline hem of its shawl of hills black-capped tern make a spring landfall, coming down on scythe-blade wings to scrape their nests in the seaward grass. As were all Highland roads not long since, these byways of the Rough Bounds are rarely wider than a single car and follow the trails cut by foot, horse and cattle. Cautionary posts mark the passing-places that inspire competitive courtesies and remind us that driving was once the civilised pleasure of motoring. Forty-seven years ago, when I rode with the carter from Acharacle to Strontian, the only vehicle we passed was a doctor's bull-nosed Morris, and even today, in late fall, I sometimes meet no one as I drive over the welcoming hills and beneath the rustling bronze of the valley trees.

It is said that Ardnamurchan's name means the land of the sea-hound, the otter, and one day I will see its brown inquisitive head breaking a circle of ripples in Glenmore Bay, or hear its shrill whistle at dusk in Borrodale. The road where this may happen goes sweetly along the timbered shore of Loch Sunart to Ardslignish, turning inland there by Ben Hiant's volcanic cone to the *ard* of the peninsula's name, the high ground of brown moors, blue lochans, and grey-ribbed hills. From the lochside there is a misted view of Mull's dark peaks to the south, and tiny islands of jewelled rock in the mouth of Sunart where Victorian sportsmen shipped oars and whistled to bring the grey seal within killing range. Ardnamurchan once belonged to the MacIains, a small branch of Clan Donald, until they were driven from it in the 17th century

Mingary Castle in Ardnamurchan. Five centuries ago James IV sat in its shadow and took the submission of a humbled Clan Donald, but he wore a coat of mail hidden beneath his scarlet cloak.

and their stronghold of Mingary was taken by the Campbells. Nearby this castle, where the western flank of Ben Hiant rises from the sea, there is said to be a cave in which some of the MacIains were smoked to death by a greenwood fire the invaders lit at its entrance. If the story is not a transplanted legend they were foolishly indifferent to precedent in their choice of a refuge, for on the island of Eigg the MacLeods had previously suffocated its population of MacDonalds in the same decisive way. Remembrance of the Ardnamurchan people was enduring, as if it were the least their misfortune deserved. When Johnson and Boswell were guests of Maclean of Lochbuie that roaring man, having been told that the Doctor was deaf, raise his stentorian voice a decibel and asked, "Are you of the Johnstons of Glencro, or of Ardnamurchan?" Johnson huffily refused to answer, leaving Boswell to explain "that he was not John*ston* but John*son*, and that he was an Englishman."*

Few travellers visit the flaked stone walls of Mingary now, except those who like driving to the end of a road for the pleasure of seeing it again on their return. On an open point of wind-bent grass, the decaying fabric of the 13th-century castle is locked in its past, pale sea-flowers like watered blood on the rock from which it appears to grow. Five hundred years ago that handsome, humane, Renaissance king, James IV, came here to accept the surrender of the Lordship of the Isles from the chiefs of Clan Donald, sitting before them in a cloak of rich scarlet, beneath banners of gold. In the late 17th century Mingary was a miserable prison for Covenanters, far from their homes in Galloway and with

* I suspect Boswell's ears were also at fault, or that he repaired his memory with Johnson's account, itself confused in hearing or recollection. Lochbuie probably did say Johnson, the English version of MacIain, and Glencoe not Glencro, the Clan Donald people of the former also being MacIains.

no comfort but an enduring faith in their harsh and unbending God. Eighty years later it was still no better than a penal settlement for the soldiers who built their wooden barracks against its curtain-walls, suffered the neglect of the Government, and watched the island seas for the ships that might – and ultimately did – bring that calamitous young Prince from France

Westward from Mingary, Ardnamurchan ends at Garbhlach Mhor, a soaring cliff against which the white Atlantic breakers can leap fifty feet and more, below coronets of circling sea-fowl. The navigation of this intractable headland is always perilous, and long-remembered when successfully made. Its changing winds almost sank the little boat that carried Johnson and Boswell from Mull to Coll, on a night dark with terror. Aware that his life depended on the skill of a one-eyed seaman at the helm, Boswell tried to compose his mind with pious thoughts, but unhappily remembered that popular theology now argued that it was "vain to hope that the petitions of an individual, or even of congregations, can have any influence with the Deity." Aboard the sloop *Johnson*, and in the same enraged waters thirty years later, James Hogg stayed below on his berth, writing a letter to Scott, he said, although I have a writer's doubt about that. He was content to trust in the skill of the master and crew until he heard the frightened helmsman shout *"Oh, my God ... my God!"* Before Hogg could reach the deck the sloop rolled over on her beam-ends, with her mainsail touching the sea, and only "A singular inter-position of Providence" brought her back on a level keel. The helmsman "thanked his Maker aloud for this signal deliverance, and indeed every heart seemed sensibly affected."

William Daniell's view of Ardnamurchan Point makes such miracles appear credible – grey-green waves heaving against the rocks, small ships fighting an inshore wind, and a Providential sword-blade of sunlight parting the clouds. Although he probably made his detailed sketches in peaceful reflection at a Tobermory inn, it is easy to think they were drawn on a wet and heeling deck, close in to that olivine altar of basalt and its black-winged acolyte gulls. My script for Mendelssohn's visit to Scotland at first began with Daniell's aquatint, dissolving to film of the Point today and as I believed the composer would have seen it on the starboard beam of the *Highlander*, but this fanciful device was abandoned when it was realised that time and need had altered the profile of the headland. Twenty years after Mendelssohn passed through the Sound, perhaps too wretched to be interested in awesome sea-scapes, a lighthouse was placed upon the Point, a stone candle designed by Stevenson's uncle and still blinking across the night-dark water to the hidden island of Coll.

There is no Highland coastline more lovely to my eye than Arisaig, the tip of Morar's finger between Ardnamurchan and Knoydart. It is fragmented into green islets past which the tide moves into its white-sand bays like the wake of invisible ships. In spring the croft-land above the tough sea-grass of the machair is veiled by the smoke of burning heather, milk-white and lazily drifting. On days of rough weather the wind from the Atlantic can be strong. Dark-headed pine lean inland before it, and the grieving rain it brings is rank with the smell of salt and kelp. And sometimes, in the tranquil dusk of autumnal evenings, greylag geese from Iceland plane down to a shoreline of yellow birch and skid across the water on the splayed web of their pink feet.

Where the road marches briefly beside the railway to Mallaig both cross the shortest river in Britain, less than half a mile and bisecting a narrow isthmus of sand and rock, oak and birch. Its clear and curling flow is the outlet of Loch Morar, the deepest water in Scotland and the legendary home of an ill-tempered monster so far ignored by publicists and post-cards. This brooding and beautiful loch was once a great glacier, four thousand feet deep and held in a bowl of mountains which now darken the water for most of the day until the westering sun ignites its cluster of islands with incandescent fire. There are no roads along its steep shores, and the remaining houses of its deserted townships can be reached by boat only, or by heather tracks from Glen Pean and Lochailort. Its remote silence, like that of many Highland glens, is deceiving, persuading the eye and mind that it was always so, but once there was a Catholic seminary here, and the residence of Hugh MacDonald, the Pope's Vicar-Apostolic in the Highlands. It was thus good theatre, perhaps, that the most notorious of Catholic chiefs – that is to say, the most guileful and double-dealing of all chiefs, who happened also to be a Catholic – took shelter on Loch Morar after Culloden and was captured there by a landing-party from H.M.S. *Furnace*, after they had dragged their long-boat over the isthmus from the sea. The fugitive chief, Simon Fraser of Lovat, was subsequently relieved of his estates and his head. The loss of the latter was scarcely regretted outside his own clan, and the former were ultimately restored to his onetime Jacobite son, perhaps because of the young man's energy as a prosecuting counsel at the trial of James Stewart of the Glen, or his greater zeal five years later when he raised fourteen hundred Highland soldiers for George II, whose right to the throne he had once disputed in arms.*

Morvern is the southern peninsula of the Rough Bounds, although some would place it outwith the *Garbhchriochan*. Behind the axe-blade edge of its coastline, slicing at the Isle of Mull, is a rising land of crumpled hills, lonely glens, and starch-white outcrops of high rock. Much of its principal highway follows the 18th-century drove-road by which some of Mull's black cattle were brought to a staging market at Strontian, below the braeside pits of the York Company's lead mine. The long-horned beasts came ashore in

---

* At the age of nineteen he commanded the Clan Fraser Regiment on his father's behalf, supporting the Jacobite cause for reasons that may have slipped his memory when he appeared before the Inveraray Assize as counsel for Glenure's widow and children. In his address to the Court he declared that the Appin Murder was "the most daring and bare-faced insult to be offered to His Majesty's authority and Government, at a time when we are reaping the fruits of his most benign reign."

Loch Aline, a sheltered bay like a notch in the axe-blade. On Ardtornish Point at its narrow entrance is the greystone rind of a castle from which John of Islay, the last MacDonald Lord of the Isles, sent envoys to England with proposals for a grand alliance against Scotland's king. They met the English commissioners at Westminster in February, 1462, and when their long arguments were over it was agreed that in return for England's help and a share in all the lands north of the Forth – which he was expected to conquer – John of Islay would become the vassal of Edward IV. The briefly-secret Treaty of Ardtornish and Westminster was the MacDonalds' greatest challenge to the Crown of Scotland, and undoubtedly their most calamitous mistake. After thirty years of intermittent conflict during which the English, fighting among themselves, did little to help their distant ally, the Lordship of the Isles was taken from Clan Donald and its humbled chiefs knelt before James IV in the midsummer shadow of Mingary Castle. Stripped of his estates and titles, a miserable pensioner now of the King he had opposed, John of Islay died at last in a Dundee lodging-house, far from the Hebrides and too poor to pay the last reckoning for his bed and board.

Loch Aline was not always as peaceful as it now appears, a green mantle of trees on the lava cliffs above its silicate shores, and its blue water dusted with white sea-fowl. The long and bloody history of Morvern, feud and foray, reached a violent climax here in March, 1746, when two of the King's sloops, one of them suitably named *Terror*, made an evening anchorage off the mouth

Ardnamurchan, by Daniell. The furthest western point of mainland Britain, and restless water where Hogg thought he might drown, and Boswell sadly remembered that prayer was now said to have no influence with the Deity.

of the loch. At dawn the next day, Captain Robert Duff landed fifty-five seamen and almost as many soldiers of the Royal Scots Fusiliers with orders "to burn the houses and destroy the effects of all such as were out in the Rebellion." By six o'clock that evening, reported the captain of the second sloop, "near 400 houses amongst which were several barns fill'd with corn, horse, cows, meal and other provisions were destroy'd by fire and fire-arms." Along fourteen miles of the coast, from Drimnin to Ardtornish at the head of Loch Aline, fifteen small townships were razed. The seamen of the *Terror* also put their torches to the natural woodlands, a wanton spite from which the trees have never fully recovered. Two weeks later another landing-party from the sloops set more houses, barns and trees aflame on the Sunart shore. All this was the bitterly-remembered "Burning of Morvern", and two generations later old men still spoke of the day when their beloved land became "one red ember".

Stevenson first saw the Morvern coast in his late teens, when he joined his father aboard the yacht *Pharos* for an inspection tour of the western lighthouses. He was more familiar with the Islands than with the mainland, the Devil's Staircase and the long track by Rannoch. He never trod that path, I think, or he would not have made Alan Breck declare that twenty squadrons of dragoons could hide in the mist of the moor, and ride down the fugitives among its bogs. But he knew the beauty of Mull, and Morvern across the Sound, and the harsh inhumanity that could violate their innocent tranquility. When he put David Balfour ashore in Loch Aline the young man saw the beach "quite black with people", and a sea-going ship taking emigrants aboard for the American colonies.

> ... and there began to come to our ears a great sound of mourning, the people on board and those on shore crying and lamenting one to another so as to pierce the heart.

This incident is irrelevant to the narrative flow of *Kidnapped*. It is also set too early in history, although it is true that here, on Loch Aline, many of Morvern's unhappy people later saw the last of their homeland, its green hills darkening to blue as their ship went out with the evening tide. Writing his novel in a yellow-brick house on a Bournemouth chine, struggling with sickness and mounting bills, Stevenson was perhaps recalling a boyhood memory, a painful experience that had long awaited relief through his creative imagination. In the year he sailed about these waters more than thirty families were evicted from the Lochaline estate by its new proprietor, the widow of a Glasgow banker. If he did not see their departure himself, as I believe he must have done, the boy undoubtedly heard about it. These were the hard days of eviction and clearance in Morvern, sadly lamented by John MacLachlan of Rahoy, a Gaelic bard and a good man who practised medicine among the people, without any formal qualifications, it would seem.

Heavy, sorrowful my heart
going through the glen ...
On an April morning I no longer hear
bird-songs or the lowing of cattle on the moor.
I hear the unpleasant noise of sheep
and the English language, dogs barking
and frightening the deer.

From the beginning of the sixteenth century, after the passing of the Lordship of the Isles, Morvern was ruled by the chiefs of Clan Maclean before the Earl of Argyll took most of it in the King's name and for his own profit. The Campbells gave it stability, reform and some prosperity until the middle decades of the last century when the estate was sold to the newly-rich from England and the Lowlands. Its history under these incomers has been admirably told in a dispassionate work by Philip Gaskell.* Although this studies one area of the Clearances without the emotion of less scholarly writers, it justifies their anger, I think. The native population of Morvern was reduced by two-thirds in the 19th century, and little if anything now remains of their small townships. But some of the great houses built by the new proprietors still stand behind their protective screens of woodland, mansard roofs lifted above the leaves, dark windows looking westward to the sea.

One of the earliest incomers was Patrick Sellar, an advocate who had abandoned Law for estate management while he was still a young man. He became a factor to the Countess of Sutherland and her English husband, the Marquess of Stafford, and cleared Strath Naver for them with a zealous brutality that led to his trial, and acquittal, on a charge of murder. Having emptied the strath, and burnt the roof-trees of its evicted people, he then took a lease on the best of its land between Ben Griam and the River Naver. With the money acquired by his success as a tenant-farmer he bought the Acharn estate in the heart of Morvern, evicted 220 people or more, and stocked the land with sheep brought from Strathnaver. Six years later he took the Ardtornish estate on the southern shore of the peninsula, and this time the outgoing proprietor was obliged to clear its encumbering people before the conveyance was completed. All this, perhaps, should be considered against Sellar's deprecatory admission that before he went to Sutherland he believed that "the growth of wool and sheep in the Highlands was one of the most abominable and detestable things possible to be imagined." Nothing redresses the misjudgements of youth so well as financial and social success in middle-age. Gaskell is critically generous to Sellar, and supporters of the sensitive House of Sutherland today maintain that he has been ill-used and misunderstood. He was clearly intelligent and industrious, amiable and agreeable among his equals, respectful to his superiors, and no doubt kind to his children. But in the Gaelic verse of the Clear-

* *Morvern Transformed*, by Philip Gaskell. C.U.P. 1968

ances, stubbornly ignored by most academic historians, he is less charitably remembered. *Nam faighinn's air an raon thu ...*

> If I had you on the field
> and men binding you,
> with my fist I would tear
> out three inches of your lungs!

Applying the wit as well as the wealth they had inherited from distilling, haberdashery, brewing and grocery, the new gentry of Morvern were instinctively more efficient than their Gaelic predecessors in the business of Improvement. Like others elsewhere in the Highlands they introduced no radical changes in the nature of land ownership, the joint holdings and co-operative sheep-herding suggested by Sir John Sinclair fifty years earlier, and they did not respond to Delane's reporter who urged them to "create employment ... make many yeomen out of one sheep-farmer." By such genuine improvements the land might have been able to support its population and avoid recurring famine and destitution. The only answer the proprietors had to these calamities was one most profitable to themselves, the removal of the people, and in that light they could sometimes think of Clearance as the solemn duty of humane landlordism. Stiff in such rectitude, and entrenched in the Victorian belief that the increasing wealth of the few must alleviate the poverty of many, they posed for photographers on the sheep-cropped lawns of their new chateaux, sitting imperially on chairs brought from within, their faces hidden by Mosaic beards or shadowed by wide sun-hats. They delighted in the romantic beauty of their mountain paradise. They read Scott and Aytoun, painted in water colours, held balls and *musicales*, hung stags'-heads and broadswords on the walls of their libraries, tramped their glens in good tweeds, filled their visitors'-books with the names of the fashionable and illustrious, and sometimes married their children to the descendants of chiefs. When the staple economy of the Highlands was weakened by the import of mutton and wool from Australasia – to which they had dispatched their unwanted Gaelic people – they were now secure enough in foreign investments to clear sheep from much of their land and turn it into a playground for deer-stalking and grouse-shooting.

Before passable roads were cut and before the railway reached the Great Glen, visitors to Morvern arrived by sea from Greenock, on elegant steamers with raking funnels, splashing side-wheels, and white awnings amidships. The little port of Lochaline has survived this busy past and is still in occasional use, piermaster's house and ticket office like an abandoned and paint-blistered railway station. It is a pleasant place to sit on an autumn evening now, with Ardtornish Castle a black silhouette on the Point, and the last ferry from Mull creaming the water of the Sound. In the silence of a closing day it is possible to think of the pier as it was when a Clyde steamer came alongside – English voices as noisy as a gathering of starlings, alpine ranges of unloaded luggage, rods and guns like stands-of-arms, spinning parasols moving toward waiting gigs, children in martial order behind their governess, a homeward soldier in scarlet and tartan, Glasgow carpenters and masons with carpet-bags of tools, a commercial traveller haggling for the hire of a horse, a wicker post-cart and canvas sacks of mail, the scent of peat-smoke, the stench of fish-boxes, the barking of game-dogs, and the music of a kilted piper, sent from Ardtornish House to greet its guests. For seventy years privileged life moved pleasantly through the seasons, and inexorably toward August, 1914, which it would survive more happily than the last of Morvern's young Highland men.

Northward between Loch Duich and Loch Hourn, Glenelg is sometimes said to have taken its name from a holy place. Once it was indeed a flourishing and devout parish, and two of its dark peaks are The Chapel and The Church. It is also thought to have belonged to Eilg, a Pictish or pre-Celtic chief. Thirdly, and more sweetly to my mind, the root of its name may be *Elgga*, a poetic term for Ireland. The old approach to this knotted peninsula goes by Glen Garry and the dammed waters of Loch Quoich, and then to the north through a narrow pass. Here it is one of the most spectacular roads in the Highlands, insanely twisting and resolutely climbing, and when it descends to Loch Hournhead it has only touched the eastern skirt of Glenelg. When I first came this way, although my mind was already stunned by the lonely majesty of the country I was still unprepared for what I saw at the end of the road. Westward in a narrow trough of mountains, the crooked bend of Loch Hourn was a dazzling blue, the tide on the turn and gently breaking the reflection of sky and clouds. During the lighting of a cigarette the surface of the water changed to violet, and then became ink-black. A storm broke in thunder along the ridge of Druim Fada, and rain came quickly from the hidden sea, grey and yellow, sweeping through the narrows at Caolasmor and masking all but the immediate stones in front of me. The air was suddenly death-cold, and there was no sound but a long drum-roll on the roof of the car. In five minutes the squall had passed, the loch was blue again, and sunlight steamed on the road. Having made its point, the thunder grumbled inland toward the glens of Lochaber.

In the days of the drovers there was a northern track from Kinloch Hourn, over the heather saddle of Buidhe Bheinn to a deep gorge below the Ben of the Sheep, turning there to the Sound of Sleat. It is scarcely visible now, but sometimes on a high point, before I come down to Loch Hourn, I believe I am not deceived by a trick of light and shadow, that I do see the clear trace of the drove-road. Because imagination is always my evocatory companion in the Highlands, I can see the slow movement of black cattle on the braes of Buidhe Bheinn, the sunlit gleam of drovers' swords. I believe that what I hear is not the keening of gulls above the tidal mud but the voices of men, calling as they approach an evening stance for their herd, rough lodgings for themselves behind the tavern and the hope of a dram from any Glengarry gentry awaiting a seaward passage to Inverie.

Glenelg was once the richest district of the Rough Bounds, rich in warriors for the rent-roll of its chiefs, in wool and mutton for their inheritors. More than two thousand people lived in its mountains, in the townships along Glen Mor and Glen Beg, and on the green and fertile urlar by Glenelg Bay. In centuries past the tip of the peninsula was the home of the MacCrimmons. Two hundred feet below the round summit of Glas Bheinn, guarding the narrows of the Sound, there is a contrived or natural heap of stones, marked on an Ordnance map as *Carn Cloinn Mhic Cruimein*. Here a party of the clan slept at peace one night, having defeated invading Mathesons in the Battle of the Archers and driven them back to their own country across the sea-water of Loch Alsh. Before dawn, the raiders returned and killed the young men as they slept. It is said that haunting pipe music is sometimes heard on the slopes of Glas Bheinn, and one should believe this, perhaps. The MacCrimmons' legendary reputation as unrivalled masters of the pipes deserves no less from the illusion of a lamenting wind.

The MacLeods of Skye had a mainland foothold on Glenelg, granted by royal charter in 1340. They successfully defended it against the piratical ambitions of Frasers and Campbells, but in the beginning of the 19th century the mounting debts of the unfortunate or improvident Laird of MacLeod compelled him to surrender the estate to southern incomers and the Great Cheviot. It was sold for £98,500 in 1811, and sold again in 1824 for £82,000. Thirteen years later at an Inverness auction its price was £77,000, but profitable sheep-farming in the intervening years no doubt repaid the proprietors for the fall in value. With each change of ownership, more of the native population were evicted, and by 1846 almost all of those remaining were living in great poverty and squalid hovels along the shore of Loch Hourn, an increasing liability under the Poor Laws. They were finally removed by the agents of the absentee landlord James Baillie, a merchant banker of Bristol who now styled himself *of Glenelg*, once *of Dochfour*. One of the social advantages of estate ownership in the Highlands was that it gave incoming proprietors the right to an ancient territorial designation, with colourful associations in romance and history, and if this did not always make them acceptable their grandchildren were assured of an influential place in society. When the name of a Highland landlord appears in the press today, dignified by territorial, military or municipal title, it sometimes pleases me to search through old notes and discover the price paid for such distinction and authority, by his grandfather or great-grandfather, and by the Gaelic people of the Highlands.

In the last great clearance of Glenelg five hundred men, women and children left for Canada on the *Liscard*, helped by £500 from the Destitution Board and £2,000 from Baillie, two-thirds of the amount the people had been led to expect from him when they agreed to accept their removal. The *Inverness Courier* praised him for his liberality in responding to the people's desire to emigrate. Thomas Mulock had a keen ear for such humbug, however distasteful his polemics are to academic scholars today. He visited Glenelg, called the heads of forty families together and asked them if they were indeed willing emigrants.

With one voice they assured me that nothing short of the impossibility of obtaining land or employment at home could drive them to seek the doubtful benefits of a foreign shore ... So far from emigration being a spontaneous movement springing out of the wishes of the peasantry, I aver it to be the product of desperation ... the calamitous light of hopeless oppression visiting their sad hearts.

No sudden storm darkening the water of Loch Hourn, and no burning sunset on Druim Fada can solace a mind angered by the knowledge of such despair. There is scarcely any part of the Highlands where the joy I take in its solitude and beauty is not sobered by the thought of the people who once lived there, and of the manner of their dispersal.

There were men who believed more might be done for Glenelg than its transformation into an uninhabited sheep-walk. Thomas Telford reported that it would always be the principal ferry-point for black cattle from Skye, and he thought the fishing-ground of Loch Hourn would develop if the military road from Loch Duich were improved. Twenty years earlier, John Knox had said "there are few places in the Highlands where the benefits of a town would be more generally felt than this place." He was writing of Glen Mor, the green valley that drops gently down from the rock-fist of Sgurr Mhic Bharraich to the crescent curve of Glenelg Bay. The land here was always of importance, as a religious centre, in clan warfare and military occupation. For more than half a century it was the lonely site of the outpost garrison of Bernera, a three-storied barrack-house largely built with stones taken from the pre-historic brochs of the glen. It was established after the abortive Jacobite Rising of 1719, and although the earth upon which it stood belonged to MacLeod of MacLeod, the Government did not ask his leave. It was thirty years before he received any payment, and while he may have been grateful for the £1,600 he was given, his agents complained that the soldiers had taken possession of a peat-moss belonging to the people, and that a salmon-fishery had been ruined by "the nastynesse which was thrown out of the barracks."

Shaded by pines, the ruin of Bernera is now a grey husk on a green meadow known as *Grund nan Righ*, the King's Ground. When I first visited it, I stood inside its fragile walls and listened to the sighing of the wind, trying to make some imaginative contact with the Englishmen who had soldiered there, until a passing voice warned me that I was putting my life at risk from falling stones. For much of its early life, Bernera was well-built and comfortable, and had to be, perhaps, for surrounded by dark and hostile hills its redcoats were far from home and the reassurance of friends. Their daily patrols left at dawn, to stumble through the rain and mist of narrow glens to the east. Young subalterns logged the passing of ships in the Sound, and successive commanders informed their masters in London of more rumours of another Rising. When that came, the soldiers might as well have been in York or Colchester. A French frigate, having brought the bonnie Prince to claim his own, sailed past Bernera without challenge and captured four English vessels in the Narrows. The garrison ended its existence in miserable decline. Where there had once been two hundred soldiers, Johnson and Boswell found only "a serjeant and a few men." Sixty years later its abandoned shell was a brief refuge for some of Baillie's evicted tenants, and when its slates were taken for the building of a Free Church its roof and floors soon collapsed. Now it is sometimes garrisoned by undisciplined crows, and once, at least, by a grey harrier which I started from the darkness of its rain-wet stones.

Despite occasional reports of its closure, there is still a summer car-ferry between Glenelg and Skye, and it is a humbling experience to watch Murdo Mackenzie's skill at the wheel of the little *Glenmallie*. The arc of the boat's crossing, dwarfed by blue and silent hills, almost doubles the breadth of the Sound at this point. The distance is no more than five hundred yards, but too wide, one might think, for the Fingalians who decided to vault it on their spears, hurrying to defend their homes in Glenelg. They were mythological giants, however, and all succeeded, except one called Reath who was drowned when his spear broke. He is remembered by the name given to the narrows, Kyle Rhea – unless one prefers to believe that it means the Strait of the Current, for the tides here are the swiftest on the coast. In the days of sail it was impossible to make the crossing when wind and tide moved in the same direction, yet this was indeed the most expedient point for ferrying stock from Skye to the mainland, and as many as seven thousand animals would be taken over in one season. At slack tide, cattle were driven down to the water by a slipway still there, but horses, said John Knox, were pushed off the rocks.

> A small boat with five men attends, four of them holding the halters of a pair on each side. When black cattle are to cross the kyle, one is tied by the horn to a boat, a second is tied to the first, and a third to the second; and so on, to eight, ten, or twelve.

The cattle were secured head to tail by a yard of stout rope, the leading strand noosed about the lower jaw, leaving the tongue free to prevent water from entering the throat. When an animal drowned, it was usually because this precaution had not been taken.

Ashore on the mainland, close-herded on the King's Ground for their evening stance, the black cattle still had one hundred and fifty miles to travel before reaching a market tryst in the Lowlands. The journey for other herds was even longer. A map of the drove-roads resembles one quarter of a spider's web, the lines joining and crossing, pulled southward to the Stirling Plain.* Great and small, the herds came from Strath Helmsdale and Strath Naver in the far north, from Scourie and Assynt in Sutherland, Loch Broom and Loch Maree in Easter Ross, the Long Isle and the Uists, Skye,

* See *The Drove Roads of Scotland*, by A. R. B. Haldane, Nelson, 1952, and also his *New Ways through the Glens*, Nelson, 1962. I owe a great debt to these books for widening my understanding of the past, and I am at a loss when I fail to take them with me to the Highlands.

Mull, Lorn and Knapdale. For much of the way they followed the valley floors, where grazing was good and freely granted in return for welcome manuring. But time and distance sometimes made it necessary to go by the high passes, a thousand feet above sea-level over Lairigmore to Kinlochleven, and thence another eighteen hundred by the Devil's Staircase to Rannoch. A higher climb yet was over the Monadhliath by the bleak pass of Corrieyairick and down to the valley of the Spey, terrace by terrace where George Wade would confidently cut his military road along much of the winding track.

According to Stevenson, the drovers lived on ewe's milk, cheese and bannocks. Perhaps they did in his youth, but a century earlier Thomas Pennant said they ate oatmeal and onions, mixed with blood drawn from a living steer. They were unwashed, bearded and unshorn. They wore homespun tweeds, coarse brown plaids, and dark bonnets of knitted wool. After the passing of the Disarming Acts, when other Highlanders were forbidden weapons, they were given licences to carry sword and dirk, pistols and musket, to protect themselves and their herds. Like the cowmen of the American West, they were stubbornly independent, offering their skill, experience and courage for the period of the drive only. They were landless men, without clan allegiance or pride, except in quarrelsome drink. When their services were not needed they were often despised and abused, and where they appear briefly in Scottish fiction they are presented as furtive and suspicious

William Daniell drew this quick sketch of Bernera Barracks in 1815. It was from here that Johnson and Boswell embarked for Skye after a miserable night at the Glenelg inn, cheered only by a local gentleman's gift of rum and sugar.

Edwin Landseer's Highland drover leaves for a cattle tryst. Almost everything is wrong, but romantic paintings like this were popular, perhaps because they anaesthetised the pain of known truth, the reality of poverty, eviction, and emigration.

animals. Yet they were entrusted with their employer's annual income in a land where cattle-thieving was an essential way of life. When the son of a chief or tacksman accompanied them on a drive, as much for adventure as the need to assure its safe arrival in Falkirk, he dressed himself with care – in tartan trews and plaid, silver buttons on his coat and a silver-hilted dirk at his hip, his bonnet cocked and a long sword slapping the flanks of his shaggy horse. This was not vanity alone. A laird who sent his son on a drive was anxious that his own dignity and station should be properly represented among the broadcloth of southern cattle-buyers and merchants. Boswell failed to understand this nicety of pride, or was derisively amused by it when he met Maclean of Lochbuie. "We were told much of a war-saddle on which this reputed Don Quixote used to be mounted, but we did not see it, for the young laird had applied it to a less noble purpose, having taken it to Falkirk fair *with a drove of black cattle*."

The herds came down to the Lowlands in August, September and October. At the height of the droving-trade, during the first years of the 19th century, more than 160,000 animals were annually gathered and sold on Stenhousemuir, two miles to the north of Falkirk. The Tuesday sales were busy, noisy and good-humoured, the moor dark with long-horned cattle and lines of carts and gigs. At dusk the light of naphtha flames glowed inside the tents of bankers, the booths of ale-sellers, tavern-masters and fairground entertainers. By 1849 droving had passed its peak, and in that year, for the first time, sheep outnumbered the black cattle brought to the tryst. Even so, cattle drives continued into this century, diminishing in size and importance. One of the last, nine years before I was born, came ashore on Glenelg Bay, moving inland by Loch Hournhead to a modest sale in Lochaber.

The first reference to a cattle-tryst, I believe, was eight hundred years ago in the records of Melrose Abbey, and it is hard to understand why the long history of Highland droving has not been a rich inspiration to Scottish literature. The great days of cattle-driving in the American West, the cutting of trails from Texas to Kansas, Wyoming and Montana, lasted no more than twenty years, from the end of the Civil War to the Great Blizzard and the fencing of open range. But they have produced a colourful balladry and mythology, a scholarly library of sober history, good as well as bad fiction, and an enduring art-form in the cinema, all of it strongly influencing the spirit of the American people and exciting the imagination of diverse nations throughout the world. Scotland's historical fiction, obsessed as much of it is with Jacobite hagiolatry and romance, has neglected the adventurous and frequently hazardous life of the Highland drover. It is too late now for that imbalance to be corrected, and long has been perhaps. The written record of the American West and its transformation into legend, the work of Ned Buntline as much as Owen Wister and Mari Sandoz, began while its inspiration was still a reality on the Great Plains beyond the Mississipppi.*

There is a small mystery in the story of Highland cattle that I have yet to see explained or acknowledged. Until the second or third decade of the 19th century all references to them carried that adjective *black*, and this was not, as I have been told, because of the peat-mud that darkened their long hair. The black bull of the Highlands, like the black herds it sired, was prized for its glossy coat, its green and waxen horns, its tapering quarters. But above all, "his colour should be black," wrote an agriculturalist in 1811, "that being reckoned the hardiest and more durable species." Hardy or not, it did not endure. By the middle of the century, artists who responded to a growing sentimental interest in the Highlands were picturing the now familiar red or red-brown animal, the pretty postcard beast still seen upon the braes. Black cattle were gone, and none can be seen today except a rare de-horned beast, forlorn among its red brethren. Perhaps I do know a common-sense explanation for their disappearance and consider it unsatisfying, preferring to believe that Providence or the like spared them from ignoble survival when the people who had depended upon them were departing, and the Great Cheviot was flooding over their valley pastures.

The only land-way to Glenelg is the road from Shiel Bridge at the head of Loch Duich, a twisting hair-pin ascent of one thousand feet to the pass of Mam Ratagan. Except for re-surfacing, it has

* Scotland's contribution to the growth of the American cattle industry was considerable, its capital heavily invested in a number of Scottish-American companies. Many of the ranch-managers, trail-bosses and cowmen were Scots, Highland or of Highland descent, like Murdo Mackenzie who built the great Matador Ranch with money from Dundee. It is not too fanciful, I think, to believe that as Highland droving declined some of the spirit and courage that had sustained it for eight centuries was reborn on the rangelands of America.

This Highland village on Loch Duich, probably at Inverinate, survived into the 19th century. It was at such a clachan in Kintail, beyond the loch, that Johnson drank frothed milk and scattered pennies among children whom Boswell thought could be wild Indians.

scarcely changed since 1809 when Telford improved the old military highway to Bernera barracks. I wish I could have climbed this road before much of it was red-walled and darkened by a forestry plantation, and thus seen the rugged mountains of Lochalsh and Kintail slowly unfolding to the north and east. But from the summit, when the road comes out of the cathedral pines, there is at last a noble view of the Five Sisters of Kintail, three times the height of Ratagan, with lakes of mist between their peaks. And westward, where the road curls down to Glenelg Bay, are the dark green waters of Kyle Rhea and the sun-hazed mountains of Skye. It was on the summit at Bealach Ratagan that I once saw an eagle *below* me in Glen Mor, the upturned fingers of its wing-feathers lightly resting on a thermal current. It hung motionless for a timeless moment and then, on one wing-beat it seemed, soared upward and lost itself in the sun.

Soon it may again be possible to look eastward to Kintail from the northern ascent to Ratagan, although the price to be paid is perhaps unacceptable. The unnatural forest has matured and is being felled. Great lorries laden with timber are breaking the road and weakening the structure of Telford's once sturdy bridges. The annual cost of repairing the road, already high, can only increase, but differences of opinion over the responsibility for its maintenance delay a practical agreement upon its future. There is no other mainland access to Glenelg. The last mail-boat visited it twenty years ago, the last Clyde steamer or coaster ten years before that. There is only the road, built for horsemen, wheeled carts and marching feet. The forest is not inexhaustible, of course, and in time the felling will stop, but by then the road may be unusable, and the little communities of Glenelg will be neglected and alone.

Boswell and Johnson passed over Mam Ratagan on their way to Skye, the Doctor riding a small grey horse that staggered under his weight and gave him unhappy thoughts about mortality above

The proper dress for a Highland chief in 1831, as suggested by James Logan in *The Scottish Gael*. Part fact, part romantic nonsense, illustrations like this set sartorial standards which still endure. Tartan, said Logan without giving proof, was a Highlander's tabard, "by which his name and clan were at once recognised."

(*Overleaf*) The head of Loch Duich and the Five Sisters of Kintail from Mam Ratagan. At such a spot on this old military road Johnson's horse staggered and he called out for John Hay to hold it. The Highlander tried to soften the Doctor's fear by talking to him as if to a child. Boswell thought this absurd, and decided that Hay was "a common, ignorant, Highland clown."

Corporal Samuel Macpherson, from the parish of Laggan on
Speyside. A leader of the Black Watch mutiny in 1743, he was shot
in the Tower of London with his cousin Malcolm MacPherson and
their comrade Farquhar Shaw. The men of the regiment who
watched the execution hid their tears behind their bonnets and plaids.

The Cuillins across Loch Scavaig. The nearest saw-tooth peak is Gars Bheinn, the first of a crescent ridge of twenty-four savage peaks. It is said that they were once a great table-land five times their present height until they were broken by the ice that covered them, or the convulsion of the earth beneath.

(*Overleaf*) The new bridge over the narrows of Loch Leven at Ballachulish. The copse of trees on the south bank covers the hill where James of the Glen recited the XXXV Psalm before his hanging. "False witnesses did rise up: they laid to my charge things that I knew not ..." A military guard was kept on the spot for seventeen months. When it was removed, a gale tore the skeleton from the gibbet.

The pleated basalt of Kilt Rock on the Trotternish coast of Skye has
made its name inevitable, with horizontal strata completing the sett
of a tartan. In the foreground here is the waterfall by which the little
Loch Mealt drains into the sea, 300 feet below.

Samuel Johnson "dressed for his Highland tour." The stout oaken staff was specially brought from London, but, said Boswell, "since his last illness he has had a weakness in his knees, and has not been able to walk easily."

a precipice. He was in a dreary humour, angered by the journey and by Boswell who had pressed on ahead, anxious to reach the inn at Glenelg. Johnson called him back with a passionate shout, saying he would rather pick a man's pocket than desert him thus. After an exchange of polite incivilities they rode on together, in friendship again and in anticipation of warm comfort at the inn. Instead of that, they found the place "damp and dirty ... a variety of bad smells ... a coarse black greasy fir table ... with not a single article we could eat or drink." After the misery of the pass, and now the thought of a night to be spent on a wretched bed of hay, Johnson was surprisingly calm. From vanity, suggested Boswell, still nettled by his companion's ill-temper that afternoon. "No, sir," said Johnson, "from philosophy."

I make no apology for my frequent references to these entertaining travellers. Their companionship in Scotland is stimulating, and Boswell's *Tour* is the best account yet written of a journey to the Highlands, or likely to be written.* They came westward to Shiel Bridge from Fort Augustus, through opening hills and narrowing glens that are the legendary hunting-ground of the Feinn. They left the fort at noon and "travelled eleven miles through a wild country" before resting for the night at the inn of Aonach in Glen Moriston. Aonach is no longer marked, or remembered perhaps, but I believe it was on the north bank of the river close to Achlain. Here the heather-hidden track of the old military road comes down the side of Druim a' Chathair to the present highway on the south bank, eleven or twelve miles across the hills from Fort Augustus. The keeper of the turf-walled inn was a MacQueen who had fought for the Pretender at Culloden, and although he was not a young man he was thinking of emigrating. "All the Laird of Glenmoriston's people would bleed for him," he said, "if they were well used." But seventy men had gone out of the glen to America and he intended to follow them now that his rent had risen to twenty pounds, twice what he could afford. Johnson was sympathetic, and wished MacQueen's landlord would go to America instead. The innkeeper said he would be sorry at that, for the Laird "could not shift for himself in America as he could do." Boswell observed that this was generously said, missing the point of MacQueen's irony, I think. Despite their approval of the innkeeper's sensibility and English pronunciation, his little shelf of books and a daughter worthy enough to be given Johnson's copy of Cocker's *Arithmetick*, both men went to bed believing MacQueen might rob and murder them in their sleep. They were perhaps ashamed of that fear in the morning, when he gave them his protective company for some miles along the road, and made Boswell weep with his account of Culloden.

They took the recently completed military route through Glen Moriston to Glenelg, the second of four roads that have been built here since 1654, when one of Cromwell's avenging generals burnt his way from Loch Ness to Loch Alsh. A good highway now makes this long approach to the Isles. It is the best of Highland roads, or so I believe until I pass again by Lochaweside. There is a fine harmony between earth and sky on the braes of Glen Moriston, a robust strength where the rolling land climbs to the clouds, stretching its limbs and opening its lungs to the winds from Knoydart and Glenelg. Five miles from Achlain at Ceannacroc, a

* They did not travel alone. They were accompanied by Boswell's servant Joseph Ritter, a Bohemian six feet tall, and as far as Glenelg by Lachlan Vass and John Hay, two Highlanders whom they employed as guides at Inverness, and from whom they rented their horses. While the travellers and Joseph rode, with a fourth horse to carry their portmanteaux, Vass and Hay ran on foot beside them. Although the Highlanders' tolerance of their employers' eccentricity and bickering must have been admirable, their presence is only briefly recorded in the books the travellers wrote. Boswell refers to them three times only, and Johnson once, approvingly but without giving their names. Since they and Ritter are often ignored in later accounts of the jaunt, this footnote is a small acknowledgement of their protective concern for their employers, and their contribution thereby to one of the great delights of English literature.

low stack above the waters of three small rivers, there is a roadside cairn for Roderick Mackenzie whose death here first inspired me to write about Scotland. And northward in the twisting glen of the River Doe is the rock-cave of Coiredhoga where the man for whom Mackenzie died was sheltered by seven outlaws. Twenty-three years ago, in the summer when *Culloden* was published, I set out to walk the rough path to the cave with my daughter. It is not far to go perhaps, but she was young, and although she would have stayed with me bravely as far as she could, it was a foolish thing to ask of her. After we had climbed a mile or so, and passed beyond a green waterfall, a shepherd came down the brae to us. He looked at my daughter and asked where we were going. When he was told, he smiled and handed her a sprig of heather, saying, "You will be walking no further this way."

Westward from Ceannacroc and in a deep brown furrow, Loch Cluanie is three miles longer and a hundred feet higher than when I first saw it, swollen now by a dam and by water that comes down from Loch Loyne through a tunnel two miles in length. Until the bespoke tailoring of the Forestry Commission has covered the shoulders of its enclosing hills, Cluanie will always appear bleak and unfinished, its shoreline so unnatural that I have been surprised to see a long-billed greenshank feeding in its shallows. It was more pleasing when there was a water-fringe of oak and birch below the hills, and yellow iris bending to the wind, the "delightful

Loch Cluanie in Glen Moriston. The level of the water has been artificially raised, and only the bare hills are as Johnson saw them when "the day was calm, the air soft, and all was rudeness."

spectacle" that Johnson saw when he paused beside it, sitting alone in thought while the horses were put to graze.

> The day was calm, the air soft, and all was rudeness, silence and solitude. Before me, and on either side, were high hills, which by hindering the eye from ranging, forced the mind to find entertainment. Whether I spent the hour well I know not; for here I first conceived the thought of this narration.

The clear recollection of inspiring time and place is beguiling, but provokes sceptical doubt. He had read Martin Martin's *Description of the Western Islands* in his youth, and carried a copy of it with him now. He had long desired to visit the Hebrides. "So long," he wrote in the opening sentence of his book, "that I scarcely remember how the wish was originally excited." He was aware that Boswell was keeping a daily journal, and it is impossible to believe that until he reached Loch Cluanie he had not once thought of writing his own account of their tour. When they resumed their journey he did not tell his companion of his momentous decision, and Boswell does not seem to have been aware of its moment of inspiration until Johnson's book was published. But they were bickering again. The Doctor was suffering from a painful stye, and was consequently in a contentious humour. When Boswell described one of the soaring peaks of the Five Sisters as a cone, Johnson said it was not, for one side was larger than the other. When the poor fellow then observed that a second mountain was immense, Johnson ended their conversation with a ponderous snub. "No, it is no more than a considerable protuberance." It is sad to think of them so out of sorts as they travelled through a country that always lifts my spirits. But I have never ridden toward the Five Sisters on the back of a Highland pony, by the rough stones of a military road, with a painful affliction and no certainty of a good inn to comfort me at dusk.

Whether or not inspiration did strike Johnson so pleasantly by the water of Loch Cluanie, I have sometimes wondered where he sat, and by what "clear rivulet." James Hogg had no doubt. In 1803 he walked over the hills from Glen Garry, crossed the River Moriston, and "joined the old military road at the very green spot where Dr Johnson rested, and first conceived the design of transmitting his tour to posterity." If my deductions from both accounts are correct, it was then half a mile up the brae from the loch, but now that has been raised it is closer to the water's edge where the little burn of Allt Coire Lundie passes under the modern road. And so, to the time and date of Johnson's professed inspiration, the morning of Wednesday, September 1, 1773, a map reference might now be added. It is 35/161107, but as to that, I could be wrong.

The considerable protuberances of the Five Sisters – a description that can destroy all aesthetic or erotic pleasure to be got from the first astonishing sight of them – are the eastern wall of Glen Shiel. Three miles westward from the head of Loch Cluanie, the valley is a narrow defile of steep mountains and dark moods, so perversely angled and shadowed that sunlight rarely touches one spot for more than a few minutes before moving to another saffron slope or high wall of blue rock. At each turn of the road, and of the storming, stony river it follows, the mountains draw in upon a traveller, and by the Bridge of Shiel the first of the Five Sisters sweeps her dark skirt to the south and almost closes the glen. The memory of defeat and despair is theatrically essential in so melancholy a place, and history supplies that here as it does elsewhere in the Highlands. On a June evening in 1719, three hundred white-coat Spaniards of the Regiment of Galicia formed their battle-line on a braeside above the stone bridge, committed by their king to the Pretender's cause and to yet another wasteful Jacobite Rebellion. They nobly stood their ground under the fire of mortar-shells, each trailing smoke from the river bank below. When their Highland allies fled, and the English and Dutch advanced against their breastwork, the Spaniards retreated to higher ground in good order. They did not surrender until the following morning, three thousand feet above the floor of the glen and in a misted hollow still known as Coirein nan Spainteach.

One can never be sure of the weather in Glen Shiel, except that whatever it may be to the east or west it will be reversed here. I left the Skye ferry-point at Lochalsh one morning in early spring, called home urgently and aware that I must make an unbroken journey of six hundred miles to the south. It was almost abandoned within the hour. The sun was warm on the Kyle when I set out, the broad windows of the hotel reflecting a blue sky and a calm sea, but as I passed by Loch Duich to the soot-black mouth of Glen Shiel a monstrous cloud was hiding the heads of the Five Sisters. The cars I now met had thick snow on their roofs and bonnets, their wind-screen wipers flapping a nervous warning. At Inver-shiel all sound and sight was lost in a whirling white screen, from which a yellow school-bus confidently emerged, bright faces singing behind its windows. Two miles on, the wind changed and improved the visibility ahead, but snow was now rolling down the flanks of the Sisters in turning waves, building drifts across the road, and at Bridge of Shiel the black and metallic river was in joyous spate. Beyond the gorge, when the hills fell back, the wind was stronger, driving the snow from the surface of the road but covering it with bright crystals of ice. I passed Loch Cluanie without being aware of it until I heard the roar of its overflowing dam, and then suddenly at Ceannacroc Bridge the snow stopped, the clouds torn northward to Affric. Sunlight glistened on the Braes of Glen Moriston, and there was a clutch of bright primroses at the foot of Mackenzie's cairn.

Glen Shiel was the land of the Macraes, the chamberlains of Kintail, its Catholic vicars and the standard-bearers of its Mackenzie lords. Their stronghold was the castle of Eilean Donan at the bent elbow of Loch Alsh and Loch Duich. It is the best known of all Highland castles, romantically placed on its saintly island at the end of a slender arched bridge. Since its first brief film appearance in *The Ghost Goes West* its varying image has decorated

Since it made its first film appearance half a century ago a view of the castle of Eilean Donan is unavoidable. This almost persuades the eye that it is real, and not a reconstruction of the stones which the Royal Navy tumbled down in 1719.

more post-cards, calendars, biscuit-tins and holiday guides than any other. But despite its arrow-slit windows, crenellated walls and crow-step gables, it is largely a 20th-century reconstruction, completed fifty years ago from the ruins of the original, destroyed by naval gunfire in 1719. Although I do not like it, or at least its artful pretensions, I remember that one thought behind its restoration was to make it a war memorial to the Macraes of Kintail, a brave people who once called themselves Mackenzie's Shirt of Mail. They suffered bitterly in three Jacobite Rebellions, but many of them were still living in Glen Shiel when Boswell and Johnson passed through on their way to Mam Ratagan. Boswell was distressed by their appearance, their black and wild faces, and said that it was like being among a tribe of Indians. "Yes, sir," agreed Johnson, "but not so terrifying." He was momentarily in a good humour, distributing pennies among the children as he sat on a turf bench, drinking frothed milk from a wooden cog. Always ready

The Canongate Tolbooth in Edinburgh as it was a century ago. In 1778 it was stormed by mutineers of Seaforth's Highlanders, mostly Macraes from Kintail who called themselves Mackenzie's Shirt of Mail. It may thus be proper that the Cross on the Canongate Church next door is supported by the antlers of a stag, the badge of the Mackenzie lords of Kintail.

to deflect his companion's critical opinion of the Scots by suggesting he had the qualities of a fine Caledonian himself, Boswell said he would make a good chief. The old man was pleased by this, but it did not blind him to the realities of such a rank.

> "Were I a chief, I would dress my servants better than myself, and knock a fellow down if he looked saucy to a Macdonald in rags; but I would not treat men as brutes."

In the winter of 1778 the Mackenzie chief, Lord Seaforth, came to Kintail and enlisted a hundred young Macraes for his regiment of Highlanders. It was not a happy battalion. The Macraes, and other men whom Seaforth had gathered from his lands in Ross and on the Long Isle, were ill-used by their brutal officers. Five hundred of them mutinied in Edinburgh, and held Arthur's Seat under arms for three days until their grievances were redressed. They had been told that they were to serve the Crown against its rebellious subjects in America, and one of the assurances now given them on Arthur's Seat was that they would not be sent to the East Indies, a station feared and detested by all soldiers. They had also been told that when its service was over the regiment would be brought home to the Highlands where they would be discharged, close to their homes. In 1781 they were sent to India, and a third of them died of fever and flux during the voyage. Three years later, the survivors of a hard and wasting war against Hyder Ali were disbanded in that country, ten thousand sea-miles from Loch Duich and the Five Sisters of Kintail. "Our discharge put in our hands," said their poet sergeant, Christopher Macrae, "free to go where we wished, and told everywhere there was no ship, nor boat nor sail . . ."

> It is a pity that I am not as light
> as the hawk, slim flying in the sky.
> I would take the desert road
> and I would not rest in the tree-tops.
> In spite of the violence of Turkey

I would pass it by like a lark in the sun,
and I would make a complaint in London
that would bring us all home.

No complaint was made in London, and few of the Macraes
came home to Kintail. *"Of the hundred of us ... only an odd one
surviving."* In 1803, James Hogg found the little townships of Glen
Shiel "mostly in ruins, the estate being all converted into sheep-
walks." He was hungry, and exhausted by a long walk on the
rough stones of the neglected military road. The remaining people
of the glen told him that they had no food to sell, but a young man
ran after him and drew him back to a cottage, giving him bread,
whey and cheese, refusing all payment. Refreshed by this, Hogg
pressed on to the inn at Invershiel. To his relief, perhaps, its
landlord was a Borderer from Annandale.

There are still Macraes in Kintail, people of the name or its
allegiance. Some hold to the old faith, my friend Rory Mackay
once told me. "They are good Gaelic speakers," he said "and fleet
of foot on the hills, which is right and proper."

O N THE GREEN FLOOR OF GLEN LYON between Keltney Burn and Fortingall, and two miles from the river gorge below Creag Mhor, there is a greystone figure of a Highlander. Masked by trees at a twist of the road it could be mistaken for one of many war memorials in the mountains, lonely reminders of a wasted generation and the last Diaspora of the Gael. Seven miles to the east, where William Adam's classical bridge arches across the Tay at Aberfeldy, there is another stone figure, in belted plaid and feathered bonnet, his musket slung, and his right hand in the basket-hilt of his sheathed broadsword. Properly set in the heart of Perthshire, and at the geographical centre of Scotland, each represents a man whose work, or short and tragic life, has diversely influenced my imagination and my writing. The first is a monument to Major-General David Stewart of Garth, at the entrance to a drive that once led to his modest home on a lower brae of Drumcharry. His *Sketches of the Character, Manners and Present State of the Highlanders*, published in 1822, are the rich source of much that has been written about the people and regiments of the Highlands, and his archetypical clansman is an amalgam of Knight Templar and Paladin from which fiction and fact make their continuing casts. The statue is perhaps his likeness, or how he might have wished to see himself, bravely posed and without his small-lensed spectacles. His kilt, plaid and sporran are in the absurd military fashion adopted by the True Highlanders, although the stone buttons on his jacket are a poor indication of the cairngorm studs he wore when he attended their inaugural meeting, leading Alasdair Ranaldson's lady into the torchlight for the first dance of the evening.

The second Highlander, above a tapering cairn of sculpted stones, stands on what was once a natural river-bank but is now a lawned and flowered garden. In May 1740, six Independent Companies of the Black Watch were embodied here as a marching-regiment of the Crown, the 43rd Highlanders. The monument is their memorial, erected by public subscription a century ago. Five hundred pounds were collected at the doors of great houses and cottages in Strathtay, and a crowd of six thousand came by special

A Highland soldier by William Adam's bridge at Aberfeldy marks the spot where the Black Watch was embodied as a marching-regiment in 1739. A tablet says the bridge was built in one summer, but it was another year before workmen erected the parapet and obelisks. The stone soldier is more than he appears; he was innocently modelled on a likeness of a Black Watch private shot for mutiny in 1743.

trains to watch the unveiling in a November mist. The ceremony was a manifestation of patriotic emotion, respect and obedience to established order, and few if any of those present, including Mr Rhind the sculptor I suspect, can have been aware of a grotesque irony in that dramatic stone figure. It had been modelled from an 18th-century engraving of a private soldier of the Forty-Third, a catch-penny sheet sold at the sign of the Black Horse in Cornhill, London. The soldier was a young drover from Rothiemurchus, Farquhar Shaw, whose dignified courage in the last week of his life moved one observer to record that he had "a generous disposition of mind seldom found among men in more elevated stations." Three years after the muster at Aberfeldy, and together with two corporals of the regiment,* he was executed for his part in a noble mutiny. They were shot by a firing-party of the Scots Guards in the Tower of London, against a blank wall of the Chapel. "There was not much blood spilt," the Governor wrote in his diary, "but what was, I ordered immediately to be covered with earth, and their graves levelled so that no remains of the execution might be perceived." Their weeping comrades buried them, each in a fifteen-shilling coffin and a few paces from the wall, and perhaps they lie there still.

The mutiny of the Black Watch was the first of sixteen major revolts in Highland regiments between 1743 and 1804, angry protests against broken promises or the Government's callous indifference to the exceptional conditions of their enlistment and their peculiar attachment to their native dress and language.

* Samuel Macpherson and Malcolm Macpherson, cousins from Breakachie and Driminard in Strathspey.

Contrary to romantic belief, the Highlander was not always a willing soldier. He was frequently recruited by threat and sold by the chiefs he trusted, and his songs regret the day he put on a red coat. *"If I were as I used to be, among the hills, I would not mount guard as long as I lived..."* The system of tenure-at-will made it easy for proprietors to force their young tenants into the regiments they were so eagerly raising, and in Sutherland this was done with despotic panache. The youths of each parish were summoned and inspected by William Wemyss, colonel of the new 93rd Regiment, and those who were offered a pinch from his snuff-mull and a dram from his flask were taken as soldiers. "I entered not as a matter of choice," wrote John Matheson who was enlisted in a Fencible regiment also raised by Wemyss, "but owing to the old feudal system of the country I was obliged to go to please the Laird. Plainly, every farmer was under the necessity of giving at least one of his sons if he had any fit for service."*

The Gaelic people's contribution to the British Army in the 18th century was grossly disproportionate. Three per cent only of the population, they nonetheless supplied the Crown with sixty-five marching and Fencible regiments, as well as independent companies, militia and volunteers. Social and political historians have been little concerned with this revealing field of research, beyond bland observations that after the last Jacobite Rebellion the *martial energy* of the Highlanders was *channelled* into the Army. They have ignored the nature of Highland recruitment, its cause and effect, as they neglected the Clearances until recent years. They are sometimes the slavish servants of prevailing authority, past and present, and in Scotland this has encouraged their indifference to Highland history, or at best a nodding acknowledgement. There is almost a sigh of relief in their writings when Culloden and the punitive Acts at last bring a proud and contradictory people within the understandable pattern of southern government, and Johnson might well have been speaking of them when he said Lowlanders were strangers to the needs of the northern people "whose life they would model, and whose evils they would remedy." There is also a lingering contempt for the Highlanders, disguised now as patronising affection but nonetheless an echo of the feelings expressed by James Wolfe when he was commanding an English regiment at Perth. Eight years later, at the moment of his death, the musketry and broadswords of the men he despised were securing his immortality, destroying the Regiments of Languedoc and La Sarre, and breaking the French advance on the Plains of Abraham. Fraser's 78th Highlanders suffered more casualties than any other British battalion that day, and none of them knew what their dying general had once thought of their race and why it should be expended in this wasteful manner.

* The 93rd Sutherland Highlanders and the Sutherland Fencibles were raised in the name of Elizabeth Gordon, Countess and later Duchess of Sutherland. Her English husband was the employer of James Loch and Patrick Sellar, architect and mason of the Policy of Improvement. In 1881 the 93rd was amalgamated with the 91st Argyll Highlanders.

They are hardy, intrepid, accustom'd to a rough Country, and no great mischief if they fall. How can you better employ a secret enemy than by making his End conducive to the common good? If this sentiment should take wind, what an execrable and bloody being shou'd I be considered here in the midst of Popery and Jacobitism, surrounded on every side as I am with this Itchy Race.*

This cynical attitude became more open toward the end of the century and was exercised in an increasing disregard for the special qualities of Highland regiments. The mutinies which resulted are the dark side of military history. Although reminders of them still provoke hostility, a study of the methods by which the regiments were recruited, and the reasons why they mutinied, is essential to an understanding of the destruction of the clan society and the dispersal of its people. When I wrote a full account of the revolts it was never my intention to devalue the achievements and valour of Highland soldiers, nor could I, having been a peripheral witness of their courage at 's-Hertogenbosch, Venlo, and the crossing of the Rhine. But one critic of the book, an officer and historian of the Black Watch, hoped "to high heaven that it will not be accepted as impartial history by the ordinary reader." Understandably, perhaps, he was particularly offended by my assertion that Highlanders were the first of Britain's colonial levies, originally used to police their own hills, and then deployed in imperial wars. That interpretation was fair, I think, and my lack of impartiality might have been shared by the remaining tenants of Sutherland in 1854. When told by their ministers and the Duke's factors that they should enlist for the Crimean War, they baa-ed in response and cried, "Since you have preferred sheep to men, let sheep defend you!"

At the time of writing *Mutiny* I regretted the absence of any reminder of the revolts on the ground where they took place – the water-orchard of Ladywood, the lochside at Linlithgow, a street in Portsmouth, Dumfries, Glasgow or Edinburgh. Military revolt is of course distasteful to all governments, however long ago it occurred, and authority in general cannot be expected to think of it with sympathy. But in one case, the mutiny of the Black Watch, I once hoped to establish some public acknowledgement of the event.

The regiment was quartered at Hampstead and Highgate in the spring of 1743. The government's intention was to send it to Flanders, but the soldiers had not been told this when they left Scotland. They thought, and were encouraged to think, that they were marching south to be reviewed by the King, after which they

---

* A double reference, no doubt, to their pride and the skin complaints from which they were believed to suffer. Wolfe's comments are taken from a letter to his friend, Captain William Rickson. His proposal for the recruitment of Highland regiments from lately disaffected clans may have been passed to the Duke of Cumberland, who in turn recommended it to William Pitt. In 1766, when the Prime Minister reminded the Commons of his own part in raising such regiments, he used words remarkably similar to Wolfe's. "I called forth and drew into your service a hardy and intrepid race of men ..."

would return to the Highlands. Their officers had also failed to explain that a marching-regiment could be sent wherever the Crown required, unlike the companies of the old Watch which had been recruited for employment in the mountains only. When told that the waiting transports at Dartford and Gravesend would take them to Flanders, many of them refused to believe it, saying "they were informed they were to be sold for slaves in the West Indies." This fear was not as nonsensical as it may now seem. The Caribbean was the nightmare of their recent history, a place of lost souls to which many of their ancestors, defeated in one rebellion or another, had been transported as felons or bonded servants. They also complained of ill-usage and arrears of pay, and in an atmosphere of growing rumour, suspicion and distrust, the response of the most resolute was simple and direct. Since they had been deceived and betrayed, they said, they were released from their enlistment and would go home to their hills. They gathered by night on Finchley Common and travelled northward for 150 miles before they were surrounded by pursuing dragoons on the timbered ridge of Ladywood, four miles to the west of Oundle. They took a defensive position within the moated enclosure of that water-orchard, near the cruciform shell of a Jacobean manor-house, Lyveden New Bield. They swore to die sword in hand rather than go to Jamaica, but toward midnight of their second day in the wood they surrendered on trust, believing they were assured of a pardon. All were court-martialled and sentenced to death, and although three only were shot the rest were sent to Georgia or the West Indies, from which pestilential garrisons few can have returned.

The National Trust now owns Lyveden New Bield, the water-orchard and the lost grave of a Highlander who died beneath the trees during the night. It seemed to me that a commemorative plaque on a pathway beside the wood would be a fitting recognition of those confused and honourable men, as well as adding to the interest of the site. I proposed this to the Trust, offering to defray any reasonable cost. I cannot remember submitting a draft

The shell of Lyveden New Bield in Northants has been uncompleted since 1605, when its owners were involved in the Gunpowder Plot. The Black Watch mutineers, retreating from London, took a defensive position here, declaring "We chuse to loose our lives in making our way if our pardon will not be granted."

of the wording that might be used, but I have a copy of it still.

> In this wood on Whitsunday, May 23, 1743, ninety-eight men of the 43rd Highland Regiment (Black Watch) at last surrendered to the King's mercy without bloodshed. Five days before, they had marched away from London in defiance of their officers, declaring that promises made to them had been broken, and that because they feared a further betrayal of trust they would return to their mountains and soldier no more. This plaque remembers all of them, and in particular
>
>
>
> Corporal Samuel Macpherson
> Corporal Malcolm Macpherson
> Private Farquhar Shaw
> shot for mutiny and desertion in the
> Tower of London, July 18, 1743
> "Sliochd fineachan uasal,
> a ghin o na tuathaich"
>
>

The Trust acknowledged the proposal with interest, but thought a plaque "might be a disruptive intervention in this isolated yet complex and imaginative architectural setting", and that a more suitable reference to the event would be an appendix to the next edition of the guide-book. After a further exchange of letters my correspondent agreed that the Trust should "consider the possibility of putting up a plaque, perhaps in the area where tickets are bought." That was eight years ago. There is as yet no plaque and no new guide-book, although I am told the latter may soon be printed.

My earliest knowledge of the Black Watch Mutiny came from a melancholy account in Stewart's *Sketches*. I first opened the two volumes of this work fifty years ago in the Reading Room of the British Museum, to which I had somehow acquired a ticket while I was still at school. They contain a history of most of the Highland regiments raised in the 18th century, much of it drawn from Stewart's personal knowledge of men and events, and it undoubtedly excited my romantic interest. This is now more realistic, I hope, but just as I am still emotionally and perversely moved by the swirl and colour of tartan, so do I respond to the story of the regiments, and I am a plodding visitor to the museums that preserve their memory, not the least at Fort George and Stirling Castle.

Before their amalgamation with the Cameron Highlanders in 1963, the Seaforths had their own depot at Fort George on a spit of land in the Moray Firth. Magnificently moated, an irregular polygon in shape, with six great bastions, lunettes, glacis and ravelin, it is one of the finest buildings of its kind in Europe, and more pleasing to me than Vauban's grey fortress at Tournai where I once spent an uncomfortable night, my last in the Army. Fort George was built after the Rebellion of 1745, when there was no great need of it, perhaps, and it now lies on the water like a stranded prehistoric animal, by the black-legged oil platforms at Ardersier. Stewart was stationed here in 1792, in *Bliadhna nan Caorach*, the Year of the Sheep, when the men of Ross tried to reverse the flow of history by driving the Cheviot from their

Johnson was unmoved by Fort George, saying he would have been surprised if it had not been extraordinary. It still has a modest military role, and is occasionally used by film-makers. Some of its vaulted chambers appeared in the television version of *Culloden*.

glens. He marched against them as a lieutenant of the Black Watch, and because many men of the regiment had been enlisted in Ross he was relieved when the affair was settled without bloodshed, "as the necessity of turning their arms against their fathers, their brothers, and their friends, must have been in the last degree painful to the feelings of the soldiers." And dangerous to their discipline, he felt obliged to add. Nineteen years earlier, Johnson and Boswell had dined at Fort George, called to the Governor's table by a beating drummer of the 37th Foot. If the diarist was so affected by the grandeur of the fort as to remember youthful ambitions and fancy himself a military man, his companion, may Reason be thanked, was properly unmoved. "It did not strike *him* as anything extraordinary," said Boswell, "if there had been less than what we found, it would have surprised him".

When I first visited Fort George, the Seaforths' museum was in an ante-room to the Officers' Mess, I think, intimate and personal like a family's loving collection of memorabilia. Its attendant and guide was an aged sergeant in scarlet sash and Mackenzie trews. At first he watched me from a discreet distance, standing to attention by the door while I studied the display of old uniforms and arms, brown photographs of bearded soldiers leaning reflectively on their muskets, fading letters, bright medals, silent timepieces, and tinted engravings of battles in which there was no noise of pain or gunfire, no stench of blood. I turned from these to the glass cases in the centre of the room, each filled with gold and silver it seemed, the shameless loot of Victoria's little wars. Now the sergeant approached me, by a well-measured pace on the polished floor. He introduced each case in a soft Highland voice that ached to lift itself across a barrack-square. "This is something our officers brought back from Lucknow ... from Delhi ... Did you know we are called The Saviours of India ...? And this from Kabul ... from Kandahar ..." As I drove westward on the Inverness

Stirling Castle became the residence of the Stuart kings, and they built a Renaissance palace within it. The sculptured statues on the wall-shafts are life-size which makes pygmies of the Highlanders in this romantic 19th century print.

road, it occurred to me that the most moving item in the museum had not been an exhibit but the pipe-clayed gaiters the sergeant wore. According to legend, they are a remembrance of the rags which Highlanders wrapped about their bleeding feet on the winter retreat to Corunna. "The soldiers suffered more from want of shoes than from any other privation," said Stewart of Garth,

> . . . and marching over mountains deeply covered with snow, their feet were torn by the ice, and their toes frost-bitten. The shoes were supplied by contract, and, as is too common in such cases, became wholly unserviceable after a few days marching.

Stirling Castle is the headquarters of the Argyll and Sutherland Highlanders, an odd Victorian hybrid uniting regiments with origins and allegiances at opposite ends of the Highlands. One November, when Edinburgh was choked by yellow fog, I asked at Waverley if Stirling was free of it, and being told it was I went there to see the Argylls' museum. I should have known the fog would be thicker on the Stirling Plain, blinding all sight and muting all sound. From the station I felt my way by foot and hand to Spittal Street, and upward there toward the Castle. A few paces ahead of me, a man and woman were walking just as cautiously, and when we reached Castle Wynd a tall sergeant stepped from the fog and assumed we were one party. He led us across the great parade and through the outer gate to a courtyard square, the fog now burning orange from lights behind the mullioned windows of King James's Palace. Before I could explain why I was there, the sergeant opened a door and brushed us into a large hall. It was brightly lit and cold. A platoon of young soldiers was at ease in

the middle of the floor, eyes to their front and pink faces lifted as they listened to an address from the commander of the Highland Brigade, a welcome to the regiment now that their initial training was over, and an unemotional recital of its history. They were watched by admiring relatives from banked rows of chairs, to the topmost and inescapable tier of which I was taken by a sergeant whose breath, as he bent to whisper guidance, was a pleasing indication that he had begun the afternoon well. When the ceremony was ended, young subalterns moved among the seated audience. How many sons, I was asked, did I have with the regiment? I apologised for my intrusion and was politely taken to the museum in the Officers' Mess. There I was left alone with the silent relics and faded honours of other young men, now long dead.

When I came down to the courtyard again it was crowded with khaki and the green tartan of the Argylls. Dusk had thickened the fog, and torchlight beams moved across a Jeep where a Regimental Sergeant-Major sat impassively erect, his wife beside him and a drawn broadsword in his hand. He was leaving the battalion and the Army, I think, honourably and traditionally escorted from the garrison. Eight sergeants pulled the Jeep away through the gate, behind a strutting piper whose brave music was soon muffled by the fog. When one of the sergeants returned, I was the first of the watchers he saw. He stopped before me, greatly moved, and it was some seconds before he said "Ye'll no see that again." I asked why, and he struck me on the chest with his fist, and more force than he intended, I hope. "Because that's Argylls!" he said, and turned away.

"Like a hawk on its basalt rock …" Stirling Castle looks over the cockpit of Scotland. It has seen the rise and fall of Wallace, the triumph of Bruce over England, and centuries of religious and political squabbles. The graveyard at its foot seems somehow appropriate.

I understood his emotion later, when I realised he must have known that his regiment might soon be disbanded. The public announcement of this was followed by a vigorous campaign to reverse the Government's decision. There was scarcely a car in Scotland, or a wall it seemed, that did not carry a sticker exhorting the country to *Save the Argylls!*, and officers of impressive rank (retired) told television cameras and radio microphones of their shock and dismay. The response was enthusiastic, arousing that admirable but wasteful passion which Scots sometimes expend upon such inconsequential matters as the flying of an incorrect standard during a Royal visit, or the lack of an anthem for sporting events, while ignoring a greater injury in authority's continuing neglect of their economy. But the Argylls were indeed saved, and the Government was no doubt pleased that the wilder anger of Scottish nationalism was so easily placated.

Although I can acknowledge the sentiment behind the campaign I was unable to feel much sympathy for it, remembering the snuff-mull and the whisky-flask, the first recruitment of Sutherland men from Strath Helmsdale, Glen Cassley and Strath Naver. And I could not help comparing it with the hurt but dignified manner in which the Cameronians had accepted their disbandment three years before. I have said earlier that this was the only Scottish regiment in the British Army to be raised by the people and not the Crown. When James II and VII abandoned the throne of Britain in December, 1688, it was four months before the Convention of the Estates in Scotland finally resolved *"That an Act be brought in from the Committee for Settling the Crown upon William and Mary, King and Queen of England."* During that uneasy interregnum Parliament House and the city of Edinburgh were protected by six thousand Presbyterian zealots. Many of them were Cameronians, so called from their attachment to the person and teaching of Richard Cameron, a field-preacher killed by dragoons on the high moorland of Aird's Moss. In April, a month before William and Mary formally accepted the Crown of Scotland, the Estates gave the Earl of Angus a commission to muster one thousand young Cameronians into a regular battalion, which he did on Tuesday, May 14.

That day and date in 1968 the regiment was disbanded by Douglas Water, in cold wind and drizzle and on the green field where it was first mustered. The ceremony was an echo of the illegal conventicles which the Cameronians had once held in the hills, under arms and protected by outposts. When he had placed his sentries about the parade, a lieutenant reported to the conducting minister, "Sir, the picquets are posted. There is no enemy in sight, the service may proceed." Two psalms were sung, as they had been sung on that distant day – *I to the hills will lift mine eyes* and *The Lord's my shepherd, I'll not want.* At the end of the service the regimental colour was laid upon the Communion Table, and the companies were given their final order. *March off!*

The first lieutenant-colonel of the Cameronians, William Cleland, is buried in Perthshire, beneath a grass floor in the ruined

There has been a Christian centre at Dunkeld for more than fourteen hundred years, and a cathedral since 1127. It was brutally gutted by the Reformers in the 16th century, and again damaged when a Presbyterian regiment defended it against the clans in 1689. The eastern gable, seen here, is still marked by the bullets of that bitter struggle.

cathedral of Dunkeld. It is an odd resting-place for so resolute an enemy of the prelacy, but he was killed here at the age of twenty-eight, three months after the regiment was raised and while it was driving Jacobite clans from the burning town. Ironic, too, that he should lie for ever in these mountains, whose people he had derisively lampooned when the King's Commissioner sent the Highland Host into the south-west to terrorise its Covenanting communities.

> It's marvellous how in such weather,
> O'er hill and hop they came together,
> How in such storms they came so far.
> The reason is they're smeared with tar,
> Which doth defend them heel and neck,
> Just as it does their sheep protect.
> But lest ye doubt that this is true,
> They're just the colour of tarr'd wool.

The history of Perthshire is largely a story of little wars, feud and foray, and since the 17th century it has contributed more men and regiments to greater conflicts than any other part of Scotland. An account of these was assembled and edited eighty years ago by Katharine, Duchess of Atholl, and it is second only to Garth's Sketches in value and importance.* I have made great use of it, with wry memories of impassioned public meetings in my youth when The Red Duchess spoke in support of the Republican Government during the Spanish Civil War. Garth would have thought her politics perverse, but he would have admired her military history of Perthshire. Its spirit and mood reflect his work and inspiration. More than any other man, even Scott, he was responsible for the conventional and enduring picture of the

---

* *A Military History of Perthshire, 1660–1902*, 2 vols, R. A. & J. Hay, Perth 1908. Edited by the Marchioness of Tullibardine, later Duchess of Atholl.

Highland clansman and soldier. He began his own military career at the age of fourteen when he became an ensign in the 77th Atholl Highlanders. "The boy is of low stature," said his father's application for the commission, "but well made and strong; others agree that he is very promising, so that want of years is a fault that is always mending." The Atholl Regiment was ignominiously disbanded before Stewart was old enough to leave Glen Lyon and carry its colours, but he later fought with the Black Watch and the Seaforths in Egypt, Spain and Italy, and was a brevet-colonel and a C.B. when he retired on half-pay in 1815. That year he became a founder-member of the Society of True Highlanders, and was later the organiser of what Scott's biographer, John Lockhart, called "an hallucination" and a "plaided panorama", the Clan Gathering for George IV's visit to Edinburgh. Other Lowlanders were more derisive in their mockery of this charade, but all the chiefs who took part were agreed that it was a splendid success. All except the Duke of Atholl, who had thought of taking his Murray clansmen out of the city when he realised that the King was wearing pink tights beneath his scarlet kilt.

Scott's choice of Garth as the organiser of the Gathering, rather than Alasdair Ranaldson (who could not have organised anything, perhaps, except grounds for litigation) was undoubtedly due to the publication of his *Sketches* that year. He had begun them in 1817 when he was asked to repair the gaps in the records of the Black Watch, most of these having been taken by the French at Helvoetsluys in 1794. As he wrote, the work became more than a duty to his old regiment, expanding to a history of other Highland battalions and a loving account of the manners and customs of the clans. I have said elsewhere that the brave romanticism of the *Sketches* anaesthetised the guilt which men of Stewart's class and sensibility may have felt for the brutality of the Clearances. In fairness, he was deeply distressed by them, and it has been said that he hoped his book would reverse the tide of removal and emigration. His loyalty to the old chiefs prevented him from condemning them in words used by Scott, who wished there could be a salutary hanging of one at least, but thirty years after *Bliadhna na Caorach* he still remembered the Men of Ross with anger and sorrow. The great Clearances in Sutherland were not yet over when he began his *Sketches* and he was dismayed by the consequent loss of what he believed to be the finest quality of the Highlanders.

> More humane measures would undoubtedly have answered every good purpose; and had such a course been pursued as an enlightened humanity would have suggested, instead of depopulated glens, and starving peasantry, alienated from their superiors, and in the exacerbation of their feelings too ready to imbibe opinions hostile to the best interests of their country, we should still have seen a high-spirited and loyal people, ready at the nod of their respected chiefs, to embody themselves into regiments with the same zeal as in former times.

He wanted the best of two worlds, of course, and worlds which had never truly existed. The loss of a docile and willing "nursery

David Stewart of Garth,
"a plain soldier
unaccustomed to
composition" who
nonetheless wrote an
enduring account of the
Highlanders, their society
and their regiments.

of soldiers" is no longer thought to be the greatest evil of the
Clearances, nor was at the time by their victims.

There is also an irony in Stewart's honest compassion for the
evicted people. He does not appear to have extended this to the
slaves on the West Indian plantation from which he received a
modest income, and toward the end of his life he too became a
Remover. After his long military career he lived quietly at Garth
House, cared for by his spinster sister. The civil engineer Joseph
Mitchell, who was once his guest, described him as "the dear old
Colonel . . . a bluff soldier . . . universally beloved, particularly by
the common people." His solacing delight was a violoncello which
he had carried with him on his campaigns, although playing it
cannot have been easy with an arm never fully recovered from a

wound he had received at Maida. In the evenings, said Mitchell, "he would send for three or four young lads, tenants' sons, who were expert fiddlers, and thus he would have two or three hours of most excellent Scotch airs, reels and strathspeys." Musical evenings in the peace of Strathtay, further writing on the customs of the Highlands, would have been a pleasant end to his life, but his genteel poverty soon became unendurable. He first raised the rents of his estate and then cleared it of some of those loving common people, a necessary "thinning" of the population he called it. The sale of the land which had supported them was still not enough to pay his debts, and he finally petitioned London for a governorship in the West Indies. Now a Major-General, he left the Highlands in 1826, "with all the spirit and gaiety of a youthful veteran," said the *Gentleman's Magazine*. He died on Saint Lucia, three years later.

The tenants he had removed were still Gaelic speakers. The language is not heard in Perthshire now, or not naturally, not part of people and place as it can be in the Isles. But the use of it stubbornly survived into the beginning of this century. It was in Glen Lyon that I first heard a story I have since heard many times elsewhere on the mainland. A woman whose ancestors had lived in the glen for generations, and may have been Stewart's tenants, told me that when her father was a boy he was whipped by his father if he spoke Gaelic. The story is part of Highland folk-lore but nonetheless true, I think. One of the most determined and sustained efforts to break the independent spirit of the High-landers was an attempt to eradicate their language and replace it with English. Even the thought of a bi-lingual people was at times intolerable to Church or State. As early as the beginning of the 17th century the Lords of the Privy Council declared Gaelic to be one of two principal causes of savagery in the Highlands (the other was strong drink), and they issued ineffectual orders requiring the chiefs to educate their sons in the Lowlands. At the time of the Jacobite Rebellions statutory prohibition of the language was seriously considered. However absurd or impracticable that may appear, it should be seen in the context of other proposals made by men like the civilised Earl of Chesterfield, who advised the Prime Minister to "Starve the country by your ships, put a price on the heads of the Chiefs, and let the Duke put all to the fire and sword." Others suggested the emasculation of all Rebels and the transportation of their children, but in a more temperate mood it was agreed that the gradual elimination of Gaelic would satisfy Christian charity and political expediency.

This work had already begun before the Rebellion of 1715, with the sympathetic approval of many Presbyterians whose Church had once encouraged the employment of Gaelic-speaking minis-ters and the printing of Gaelic Testaments as part of its evangeli-sing mission to convert the clans from Popery. For almost sixty years the speaking and teaching of Gaelic was forbidden in all Highland schools established by the Society for the Propagation of Christian Knowledge, the only positive result of which was that

Loch Lyon, in the mountains to the south of Rannoch Moor, has been enlarged by a dam. Its waters have hidden the old drove-road, and the raiding-road by which the MacDonalds of Glencoe and Keppoch entered the rich Campbell lands of Breadalbane.

the children were robbed of an ability to express themselves fully in Gaelic or English. That sensible men and women in the south could approve of this idiocy is partly explained by their continuing fear of another armed rising in the mountains, and partly by their belief that the disappearance of Gaelic would be no great loss. Johnson said it was the rude speech of a barbaric people who had "few thoughts to express, and were content, as they conceived grossly, to be grossly understood." But this, he admitted, was what he had been told by others. His own opinion, not of the language but of the right of the people to speak and read it if they wished, was more sympathetic.

> Of what they had before the late conquest of their country, there remain only their language and their poverty. Their language is attacked on every side. Schools are erected, in which *English* only is taught, and there were lately some who thought it reasonable to refuse them a version of the holy scriptures, that they might have no monument of their mother-tongue.

The Society's prohibition was finally abandoned in 1766, four years after James Macpherson had published his spurious translation of Ossianic verse, persuading susceptible minds that there was a Gaelic mythology and literature comparable with ancient Greece. At the beginning of the 19th century the teaching of Gaelic was revitalised by the founding of the Gaelic Schools Society and the distribution of Testaments in that language by the British and Foreign Bible Society and the now contrite SPCK. This was part of and an encouragement to the rise of religious revivalism in the Highlands, alarming Presbyterian moderates and foreshadowing the great schism of 1843. Inspired by wandering preachers, the people may have turned to this new frenzy of faith as an escape from the confusion and decay of their society, but there can be no doubt of the joy they felt in once more speaking to God and listening to His Word in their own language. Had this encouragement of Gaelic been allowed to develop it might well have survived as the dominant tongue of the Highlands, but within four decades the Clearances had winnowed or dispersed the revivalists. It is not surprising that the strongest attachment to the language, and the inspirational use of it, should now be in the maritime provinces of Canada. The evicted people of the *Gaidhealtachd* who first settled there in the 18th century, and the revivalists who joined them later, left their homeland before a southern ascendancy finally persuaded them that their culture and their language were barbaric, and that only by military service could they earn the approval of the inheritors of their hills. And those who remained, still influenced by the malevolent spirit of that original ban, were sometimes convinced that dependence upon their ancient tongue would not only disadvantage their children in later life but was also sinful before God and thus deserving of a whipping.

There is a point beyond which the decline of a living language becomes irreversible, and it is hard not to believe that this was long since reached in the Highlands and the Isles. Gaelic continues as the natural tongue of some communities, but they are diminishing with the wasting of the economy that once supported them, and might still sustain them if successive Governments were not indifferent to them and their language. It is taught in island schools, in villages on the west coast, but their teachers sometimes bitterly admit that they are required to educate children for emigration to the mainland or the south. The voice and character of an alien and increasingly dominant culture is English and metropolitan, and as the widening range of television transmission carries it beyond Skye and the mountains of Kintail it becomes irresistible. It is true that there is a growing use of Gaelic by the valiant *West Highland Free Press* and other regional papers, and resolute efforts are made by Gaelic societies, largely urban and middle-class in direction, to encourage the learning and speaking of the language and its publication as literature. But all this is perhaps fertilising a ground in which there may no longer be roots capable of survival.

There is, of course, no guarantee of perpetuity for any race or society. The Gaels and their language occupy less than half of Perthshire's recorded history, and little survives of the people they overwhelmed and absorbed. There is no substantial record of the laws and customs of the Picts, their legends or their religion, no enlightening sentence in their language, only their lovely symbol-stones and the lonely remains of their hill-forts. But they were the Painted Ones, the Caledonii whom the Romans failed to subdue eight centuries before Kenneth MacAlpine made himself *Ard-righ Albainn*, and the seat of the Dalriadic kings was moved eastward from Dunadd to Scone. Perthshire was the northern frontier of Roman conquest, and from their great encampment of Pinnata Castra at Inchtuthill their legions and their patrols marched into and retired from the mountain wilderness to the north. Somewhere in the Grampians or the Monadhliath they fought a bloody battle against an army of tall, red-haired men led by Calgacus the Swordsman. If he was not the invention of Tacitus, he was the first inhabitant of Scotland to be given a name in its history. His defiance on the eve of the battle in which he died was also the first recorded voice of Scotland, condemning its enemies in a sentence that was subsequently used to describe the punitive battalions of Cumberland and the evicting sheep-fanciers of Improvement.

> At the furthest limits of both land and liberty, we have been defended until this day by the remoteness of our situation and our fame ... The plunderers of the world devastate the land and rifle the ocean, provoked by avarice to ravage and slaughter, and *where they create a desert, they call it peace* ... We fight not for gain but for liberty, shall we not show what men Caledonia has for her defence ... ?

Tacitus probably composed this himself, from hearsay or his own imagination, thinking it proper for Rome to have such brave and noble opponents. But the spirit of The Swordsman's declamation was enduring, and twelve and a half centuries later his words may have inspired the Chancellor of Scotland, Bernard de Linton, for there is a curious similarity between them and the phrasing of the Declaration of Arbroath, which he is believed to have written.*

When the Romans withdrew from Perthshire, southward to the Antonine Wall and thence to the Cheviots, memories of their occupation were perhaps woven into the mythology of the Picts and later inherited by the incoming Scots. Stories of the legionaries who marched by Creag Mhor to Rannoch could have become entwined with the legends of the Fingalians who sleep on their shields in the high corries of Glen Lyon. Rome's footprints at the mouth of this long valley survive in distorted history and nonsense tales. A rectangular site on the bank of the Lyon at Fortingall, close to a 14th-century plague-pit, is known as the Praetorium, and past scholars who found silver denarii and discoloured potsherds in the vicinity decided that it was once a Roman garrison. Perhaps it was, but the surface mound today is the remains of a medieval building whose last residents could be lying in the plague-pit, below a stone pillar where cattle ease their itching flanks on the surrounding barbed wire. The victims of the pestilence were taken to burial on a sled drawn by a white horse, an old woman leading. Horse, sled and woman still make this nightly journey, and will do so for as long as anybody is willing to believe it possible.

In the walled churchyard of Fortingall there is an ancient yew-tree, still great in size but smaller than it was when the MacGregors of Roro made bow-staves from its branches, or when Pennant estimated its girth to be fifty-six feet. Guide-books say it was already growing when Fortingall was the birthplace of Pontius Pilate, "whose father may have been an ambassador in North Britain during the Roman occupation." At one time a belief in this beguiling story was encouraged by the Yorkshire barman of the hotel, with elaborations of his own that grew more fanciful as he left his side of the bar to sit in jovial fellowship with the uneasy guests. He was much too intelligent to believe it himself, but he enjoyed the credulity of others, and I regret the day I spoilt his pleasure by asking how any Roman could have been born here half a century at least before Claudius began the conquest of Britain,

* Cf. page 116

Loch Tummel in Perthshire looking westward to Loch Rannoch, and beyond the low mists to the Moor and the mountain gateway of Glencoe.

and seventy-five years before the first legions entered Scotland.

Glen Lyon is a long and crooked pleat in the rolling hills of Breadalbane, the greatest district of Perthshire, once ninety miles from the Braes of Atholl to Argyll, and as many again from the Grampians to the hills above the Stirling Plain. When Breadalbane was ruled by despotic Campbell lords it took them three days to ride from one border of their ground to another, but when the summons of their fiery cross was carried by relays of runners it could pass from Kenmore to Kilchurn in one night. The land rises northward from Loch Tay in a great stairway of hills, by the blue crown of Ben Lawers and the maiden's breast of Schiehallion to Loch Tummel and Loch Rannoch, and the limitless mountains beyond. In 1777 the Astronomer Royal, Nevil Maskelyne, built an observatory hut below the nipple of Schiehallion, and was watched with suspicion by the people until they decided he was looking for a lost star. Had they known he was trying to calculate the weight of the earth they might have burnt his hut, that being the Highlanders' old way of acquainting unnatural incomers with their disapproval. Wade's military road went by the shadow of Schiehallion, northward to Dalnacardoch, Dalwhinnie, Corrieyairack and the Great Glen. He directed its progress from the inn at Weem, half a mile from William Adam's bridge which he had built, he said, "to set the rapacious ferryman and his boats on dry

land." He cut the road along the flat carse of the River Tay toward the mouth of Glen Lyon, and then up the narrow gorge of Keltney Burn. It is still the shortest route from Strathtay to Rannoch, climbing steeply by the burn until it looks down on the square keep of Garth Castle, one of a dozen bleak strongholds built six hundred years ago by the Wolf of Badenoch, a royal Stewart, one of Robert II's numberless bastards and a bloody man.

Schiehallion, the Maiden's Breast, across the water of Loch Rannoch. The name is also said to mean a fairy hill, but neither need cancel out the other.

The view from Tomphubil, the tented hill at the top of the Keltney gorge, is one of the finest in the Highlands, two hundred feet above the serene waters of Loch Tummel and Loch Rannoch. Northward are the rolling combers of the Grampians, and thirty miles to the west the guardian peaks of Glencoe. The land here is open, the air clear and invigorating, and one breath-taking arc can sometimes encompass sunshine and storm, mist and rainbow. The basins of the lochs, and the wasteland of the moor from which they drain some of their peat-brown water, were once a great forest, the home of the wild beasts of pre-history. Bear and wolf, elk and boar are now long gone and only remembered in the badges of the clans and the arms of the chiefs. Some of the ancient pines, red-trunked and dark-headed, still survive in the Black Wood along the southern shore of Loch Rannoch. Protected and re-seeded by the Forestry Commission, they are a pleasing compensation for its more usual pre-occupation with Sitka spruce.

It was on the braes of Schiehallion, where the road forks westward from Tomphubil to Kinlochrannoch, that David Stewart's uncle, a captain of the Atholl Highlanders, trained two or three of Garth's young tenants to be pipers for the regiment. Some years ago on this road, a mile or two from Kinlochrannoch and by a golden stand of birch, I stopped to listen to a hedge-piper. He was an old man and a wild man. His clothes were held together by safety-pins and cunning knots of string, and the bright orange bag of his pipes appeared to have been made from an inner-tube. Whether he was a good piper or not, I cannot say. He told me that he had been taught by John MacDonald from Glencoe, and since I was the only person who had stopped and spoken to him that day he obligingly played for me as long as I wished. The music was unfamiliar but had once been well-known in his tutor's glen, he said.

Before I left him, I asked where he lived. He moved his arm in a wide sweep, the land was his house and his bed. At dusk, he said, he would go over to Glen Lyon and spend the night within the walls of Garth Castle. It was then a ruin, but it has since been roofed, floored, plumbed and wired to make it a residence again. Breadalbane's past, preserved in such imperishable stone, is not always as plain to the eye as the Wolf of Badenoch's stronghold. Screens of beech and alder hide the stumps of other fortresses, and quilts of belled heather cover the braeside cells of the missionaries who came from Ireland and Iona. Below the clear inshore water of Loch Tay, and sometimes breaking its surface, are the whitestone crusts of lonely crannogs, man-made islets of brushwood and gravel upon which an early Celtic people built their homes. The beautiful glen of the River Lyon, twenty-five curling miles from Keltney Burn to the south-eastern march of Rannoch Moor, is studded with the ruins or levelled sites of chapels, keeps and circular forts. "Twelve castles had Fionn MacCumhail," said an old legend, "in the dark glen of the crooked stones." In the 7th century Saint Adamnan, abbot of Iona and biographer of Columba, built a church and a school here, and a corn-mill which survives in the hamlet name of Milton where Allt Bail a' Mhuillin, the milltown stream, comes down to Bridge of Balgie. Eight hundred years later, Black Colin Campbell of Glenorchy took the glen from the Stewarts of Garth and gave it to his younger son, whose descendants built almost as many castles as Fionn MacCumhail and graced their approaches with avenues of yellow sycamore.

I spent many days in this valley when I was writing *Glencoe*, for Robert Campbell of Glenlyon was the commander of the Argyll soldiers sent to destroy MacIain and his people. Drunken and improvident, a gambler and a wastrel, attractive to women even in his seventh decade, he was the last notorious member of his family, and in his defence it might be said that he and they had suffered bitterly from the raiding and thieving of the MacDonalds of Lochaber. The Lairds of Glenlyon had always answered force with force, so arrogant and secure in their isolation that they sometimes hanged a King's Messenger at the door of Meggernie

Castle, or used their fine trees as gibbets for the Lochaber Men. The third laird, whose wits had never recovered from a blow on the head in his youth, once captured thirty-six MacDonalds, pistolled their leader and hanged the rest. When an outraged Privy Council in Edinburgh ordered Mad Colin to put his hand to a deed swearing that he had executed them in defiance of proper justice, he said he would put his foot on it as well, for the raiders had come to his land

> ... with bow, quiver and other weapons invasive, upon the 24th of June last by the break of day, and masterfully reft, spulzied and took away from the said complainer and his servants, four score head of kye, eleven horses and mares, together with the whole insight and plenishings of their houses; and also not satisfied with the said oppression committed by them as said is, struck and dang the women of the said lands and cutted the hair of their heads.

For a century and more the road which once passed by the door of Mad Colin's dark keep has been deflected to a loop track on the northern brae. A straddling lodge-house of Arthurian design bars the old road, and when I rang its bell a decade ago I was told that casual visitors were not welcome at Meggernie Castle, wherein a tobacco magnate now lived unreft and unspulzied.

Before the end of the 18th century the Campbells were gone from Glen Lyon, their line at last extinguished by the Curse of Glencoe it was said.* They were followed by more gentle proprietors. One of these, James Menzies of Culdares, maintained their interest in arboriculture and was among the first to introduce the larch to Scotland, bringing it from Tyrol where its red-brown bark and bright green needles had solaced his years as a Jacobite exile. Seedlings from his trees were sown throughout Perthshire, and eighty years ago they developed a hybrid now known as the Dunkeld Larch. If I am asked why I am not as disapproving of the Tyrolean larch as I am of the equally alien Canadian spruce, it may be because one is less obtrusive than the other, and the spruce is not here because it once reminded an unhappy exile of the dark forests of his homeland.

There are tall stands of Dunkeld Larch on the wooded hills above Kenmore. Here the River Tay takes bright water from the loch of that name, drawing it eastward under the fine arch of a bridge that was built with the rents of forfeited Jacobite estates. Loch Tay is a majestic water, wide and long, embraced by noble hills. In the 18th and 19th centuries the Earls of Breadalbane turned its banks into broad farms and parklands, creating a tranquil landscape where there had once been a bloody amphitheatre of wasting conflict. When their Improving transformation began, the loch itself seemed to protest, the restless rock stirring below its deep basin. There were many witnesses of this phenomenon, the first being the blacksmith of Kenmore who had gone down

* The designation "of Glenlyon" continues in a viscountcy held by the Dukes of Atholl, an irony less astringent than the Barony of Culloden, a royal title borne by the Dukes of Gloucester.

to the lochside to wash his face and hands, early in the morning of Sunday, September 12, 1784. As he knelt and bent his back, the water suddenly receded from him, leaving the bay empty for a distance of three hundred feet. The surface wave moved westward for another hundred yards until it met a second moving east, both colliding in a foaming wall, four feet high. The ebb and flow of the waves continued for an hour and a half during which there was no wind, no disturbance of the still air, and when the water was at its lowest ebb the River Tay flowed backward under the bridge and into the loch. This strange occurence was repeated the next morning, and again on Tuesday, an hour later and to a lessening degree.

On each occasion a small, wooded island in the bay appeared to rise and fall like a ship on an ocean swell. It is *Eilean nan Ban Naomh*, the Island of the Holy Woman, and because I am English I have a particular affection for it. It is a reminder of the long and sometimes bitter-sweet affinity between the country of my birth and the northern land I love. Its trees, seemingly growing from the water, now hide the few remaining stones of an ancient priory and also the grave of Queen Sibylla who was buried here eight and a half centuries ago. She was the English wife of Alexander I of Scotland, and the natural daughter of Henry I of England. Alexander was perhaps more Saxon than his queen or his father-in-law, being the grandson of Edgar Atheling, king-elect of England until his reluctant submission to the Conqueror. Schooled by the example of their saintly mother Margaret, Alexander and his brothers began the anglicising of their Celtic kingdom, a slow but relentlessly inexorable process still continuing. Of the childless Sibylla little is known, her memory preserved in this quiet island and in a charter by which her husband gave it to the monks of Scone "so that a church may be built there for me, and for the soul of the Queen there deceased."

Until the 18th century Breadalbane was a turbulent and tumultuous land, ruled by Glenorchy Campbells who took it from the MacGregors, the Stewarts and the Menzies, and held it against frequent forays by the Lochaber Men. Hoping to outmatch their cousins of Argyll, whose leadership of Clan Diarmid they enviously coveted, they rose by one leap from a baronetcy to an earldom, and then higher to a marquesate. When that line was exhausted, another branch of the teeming family came forward to claim and win the earldom. This dubious evasion of primogeniture had been made possible by the first earl, who had secured the King's agreement that the title would not only pass to his children's children but also to those of his collateral ancestors should his own line become extinct.* By the middle of the 19th century the second Marquis and fifth Earl of Breadalbane was as rich and

---

* Sir John Campbell, 11th Laird of Glenorchy and 1st Earl of Breadalbane (1635–1717). Known as *Iain Glas*, Grey John, "cunning as a fox, wise as a serpent, slippery as an eel", he was one of the principal figures in the dark plotting that led to the Massacre of Glencoe, although he has taken more blame for that than he deserved.

powerful as the Duke of Argyll, and if he could not marry a son into the Royal Family he was determined to outmatch Inveraray in Highland hospitality to the Queen. Victoria and Albert came to Breadalbane in September, the loveliest month in Strathtay. They rode by carriage on the high road from Atholl to Aberfeldy and thence through groves of larch and oak to his lordship's greystone castle in a horse-shoe bend of the River Tay. The original slit-eyed, black and square fortress of Balloch had been transformed by the Earl's father into a Gothic nightmare – great rooms and great halls, great doors and a great stone stairway down which the 4th Earl could have marched his Breadalbane Fencibles six abreast, and might well have done had they not been disbanded after a riotous mutiny in Glasgow. Lance-headed windows looked out to noble braes of oak, lime, chestnut and pine. The walls of the library were elaborately and expensively panelled, and it had taken seven years to paint the ceilings of the state rooms in the style of a medieval illuminated manuscript.

Victoria was as deeply impressed by this mountain splendour ("The *coup d'oeil* was indescribable") as she was by the gentry and tenantry assembled to greet her, Campbells in green tartan, Menzies in red and white, and a company of the 92nd Highlanders presenting arms in a cloud of pipe-clay dust. Cannon were fired in salute as her carriage reached the castle doors, and the cathedral transept within was lined with more kilted tenants. "Keeper," she said to the Earl, entering into the spirit of the day, "what a quantity of fine Highlandmen you have got." When she dined at eight that evening it was with some of the best of Scotland's nobility, in tartan, velvet and lace. It was all grand theatre and had nothing to do with the reality of Highland life, in that year or yester-year,

"O'er many a winding dale and painful steep, Th' abodes of covey'd grouse and timid sheep, My savage journey, curious, I pursue, Till fam'd Breadalbane opens to my view." Burns wrote that and more (with subsequent regret, it may be hoped) on the chimney-piece of the Kenmore Inn, the gable of which is just visible on the far right of this 18th-century prospect of Loch Tay.

Taymouth Castle in its
early years, an ornate
shell which 19th-century
Breadalbane lords placed
over the black keep of
their ancestors. Victoria
was welcomed here, she
said, "as if a great
chieftain of olden times
was receiving his
sovereign."

but the Queen's sentimental ignorance protected her from this
harsh truth. "It seemed," she told her diary, "as if a great chieftain
in olden feudal times was receiving his sovereign". When she
retired to bed, in a wing specially built for her visit, one of the
Earl's nine pipers played her to rest, beacon fires burned on
Drummond Hill, and about the railings of the castle lawn a chain
of lamps spelt out a glowing message *Welcome Victoria – Albert*.
And in the morning, perhaps, the capercailzie which the Earl was
successfully reintroducing to Scotland broke the dawn silence of
the pine-woods with its singular but not inappropriate imitation
of a cork being drawn and liquid gurgling from the neck of a
bottle.

Such a world must have seemed indestructible, its people enduring in their love and loyalty. It was charming to see the surprise
of a plump cottage-wife when she was given money for presenting
the Queen with a handful of garden flowers. Or to watch another
standing in a burn, her skirt tucked high to her knees as she bent
to wash a pan of potatoes. And doubly pleasing, no doubt, to
reflect that Albert was sharing such rude simplicities, wading
through rough bogs below Schiehallion, and coming back to the
castle with nine brace of grouse he had brought down with his
fowling-piece.

Breadalbane earls no longer own a blade of grass in Strathtay,
and it is more than a quarter of a century since I was sent to
interview the last heir to the title, then entertaining himself and
others by playing the pipes in a London public-house. Taymouth

Castle is empty, abandoned now by the Government ministry which once occupied it, and there is a happy school and an 18-hole golf course in the grounds. The gentry who once supported the eminence of the earldom, as the base of a pyramid carries its peak, have also gone, or remain in discreet isolation within their ancient homes. The castle at Weem is no longer sustained by the fortune which one of its Menzies chiefs brought home from the West Indies. It survives as a clan museum, struggling against wood-rot and crumbling stone, and its doors are sometimes opened at the promised hour and sometimes not at all. The changes which Improvement brought to Strathtay remain perversely Anglo-Saxon. Fortingall and Kenmore were rebuilt to resemble the half-timbers or thatched roofs of an English village. The agreeable hotel at Kenmore, which was The Breadalbane Arms when there was an earl in the castle, is said to be the oldest inn in Scotland, but despite the Campbell tartan on its benches and chairs it would not be out of place in Sussex. It is no longer possible to find a window at which Dorothy Wordsworth may have sat, and looked out in happiness to "a very beautiful prospect". Behind a protective sheet of glass in Archie's snug there is a verse which Burns pencilled on the plaster, but he wrote it in English not Scots. It is thus no indication of his genius, and some lines are perilously close to McGonagall. *Admiring Nature in her wildest grace, these northern scenes with weary feet I trace ...*

Victoria and Albert had come to Kenmore from Dunkeld, where Lord Glenlyon welcomed them beneath a ceremonial arch,

Much of the ritual of Royal visits to Scotland is based upon precedents made by Victoria and her family, not the least the ceremony of their arrival. Scott's great work had made it easy for many Scots to see this young woman as a proper replacement for the tragic Stuarts in romantic sentiment. She would not have disputed that.

with pipers of the Atholl Highlanders, an alfresco luncheon, sword-dances and reels. His uncle, the 5th Duke of Atholl, was then at the height of his family's fortune and influence, comfortably lodged in his castle of Blair and enjoying the grandeur of the magnificent estate his father had created. In fifty years the 4th Duke had changed the face and nature of Atholl, replacing its wild woodlands with parkland and forests, draining river-floors, cutting roads, building farms, follies and sylvan temples, making sure that no English peer would have reason to look down his nose at the property of a Highland duke. His pride in being *Am Moireach Mor*, and his youthful happiness in domestic bliss, were captured by David Allan in one of Scotland's earliest conversation-paintings. He stands on the Hill of Lude, I think, surrounded by his wife, his children, a kneeling gillie, the carcass of a twelve-pointer and sundry game-dogs. He wears a high-crowned bonnet with a curling black plume, a brown sporting-jacket and a little kilt of the tartan which Major Dalrymple had selected for the Atholl Highlanders. The Duke's double-barrelled sporting-gun is tucked beneath his right arm-pit, and his left hand holds a splendid blackcock above the eager reach of his son and heir, a smiling cherub in a white dress and pink sash. The landscape of the painting is conventionally contrived, but is recognisable as the valley of the River Garry, and in the middle background the white block of Blair Castle holds the composition together like a linch-pin. At the left of the canvas, and creating cunning perspective points, are two trees. The first is a Tyrolean larch, and the second is the most gentle and natural of all Highland trees. James Hogg thought so too. When he came here in 1802 he had expected to see a wilderness "instead of which, every opening shewed me so much more of a paradise." He was entranced by the landscaped woodlands, tall cedars, straight-backed pines, and flourishing larch. But this one tree particularly pleased him, although his description of it barely survives his strangled syntax.

> The weeping birch hangs her beautiful tresses all around her white stem in the most graceful attitude imaginable. Sure the vegetable creation cannot produce her equal, especially high in Atholl where she seems to arrive at the most perfect stature: with such an easy modesty does her small boughs descend and kiss each other, the lowest branches often reaching to the ground, the next to these, and so on to the top, while "one blast of the southland wind" causeth the most graceful sweep through all the wood. I could not help viewing her as the queen of the forest, whose modest deportment all the rest of the trees strove to imitate.

I think he was himself striving to imitate the descriptive power of Scott, to whom this was addressed, but I understand his feelings. I turned to word-painting in my youth when I realised I had no talent to be an artist, but writing is a poor way of conveying the beauty of the Highlands, and a dependence upon metaphor and simile leads to unhappy excess. If Hogg's prose is sometimes self-destructive, its breathless fervour matched the Gothic inspiration of his time, a love of melancholy landscapes, dark mountain-heads, ruined turrets and forest glades. In the engravings and canvases that were now popularising the Highlands there was also a deliberate exaggeration of natural proportions. Mountain ranges became alpine peaks, the valleys deep canyons of mist and torrent, and the inhabitants, where they appeared at all, were tiny mannikins, crawling like insects over the monumental rocks.

The reality behind such romantic exaggeration became increasingly accessible with the building or improvement of carriage-roads, the establishment of comfortable inns and tolerable lodging-houses. The growing number of tourists, once the French wars were over, produced a steady flow of guide-books, more easily read and less cumbersome to carry than Boswell or Pennant, but inspired by their example and by the remarkable Mrs Murray who had published her account of a tour through the Highlands and Inner Hebrides "because I think my Guide will be really useful to travellers who may follow my foot-steps."* One of the first of the new guide-books was *The Scottish Tour and Itinerary*, rightly dedicated to Scott "whose fascinating works have spread the fame of this country far and wide." The publishers, it said, had spared neither pains nor expense to "combine simplicity of arrangement with accuracy of detail", and while it directed the travellers' attention to "the scenery, antiquities, and principal steam-boat tours", the location of change-houses, the height of mountains and the depth of lochs, it also reminded them that there was more to touring than the hedonistic pursuit of enjoyment.

> To the philosopher, Scotland is perhaps now more interesting than at any former period, owing to the rapid strides made in the arts and improvements of every kind; also in the acquirement of wealth, the result of the industry, the ingenuity, and enterprise of her inhabitants.

The *Scottish Tour* was reprinted eight times in as many years, and others more successful galloped through nineteen or twenty editions. Before the middle of the century their pot-boiling publishers had realised that the new traveller of the Industrial Age was no longer an itinerant philosopher and was less interested in arts and improvements than he was in how much he would have to pay for his northern jaunt. "The expenses necessarily attendant upon travelling," said the eleventh edition of *Black's Picturesque Tourist of Scotland*, in a mournful comment still applicable, "must be admitted to be a considerable drawback from its pleasure. Still, the evil is inevitable." Before the reader began the first chapter of this guide (*Rivers, Lakes, Mineral Produce and Springs . . .*), he was told that a riding-horse could be hired for six shillings a day, a four-wheeled carriage for fifteen. A room in a reasonable hotel would cost him half-a-crown a night, twice that if double-bedded, and the

---

* *A Companion and Useful Guide to the Beauties of Scotland*, Sarah Murray, 1799 and 1803. She was a redoubtable widow of 52 when she made her tour in the summer of 1796, travelling two thousand miles with only her maid and coachman for companionship. Her *Guide*, recently republished by Byway Books, is among the most delightful of all travel books, and it has the best opening sentence of any before or since. "Provide yourself with a strong roomy carriage, and have the springs well corded."

use of a parlour was five shillings more. He should be willing to pay two shillings for his breakfast, sixpence or a shilling for lunch, from two to three shillings for dinner, and eighteenpence for supper. Whisky was ninepence per gill, brandy eighteenpence, beer, ale, and porter sixpence a bottle, and a pint of tolerable port or sherry was three shillings. "The payment of gratuities to hotel servants is a source of great annoyance to travellers," but this too was an inevitable evil, and the *Picturesque Tourist* offered sympathetic guidance.

> A gentleman and his wife, occupying a sitting-room and bedroom, 2s. 6d. to 3s. 6d. per night for Waiter, Chambermaid, Porter and Boots. If accompanied by sons or daughters, or other relatives, half this rate from each; but no charge for children under nine years of age. A party of four or six for one night, about 1s.6d. each.

Any nostalgic longing these charges may excite should be tempered by the knowledge that while the Duke of Sutherland's annual income was £300,000, lesser men lived comfortably on £250, and the miserable weekly wage of a labourer was counted in pence.

I sometimes take these old guide-books with me to the Highlands. Imposed upon the present, they have the charm and irony of a film twice exposed. They contain nothing that would have disturbed a 19th-century traveller's contentment or ruffled his conscience. There is no reference in any of them to the great changes then taking place, no mention of cholera and recurrent famine, of clearance, eviction and sorrowful emigration, and only hindsight gives poignancy to one bland sentence in the *Picturesque Tourist*. "The extensive county of Sutherland," wrote its anonymous author, "presents the striking peculiarity of having the whole of its 1800 square miles under sheep." Earlier in the century, Hogg touched upon the darker side of the paradise he found in Perthshire, but having discovered it, seemed anxious to close a door upon it. The 4th Duke of Atholl, he said, "was loved by his people in general." That qualification *in general* may have been added in doubt, the result of a disarming meeting with one of the Duke's former tenants.

> He was one of nineteen farmers who were removed from the Duke's land to make way for one man, who now possessed the whole of what they, and their families, lived happily upon. On expressing my astonishment what could move his Grace to such a proceeding, he replied, "Ah! Cot pless him, hit pe nane of his doings."

It was, of course, and the man surely knew it. There is perhaps a need for an academic study of the relationship between the human effect of the Duke's land reforms and the violent revolt of his tenants five years before Hogg's visit. There is no reference to this in Hogg's letters, although it cannot have been forgotten by the people he met, and there is no mention of it in the guide-books now sold at Blair Castle. In September, 1797, sixteen thousand people of Strathtay and the Braes of Atholl gathered in protest

Blair Castle in the vale of the River Garry. The landscape is man-made by the Dukes of Atholl, and the handsome castle one of several mutations. The medieval fortress was turned into a Georgian mansion in the 18th century, and in the next was reconstructed in "Scottish baronial". James Hogg wondered what Johnson would have made of Atholl, and so do I.

against the imposition of Militia Act. Of these, six hundred men and seven hundred women marched upon Blair, determined to have the Duke's written assurance that their sons would not be taken into the Militia. They barred all approaches to the Castle, holding it under siege, and as they lit their evening fires about the kirk-yard on Banavie Burn their leaders composed a petition to the Duke.

We your dutiful Tenants and all the country people round about, do not at all approve of Militia in Scotland, whatever encouragement you may show us; because we do not at all wish to serve against our inclinations, because our most brave ancestors and forefathers would not suffer such usage; and we your above-named are surprised that you endeavour to make slaves of brave Atholl Highlanders. May it therefore please your Grace to abolish this Act from us, and give security for it, as we will lose the last drop of our blood before we yield to such oppression.

This was delivered to the Duke at noon the next day, and two hours later the people advanced upon the Castle. The women, he was told, were in the van, and many had removed their stockings, filling the feet with stones and broken glass. Alarmed by such threatening anger, and because he had less than two hundred loyal tenants to defend him, he signed the papers presented to him. That evening, as the rioters celebrated by the inn at Blair, he wrote to the Lord Advocate, asking for dragoons to protect him and all men of property. The soldiers came, English horsemen and Highland Fencibles from Sutherland, and the revolt ended with the arrest of its principal leaders and the dispersal of their dismayed followers. But for one terrifying week, during which their beacons and their torches had burned from Blairgowrie to Bridge of Orchy, from Loch Rannoch to Strathearn, they had badly frightened the gentry of Perthshire, persuading it that the radical teachings of Tom Paine and the evil example of the French Revolution had at last reached the Highlands.

The story of the Perthshire riots is rarely told, and then only as part of a wider resistance to the Militia Act, the climax of which was the bloody suppression of a colliers' revolt in the Lowlands, but the Highlanders' protest should perhaps be seen in its own particular perspective. The wording of their petition to Atholl suggests there was more to their discontent. Eviction was already undermining their security and self-respect, past betrayal had weakened their loyalty to vestigial clan ties. There was also a sullen resentment of the proprietors' power to demand military service as a condition of tenure, and the Highlander's presumed warrior zeal had already been in decline before the Rebellion of 1745. The Atholl Brigade was one of the strongest clan formations in the last Jacobite Army, but despite its suicidal courage at Culloden it had been largely recruited by threat and had the highest rate of desertion. When the rioters recalled their ancestors and told the Duke that he should not "make slaves of brave Atholl Highlanders" they were reminding him of those bloody months of rebellion, and of a later year more wounding to his pride.

In 1778 he had raised a marching-regiment for the Crown, the 77th Atholl Highlanders. Like other battalions then formed, the men were engaged for the duration of the American Revolution only, but when that was over Britain had another, unfinished war in the Far East. The news of the peace treaty was not made public for six days, and in that time the Atholl Highlanders and other regiments quartered near Portsmouth were ordered to embark for India. The Highlanders were at first willing to go, but when the Lord Mayor of Portsmouth let slip the news of peace their anger was immediate and violent. They drove their officers from the city and held it under arms for a week until Parliament forced the Secretary at War to give them their discharge. They were marched to Berwick and there, at the border of their own country, they were dismissed with ignominy, their officers complaining that they were "insolent cowards . . . scoundrels divested of Principle." But as the men walked northward through the Lammermuirs, and across the Forth towards the Braes of Atholl, they sang their own derisive valediction.

> We Atholl men go home to rest,
> For sure we are we've done our best,
> But her nainsel* has been opprest
> By Murray who fairly sold us!

History would have been charitable to their memory if that were the last record of them. In 1822, however, the aging Duke resurrected the ghost of the regiment to represent him and his clan at the Gathering in Edinburgh. Seventeen years later, his successor mustered a company of Atholl Highlanders for his contribution to the musical-comedy Tournament of Eglinton.

---

* One's ownself, a common reference to a Highlander. The song was written in a Portsmouth tavern during the mutiny, and sung to the music of the Jacobite rant *Hey, Johnnie Cope!*

They were thereafter maintained as a ceremonial house-guard, delighting a romantic Queen who presented them with a pair of Colours and presumably her permission to carry arms denied her other subjects. When "the only private army in Britain" now parades at Blair Atholl with plaid, kilt, ribboned bonnets and old Lee-Enfield rifles, only a malcontent would remember those angry and embittered soldiers in Portsmouth two hundred years ago. Or recall the warning they sent to their lieutenant-colonel when they discovered the shabby trick that would have put them aboard ship for India. *"You need not doubt, but we'll do for you if we go, and before we go!"*

It was a spring afternoon when I first visited the church at Croick, on a river-bend where Strath Cuileannach joins the wider, greener floor of Strathcarron. There was still snow on Diebidale Ridge above dark braes of bracken and heather, and the air was noisy with the cold sound of hastening water. The twisting glens of Cuileannach, Alladale and Calvie are talons on the extended arm of Strathcarron, clawing at the mountain hide of central Ross. They are also narrow airways down which winter-visiting greylag come to the alder-woods and farmland fields along the Dornoch Firth. A northward skein was returning to Iceland when I reached the church-yard wall, and I watched them until they were lost against the leaf-brown hills. I remember them clearly, and not only because they recalled a boyhood memory of wavering arrow-heads in a prairie sky. I remember them because of the native greylag which James kept on the shore of the firth, and because the book that took me to Croick also brought me his friendship.

I went to Spinningdale at his invitation three months after my account of the Clearances was published. I went in December and by train from Inverness. There were leaden snow-clouds upon Ben Wyvis, hoar frost like dusted sugar on the Muir of Ord and the furrowed fields of Cromarty, but at Bonar Bridge the sky was clear, roses and lupins flowered in a cottage garden, and the warm hills were glazed in sunlight. I was the only passenger to alight, the carriage door held by a porter who told me that Dr Robertson-Justice had just arrived to collect me. And there he was with an outstretched hand and a welcome in Gaelic, tweed cap and cape, and a swathe of red Clan Donnachaidh tartan about his waist. At Spinningdale, which he reached with skilful speed in a Mini, he took me first to the oak-wood that marched with his policies, naming plant, bird, lichen and insect with encyclopaedic brevity. With two pointers and Irena's Jack Russell at our heels we went to the ruin of a cotton-mill above the inlet. It was built by an improving Dempster laird in 1791, inspired by Richard Ark-

wright's mills at New Lanark. It was never a success, and when fire destroyed its timbers it was abandoned, time and erosion changing it to the ancient fortress most travellers presume it to be. I asked if it explained Spinningdale's name, and James's answer disturbed the rooks above us. "*Spanzidaill* ... not Spinningdale!" The word is Norse, meaning a place for spinning, perhaps, but we later agreed that another derivation was more to our taste – *spanning-daill* the vale of temptation.

That night we talked until first-light touched the head of Struie across the Firth, and a silent tide ebbed from silver to gold. We built walls of reference-books at our feet – Brewer, Roget and Burke, Ruvigny's Jacobite Peerage, Haydn's Dignitaries and Cruden's Concordance, gazetters, dictionaries of etymology, place-names and quotations. We talked of the clans and the Clearances, of falcons and the marital fidelity of greylag geese, of moths and butterflies, Bach, Mozart and Robert Louis Stevenson, salmon, seal and seine-netters, London before the war, journalism, socialism, brave soldiers and their obscene trade, the Spanish Civil War and Belsen. We discovered a mutual pleasure in serendipity, and decided that it was not so much a faculty as a faery gift. We shared an admiration for Alexander Mackenzie from Stornoway, the first white man to cross the Canadian Rockies, and we decided to visit his grave not far away at Avoch on the Black Isle, but we never did. We talked of the white-lipped bay of Calgary on the west coast of Mull, and the redcoat Mounted Police Commissioner, James MacLeod, who gave its name to a settlement in Alberta, not

Croick graveyard in Easter Ross where the evicted people of Glen Calvie took shelter in 1845. "For what is this virtuous and contented community to be scattered and driven into destitution?" asked an angry *Times* reporter. The answer was sheep, and the higher rental therefrom.

long before he and his small patrol took Sitting Bull and the Sioux nation under the protection of the British Crown.

We also talked of Croick Church which he had never seen, although we went there together in later years. Plain-walled, rectangular and functional, screened by a wind-break of fir, it is one of a hundred and more Parliamentary Churches built by Thomas Telford. At the beginning of the last century it served the ninety people who lived in Glen Calvie, tenants and sub-tenants of William Robertson of Kindeace. They were able to support a poor teacher for their children's education, albeit in English, and until many of them joined the newly-established Free Church their spiritual needs were answered by a sympathetic minister, Gustavus Aird. In 1842, two years before his death, Robertson decided to clear them from the estate and offer it on lease as one farm, leaving the troublesome details to his factor, James Falconer Gillanders. This resolute man was the third generation of a family of factors who rose in station and wealth by the leases they took upon the land they cleared for their employers. The first was George Gillanders who managed Lord Seaforth's estate on the Long Isle, where the people endured epidemic fevers, recurrent crop failures and predatory raids by emigration agents. Gillanders' factorship gave him a trading monopoly in black cattle, white fish, grain and meal, and he increased this comfortable income by selling back to the people any surplus of the firing they were obliged to collect for his use. He conducted his own affairs as prudently as he managed those of his master, and soon accumulated a capital of £20,000 with which he bought an estate at Highfield in Easter Ross. When he retired to this, his son Alexander succeeded him in Seaforth's employ and did so well at the tenants' expense, it was said, that he became richer than many Highland proprietors. The grandson James was the most successful of the three, and like Patrick Sellar he was respected by his superiors, admired by his peers, loved by his family, and hated by the people.

> James has shown by his nature
> that he is a brutal chamberlain
> like his grandfather before him,
> wasting and stripping the poor.
> He is a poor creature without responsibility,
> without honour, understanding or shame.
> An unpleasant boor, he will be
> doubly judged for driving
> away the Rosses of Glencalvie.

Writs of eviction were issued against the Glencalvie people at Whitsuntide in 1845. Before they were executed, concern for the distress and destitution they would cause prompted some northern gentlemen to establish a relief fund. When *The Times* was asked to publish their advertisement appealing for subscriptions "to cheer the sufferers amidst their cloudy prospects", John Delane recognised that there was more to this matter than a modest source of advertising revenue. The anonymous correspondent he accordingly sent to Ross was probably the legal writer Thomas Campbell

Foster, an ardent and compassionate man who later reported the Irish Famine for *The Times*. Witnessing the removal of eighteen families from Glen Calvie, he wrote one of the most vivid accounts of eviction, with a precise understanding of the suffering and responsibilities involved. His first dispatch, written at the inn of Ardgay on the evening of his first day in Ross, began as angrily and as trenchantly as it continued.

> Those who remember the misery and destitution into which large masses of the population were thrown by the systematic "clearances" (as they are here called) carried on in Sutherlandshire some 25 years ago under the direction and on the estate of the late Marchioness of Stafford* – those who have not forgotten to what an extent the ancient ties which bound clansmen to their chiefs were then torn asunder – will regret to learn that the heartless course, with all its sequences of misery, of destitution, and of crime, is again being resorted to in Ross-shire.

That morning Gustavus Aird had taken Foster to Glen Calvie. All the cottages were now empty except one in which Hugh Ross, an old military pensioner, was dying. The people were standing on the open hillside, "the women all neatly dressed in net caps and wearing scarlet or plaid shawls, the men wearing blue bonnets and have their shepherds' plaids wrapped about them." When the

Society outside the Highlands was not unaware of the Clearances, but the tragedy of them was softened into the cloying sentiment of the day. In this painting, "The Last of the Clan", eviction and exile appear sad but inevitable, cruel but romantic.

* Elizabeth Gordon, Countess of Sutherland, Marchioness of Stafford and Duchess of Sutherland. The events referred to by Foster are the clearances in Strath Naver and Strath Helmsdale as part of James Loch's Policy of Improvement.

Times man arrived they were singing the 145th Psalm, *The eyes of all things wait on Thee, the Giver of all good.* Two days later they moved to the churchyard at Croick, making tents from tarpaulins, blankets and plaids, "the poor children thoughtlessly playing round the fire, pleased with the novelty of all around them." There were twenty-seven children, all under ten, and seven were ill. There were also some young and unmarried men and women, but most were married and over forty. When Aird told them why Foster was there they gathered about the *Times* man, shaking his hand. "Their Gaelic I could not understand," he told Delane, "but their eyes beamed with gratitude. This unbought, spontaneous and grateful expression of feeling to you for being their friend is what their natural protector – their chieftain – never saw, and what his factor need never hope for." Why, he asked, were the Highland people reduced from comfort to beggary?

> I confess I can find no answer. It is said that the factors would rather have one tenant than many, as it saves them trouble. But so long as the rent is punctually paid, as this has been, it is contrary to all experience to suppose that one large tenant will pay more than many small ones or that a sheep walk can pay more rent than cultivated land. Now, no doubt there is an object in driving off the people – namely fear of the New Scotch Poor Law, compelling the heritors to pay toward the support of those who cannot support themselves.

He was wrong in believing that sheep were not more profitable than cultivated land, but he was right to accuse Highland proprietors of being unwilling to pay their share under the Poor Law. The lairds of Kindeace, he said, "never gave one farthing, the poor supported their own helpless poor, the wealthy let them do so unassisted." Major Charles Robertson, the new proprietor, was not in Ross to answer this charge, or watch the energy with which Gillanders cleared his estate, and I know of no record of his thoughts and feelings at this time. Like other proprietors, he was protected by his factor who no doubt willingly accepted all the hatred and obloquy that Kindeace and his father should have shared.

The leaders of the Glen Calvie community, those named as tenants in the writs of eviction, were a teeming family described as "Ross alias *Greishich*", a variant spelling of *greusaich*, a shoe-maker. On the day following my first visit to Croick I found the writs in the Tolbooth at Tain, in a high tower room above the cells of the old gaol. It was used to store burghal documents and was now rarely entered. Yellow columns of papers, tied with pink tape, were shrouded in dust-heavy cobwebs upon which black spiders hung like beads of shining jet. There was a rough order in the storing – if only that those papers nearest the door were the latest in time – and it was not too difficult to find the writs I wanted and read the fine cursive handwriting that required the Shoemakers

> ... to flit and Remove themselves, Bairns, Family, servants, sub-tenants, Cottars and dependants, Cattle, Goods, and gear forth and from possession of the said Subjects above described with the perti-

nents respectively occupied by them as aforesaid, and to leave the same void, redd and patent, at the respective terms of Removal above specified, that the Pursuer or others in his name may then enter thereto and peaceably possess, occupy and enjoy the same in time coming.

Within two weeks of the eviction the people of Glen Calvie were gone from the cold shelter of the churchyard. Gillanders claimed that he had resettled six of the families, and the *Times* man followed them. David Ross *Greishich* Senior, David Ross *Greishich* Junior, and Alexander Ross *Greishich* "got a piece of black moor near Tain, twenty-five miles off, without any house or shed, out of which they hope to obtain subsistence." The other three families were given turf huts near Bonar Bridge, but "the rest are hopeless, helpless." The short-lived Society for the Protection of the Poor, inspired by the northern gentlemen's concern and by Foster's reports, could do little to aid them or prevent further evictions on the Kindeace estate, and they were soon gone to the south and ultimately, perhaps, to Australia. There is nothing now on that piece of black moor to show that the Shoemakers settled there, and for some years I believed that they too had left the land of their birth. But not long ago, in a kirkyard near the tidal flat of Edderton sands, I found some of their graves. They had not lived long after their eviction.

Before they left Croick, a few of the Glencalvie people scratched their names and sorrowful messages on the eastern window of the church, the most moving evidence of the Clearances that I know.

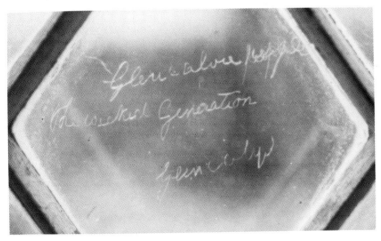

Before the people left the graveyard at Croick some of them scratched their confusion and grief on the windows of the church.

This was what I came to see that Spring day twenty-two years ago, walking over the long yellow grass of the grave-yard, by stark headstones and glass bowls of skull-white porcelain flowers. The diamond panes of the window were thick with grime, and even when I wiped them clean with my hand the oblique fall of the afternoon light made reading difficult. A woman I had not seen in the churchyard now came round a corner and offered me face-powder from her hand-bag. I rubbed it on the window, and immediately the writing became clear, slanting across the glass. The messages are in English, for although the people were Gaelic speakers none of them had been taught to write in their own tongue.

> Glencalvie people was in the church here May 24 1845 ... Glencalvie people the wicked generation ... John Ross shepherd ... Glencalvie people was here ... Amy Ross ... Glencalvie is a wilderness blow ship them to the colony ... The Glencalvie Rosses ...

Since I recorded these inscriptions in my book a protective grating has been placed over the window, too late to prevent some unthinking visitors from adding their own names, and for that I feel a sad responsibility.

In 1854 James Gillanders, now married to Kindeace's daughter, cleared the Greenyards estate in Strathcarron, and this time the people did not submit without protest. When a Sheriff-Officer brought the writs of eviction they were torn from his hand and burnt, and a crowd of women and boys stripped him and his companion of their clothes and drove them from the glen. Three weeks later the Sheriff-Substitute and the Procurator-Fiscal came with new writs, and escorted by thirty-five constables who had drunk "several bottles of ale, porter and whisky" at the inn of Midfearn. Entering the strath shortly after dawn they heard firing and whistles blowing, but Sheriff Taylor put his head out of his carriage and told the constables to be of easy mind, this was the Rosses' usual method of warning. As they came through the wood at Greenyards they found the road blocked by sixty or seventy women with red shawls over their heads. Behind them were less than a dozen men and boys. All were dispersed by a savage baton charge. "The police struck with all their force," wrote the advocate journalist Donald Ross,

> ... not only when knocking down, but after the females were on the ground. They beat and kicked them while lying weltering in their blood. Such was the brutality with which this tragedy was carried through, that more than twenty females were carried off the field in blankets and litters, and the appearance they presented, with their heads cut and bruised, their limbs mangled, and their clothes clotted with blood, was such as would horrify any savage ... Dirty work must be done by dirty hands, and a cruel business is most generally entrusted to cruel hearts and ferocious dispositions.

Four women and a boy, whom the Sheriff described as "ringleaders in the riot and mobbing", were dragged to Tain and locked in the Tolbooth below the room where I read the Glencalvie writs. One of the women and the boy were later brought to trial at Inverness, and upon the advice of their counsel, who hoped thereby for the leniency of the Court, they pleaded guilty to the lesser offence of a breach of the peace. Lord Justice-Clerk Hope, coming to the Court from a shooting-holiday on his son's estate in Sutherland, addressed the prisoners in English, which they may have had some difficulty in understanding, but he was perhaps less concerned with them than he was with the riotous and presumptuous spirit of the commonality in general. The course of Law, he said, must protect all persons high and low, and all persons, whatever their feelings or perverted notions of right and wrong, must submit to the authority of the Law.

It is quite essential therefore, that such a spirit as that which these pannels exhibited should be repressed. Neither they nor their neighbours can be allowed to suppose that they can live in this kind of wicked and rebellious spirit against the Law. They must be taught submission in the very first instance.

The woman was sent to prison for twelve months, and the boy for eighteen. Thanking the jury for their attendance, Lord Hope said that they had performed a most important duty in ensuring the conviction of Ann Ross and Peter Ross. They were aware, he said, of the singular and perverted feeling of insubordination in some districts of the Highlands against the execution of civil processes in the removal of tenants. "This feeling is most prejudicial to the interest of all, and it is absolutely necessary to suppress it."

I have sometimes sat by the roadside at Greenyards, listening to the distant sound of gulls above a moving plough. I have walked by the river at Braelangwell where the wife of William Ross tore her apron into strips for bandages, and was herself clubbed into the water. Foolishly, I once stood on the spot where Sheriff Taylor waved his cane like a sword, and I shouted his orders at the empty road, *"Clear the way . . .! Knock them down . . .!"* But it has always been difficult to *see* the strath as it was on that cold March day, the red shawls of the women, the white paper of the Riot Act in the angry Sheriff's hand, the frosting breath of the coach-horses and the marching constables, and I cannot hear the shouts and the screaming cries of pain. The recreative faculty which serves me well at Glencoe, Strath Naver, Kintail and Culloden is unresponsive here.

Strathcarron is now too lovely, perhaps, too serene and gentle to be recognised as an arena for bloody violence, and time has grown a scar tissue over memory and concern. Some years ago, when I was staying at Spinningdale, I drove again to Braelangwell and walked by the river. The afternoon was warm and sunlit. Smoke scarcely moved above a field of burning stubble, and in the silence the hum of a single insect was like the throb of a cello string. A man came from the road and said that if I wished to cross the water there was a bridge further up the glen by Anat. I said I was content, and explained why I was there. He had only a fragmentary knowledge of "The Massacre of the Rosses", his family had been incomers at the end of the last century, but he remembered an old woman who had once spoken of Gillanders. A bad man was he now, he asked, and I said it seemed so. They were hard times for all, he said. He was attached to the land, and like many of the Strathcarron men two hundred years ago he and his father had soldiered in a Highland regiment. I saw him again later that month, in the noisy motor-inn at Ardgay. We took a dram together and talked briefly, not of the Strathcarron evictions but of winter days on the Maas, the Hochwald in the spring of 1945, and Canadian flame-throwers burning the last German trenches on the west bank of the Rhine at Xanten.

The Clearances in Ross and elsewhere are said to have been foreseen three centuries ago by the Brahan Seer. He was *Coinneach Odhar Fiosaiche*, Sallow Kenneth the Soothsayer, an Islesman by birth but working as a farm-labourer in Strath Conon near the Mackenzie stronghold of Brahan Castle. In his youth the gift of a magic blue stone brought him the power of *taibhsearachd*, second-sight, and he prophesied many calamities great and small, domestic, local and national, including a few yet to come – such as the "horrid black rains" which some believers say will be radio-active fall-out, and others the result of a monstrous explosion in the oil fields of the North Sea. He had a vision of Drummossie Moor at Culloden "stained with the best of Highland blood . . . no mercy will be shown or quarter given." He forecast mountain roads from sea to sea, bridges over every stream, dram-shops "at the head of every plough-furrow", and policemen so common that they would be met on every street-corner in every town. He saw the coming of the railway in "a fiery chariot" and "long strings of carriages", and may have had his finest moment of precognition in a terrifying vision of the automobile age, declaring that he would not like to be alive when "a black bridleless horse passes through the Muir of Ord."

Most of the understandable predictions of this Gaelic Nostra-damus were concerned with parochial affairs or the misfortunes awaiting the Mackenzie chiefs and their wives, one of whom ultimately ordered him to be burnt for witchcraft. The prophecies are often clothed in an imagery that easily fits subsequent events, but in their forecasts of the Clearances the language is blunt and clear. The Big Sheep will over-run the country and the disheart-ened clans will flee before it, across the sea to islands as yet undiscovered. The land will pass into the possession of strangers and become so desolate that no cocks will crow in the glens north of Drumochter. The price of sheep will rise and then fall, and in time they too will disappear and be forgotten. Some comfort is offered, if not altogether reassuringly, in a promise that after the horrid black rains have destroyed all wild life, and turned the mountains brown, the people will return. Credulous belief in these prophecies should perhaps be qualified by the knowledge that until they were published a century ago* they were oral folklore, and there is little or no documentary evidence of them before the events they predict. A churlish mind might therefore conclude that the Brahan Seer's reputation as a prophet depends less upon his remarkable second-sight than on the inventive hind-sight of others.

* *The Prophecies of the Brahan Seer*, by Alexander Mackenzie, 1881. Mackenzie was the editor of *The Celtic Magazine*, and the author of *The History of the Highland Clearances*, 1882. He appears to have given Kenneth Odhar the title of The Brahan Seer.

Osgood Mackenzie was twenty-two when he started his garden at
Inverewe in 1862, "and perfectly ignorant," he said, "of everything
connected with forestry and gardening." Within his lifetime the bleak
and barren ground of Am Ploc Ard was miraculously transformed.
Today there are almost 3000 species growing in its forty-eight acres
of woodland and garden.

Thomas Sandby, Cumberland's private secretary, painted this view of the Duke's camp outside the breached walls and roofless houses of Fort Augustus in July, 1746. There was a garrison here until 1867 when the Government sold the site for £4,000 to the 12th Lord Lovat. To the dismay of those who hoped he had seen the Protestant light, he bequeathed it to the Benedictine order. The fort was replaced, at a cost of £40,000, by a monastery "for the education of higher-class Catholic youths", but some of its stones survive in the walls.

The eroded escarpment of Stac Polly on the road by Loch Lurgain to
Achiltibuie. Despite its forbidding appearance, "visitors of any age
may reach its summit ridge", or so experienced climbers say.

The lonely ferry at Kylesku on the north-western coast of
Sutherland, with Loch Glencoul and the shoulder of Glasven beyond.
There has been an inn here since droving days, when the cattle of
Lord Reay's country were gathered on the shore of Eddrachillis Bay.

(*Previous page*) Canisp and Suilven, lone companions on the western littoral of Sutherland. Suilven is the most eccentric mountain in the Highlands. Behind its round helmet of grey gneiss is a sharp hog-back one and a half miles in length.

Ardvreck Castle on Loch Assynt. There is now a modest and scholarly wish to exculpate Neil MacLeod whose stronghold this was in 1650. Whether he did, or did not, betray the Marquis of Montrose to the King's enemies for money and meal, his envious neighbours, the Mackenzies, were untroubled by doubt. They subsequently stole ten thousand head of his stock, and then drove him out of Assynt for ever.

Balnagowan Castle, home of the lords of Ross and later of Vice-Admiral Sir John Lockhart Ross, who brought sturdy sheep to the Highlands, with the best of intentions. The castle has long since passed into other hands, one of whom equipped it with sixteen sunken bathrooms of blue mosaic.

One of these was perhaps the old man who was said to have wandered from township to township in Ross in the last quarter of the 18th century, crying *"Mo thruaighe ort a thir, tha'n caoraich mhor a' teachd!"* Woe to thee, oh land, the Great Sheep is coming! This has been taken to mean the Cheviot which was brought to Easter Ross in 1790, but profitable sheep-farming was already flourishing there long before that, and before the old man had his melancholy vision. In 1762 Admiral Sir John Lockhart inherited the medieval castle and forty-eight properties of the Balnagowan estate. Since his tortuous descent from the Celtic Earls of Ross also gave him claim to the disputed leadership of Clann Aindrea, he hyphenated his surname with Ross, took pleasure and pride in his inheritance, and began his shore life as a successful Improver. He enclosed and cultivated neglected land, drained marshes, raised rents, gave leases to southern graziers, and put black-faced Lintons on the hills. A resentful people sometimes shot or drowned these placid animals, and in *Bliadhna nan Caorach* two years after Sir John's death they attempted to drive them all from Ross, but nothing could halt the changes the Admiral had begun. The prosperity of his family, founded upon prize-money and Linton sheep, continued for another century until the baronetcy expired with the entertaining inventor of the Ross rifle, a weapon I still remember with astonished dismay. For two dark nights during an invasion-scare in 1940 I sat on the beach at Pensarn in North Wales, holding it between my knees and wondering what use I could be with five rounds of ammunition only, and those too large for the rifle's breech. There are few sheep on Balnagowan now, and much of it is a sporting estate for foreign guns. The turreted castle above the road to Tain is the Highland seat of an absent Arab sheik, and its sixteen sunken baths of pale blue mosaic are a marvel unforeseen by the Brahan Seer.

Westward from the low hills and fertile ground between the

Loch Maree, one of the most beautiful in Wester Ross, probably takes its name from a saint who came here from Ireland thirteen centuries ago. Its lochside road was one of several built to relieve destitution during the Potato Famine of 1846.

Dornoch and Cromarty Firths the county of Ross stretches across the Northern Highlands from sea to sea, and beneath the black soil of some of its glens are the pebbled beaches of their long-receded tides. It is a land of magnificent peaks, dark bogs, grieving survivors of once-great forests, and moorland tarns like burnished shields. Its high-coned mountain wall on the western coast is lofty and indifferent, facing the grey Atlantic from which it arose as part of the first crust of the planet. Inland is another ocean of heaving earth and eroded rocks, tumultuous but immobile, empty of man but rich in the wild-life he now makes a brave effort to preserve – red deer and roe, fox and pine-marten, otters moving at dusk, ravens clearing their throats on moss-green outcrops, snow buntings on the cold high braes, red grouse in the heather, warblers among stands of white birch, a lone eagle, a stooping peregrine below scudding clouds.

The complex and magical beauty of Ross numbs the imagination and mocks all attempts to describe it. In the first moments of an early dawn its great wastes and upthrust hills are grey with the pain of their solitude, and night-shadows still deepen the parallel lines on the troubled face of Liathach. The rising sun warms and enlivens, and at noon it glistens on the white quartzite head of Beinn Eighe. With the passing of day the ice-hewn spearheads on the side of Slioch are a gentle rose-pink above the blue mirror of Loch Maree, but southward the scarred sandstone flank of Beinn Alligin drips blood into the darkness of Torridon. The seasons change colour and metaphor. When spring has melted its last corrie of snow the amethyst escarpment of Ben More Coigach is a cloud city above the dark gateway to Loch Broom. In summer,

when they are seen from the narrow coast-road to Diabaig, the round heads of the Beinn Damh range become gossiping women in purple shawls. The ochrous light of an autumn evening changes the jagged ridge of Stac Polly into the broken wall of a beleaguered Andalusian castle. In winter all can be hidden by a frozen mist. When that is lifted, by sun or wind, mountain and moor are chalk-white and ink-black against a blue sky.

It would be easy to believe that this land was always empty, but every glen, rock-face, mountain and lochan has a Gaelic name, remembering an imaginative society long since devoured by sheep. Most of its Mackenzie lairds were glad to be quit of it before the middle of the last century, but while they enjoyed their property they did so in style. On a June Monday in 1803, James Hogg stepped ashore from the *Isabella* at the head of Little Loch Broom to be the guest of George Mackenzie of Dundonnell. He was royally entertained, keeping his host company at the punch-bowl until they heard the dawn song of a blackbird beyond the window. Mackenzie lived well on his twenty thousand acres, employing one tutor in mathematics for his children, another in languages, and a third in music. With a Borderer's keen eye for bad husbandry, Hogg thought the estate was dismally managed, and although it was "crammed full of stout, able-bodied men and women" the glens were impoverished by perpetual cropping. Mackenzie asked what the land might produce if let as sheep-walks, and Hogg thought its rental could not be less than £2,000. Mackenzie said his people would never pay that. "He was loath to chase them all away to America, but at present they did not pay him above £700." Hogg liked Mackenzie, his good humour, the rich table he kept,

Stac Polly and Cul Beag, eroded sandstone ridges among the lochans of Coigach, where the coast of Wester Ross fragments into the Summer Isles, and the wind comes unbroken from the bitter Atlantic.

the civility of his family, their musical evenings and their delighted applause when their visitor played upon the fiddle. And if the laird was not making as much as he might of his lands

> He hath, however, the pleasure of absolute sway. He is even more so in his domains than Bonaparte is in France. I saw him call two men from their labour, a full mile, to carry us through the water. I told him he must not expect to be served thus by the shepherds if once he had given them possession.

When the dawn breaks on An Teallach the blackbird may still sing in the dark trees of Dundonnell, but the stout, able-bodied people are long gone. They are gone from all the sea-torn coast of Ross, the small townships that once supplied the Royal Navy and the fishery fleets with ten thousand men. They are gone from Strath Conon and Applecross, from Glen Torridon and from Loch Carronside where Hogg saw many villages, and where he lost his temper when he asked for more meat and was given whisky. On the peninsula coast of Coigach, looking out to the Summer Isles, there are a few white cottages and a good inn for those taking the twisting single-track by the ox-bow bend of Loch Lurgain. This was once a thickly populated estate, but in 1852 it became the property and responsibility of the young Marquess of Stafford who had ambitions to be as great an Improver as his grandfather, the first Duke of Sutherland. The land came to him as part of the property of his bride, Ann Hay-Mackenzie of Newhall and Cromartie, and it was in their joint names soon after their marriage that his agents issued writs of eviction upon its people. But the women of Achiltibuie, Polgass and Achabraighe were strong in spirit, and their defiance may have encouraged the women of Strathcarron two years later. They burnt the writs and drove the agents and Sheriff's officers back to the boats that had brought them from Ullapool. "It was a distinguished triumph of brute force over Law and Order," the agents told the Marquess, "and while it continues in the ascendant, the rights of the proprietors must remain in abeyance." And so they did, but not for long.

To the south of Coigach, across the wide mouth of Loch Broom, the inheritors of the Mackenzie lairds of Gruinard also dispersed its tenants and sub-tenants, and a scattering of stones is all that is left of their township on Gruinard Bay. This is one of the finest inlets on that beautiful coast and deserves its Norse name, the fjord of green shallows. Its green-blue water is held in a bowl of rounded rock. There is a green belt of earth above the white stones of its shore, a plaid of green timber upon the gently rising hills. Black cattle from Lewis, brought over the North Minch, were once landed here and driven eastward up the river to the Glen of Hunting, by the black shadow of An Teallach to Dundonnell Garve and the Muir of Ord. Joy in the solitude of Gruinard would be a kindness to the people who left it in sorrow, were not its beauty imperceptibly but nonetheless obscenely marred. There is a tear-drop island on the water, and although it is green with trees it is dead, all animal life still poisoned by the anthrax which military scientists placed there forty years ago.

The Gulf Stream warms the coastal waters of Wester Ross, curling in from the Rockall Deep. Without this, Osgood Mackenzie would have been unable to create his wonder-garden on the same latitude as Hudson Bay and the Bering Sea. He began it in 1864 on an old sea-beach, twenty-four acres of a bleak peninsula in Loch Ewe, a rock of red Torridon sandstone known as *Am Ploc Ard*, the High Lump. Nothing was growing there but heather, crowberry and a single dwarf willow three feet high, and much of its surface peat, varying in depth from an inch to two feet, had been taken for fuel. Westward from the mouth of Loch Ewe is the Long Isle and then the broad Atlantic and until Mackenzie planted a wind-break of trees the "exposure was awful, catching as it did nearly every gale that blew". He knew little of gardening when he began but he had inherited a love of it from his father, the fifth baronet of Gairloch. He learnt as he laboured, and after four years, during which black grouse, hare and red deer ate the young shoots of the trees and shrubs he planted, the land at last responded to his love. "Now came the real pleasure," he wrote, "of watching the fruit of all our labour and anxiety." He grew rhododendrons of wondrous size and colour, magnolias, azaleas and wistarias, camellias and cyclamens, spring, summer and autumn flowers, great shrubs and noble trees from two hemispheres, Bon Chrétien pears "as luscious as any that could be bought in Covent Garden", plums and apples, orange-flowered ixias, scarlet lobelias and great lilies.

When he died in 1924 his work was continued by his daughter, and thirty years later it passed into the care of the National Trust.

Dundonnell House below the great smithy of An Teallach, as seen by Moses Griffith in 1771. It looked much the same, no doubt when James Hogg was later the guest of its Mackenzie laird, drinking punch until the blackbird's dawn song.

One hundred thousand people visit it every year, and in their proper admiration for Mackenzie's achievements I hope they give some thought to how the garden at Inverewe acquired its present bed of black and fertile soil. The thin ground of the original sea-beach was first cleared by children who hand-picked it clean of pebbles. New earth was then brought by an old man, in a creel and upon his back. Later, others carried more soil in creels and carts, bringing it from the moors and from an abandoned turf-dyke. These people, unnamed in Mackenzie's brief history of the garden,* were no doubt glad of the work. In a contemporary reference to Gairloch, Black's *Picturesque Tourist* said "Extensive experiments have been tried to introduce the turnip husbandry among the crofters and tenantry, but not with any decided success as to the Landlord's rental or the increased comforts of the people".

There are two roads only through the central massif of Ross, from Strath Conon to the west coast. They begin as one on the Muir of Ord, dividing at Garve below the aloof shoulder of Ben Wyvis, and they follow the course of the old droving paths. The north fork goes by Strathvaich to Loch Broom and Ullapool, the second westward through Strath Bran to Achnasheen, Loch Maree and Gair Loch. At Achnasheen there is a southern branch to Loch Carron and the Skye ferry on the Kyle of Lochalsh. Each of these highways has sometimes been called Destitution or Desolation Road, although that title was originally given to a short stretch above Dundonnell, built to give employment in the years following the Potato Famine of 1846. But as the roads were used by the evicted people of the west, moving from their homes to the emigrant ships at Inverness, the name was applied to one or all with more sorrowful significance.

The northern road to the long sword-blade of Loch Broom was built to serve the new village which the British Fisheries Society was establishing at Ullapool, a planned and orderly assembly of parallel streets and a hundred houses, well-slated or thatched with turf and heather. Time has changed it and it has grown in size, but with Inveraray and Lochgilphead it is still an example of what other Highland towns might have become, had the good taste of the 18th century directed their growth. John Knox recommended the site to the Society, not only for the white fish in the ocean beyond the Summer Isles but also because of the abundance of herring at the mouth of the loch, "remarkable for their large size as well as their richness and flavour." In 1786 there was only a droving-path to the east, "the track of a road" he called it, and because he could find no one to guide him along it, or none who could speak English, he wisely continued his tour by boat. A new road was surveyed four years after his visit and was finished in 1797 by Kenneth Mackenzie the laird of Torridon, inspired to this undertaking, he said, by the poor people's needs and their "avidity for labour." He built the road for considerably less than the £8,000 estimated, and should perhaps have been less cautious with the

* Chapter XVIII of *A Hundred Years in the Highlands*, by Osgood Mackenzie, 1921.

subscribers' money, for by 1809 the highway was in such disrepair as to be almost impassable along some stretches. In that year Telford began the southern road by Achnasheen to Loch Carron. There were long and frustrating delays, much anguish of his spirit and mind, before it was last completed, and Robert Southey's carriage was the first to arrive at Strome Ferry. There the poet dined well at the inn on a choice of mutton chops, herrings, good potatoes, bannocks, cream and butter, as well as smuggled whisky.

Knox and Southey came to Wester Ross in autumn, when it burns with the red and brown, the bright orange of leaves inflamed by the first warning frost of winter. Southey saw the mountains and the glens "drest with sunshine" as I have often seen them, and always long to see them again. It was on such a golden day in late October that I once left Ullapool for Inverness. We had been filming *The Three Hostages* in Glen Achall, and that morning at the head of its lonely loch we had shot the last scene, Dominic Medina's fall to his death as he slips from Richard Hannay's grasp. On our drive eastward the high braes of Strathvaich were already touched with snow, but along the artificial loch of Glascarnoch the air was sunlit, the moorland heather bright with beaded rain. Beyond the dam we stopped at the inn of Altguish, a hotel now but once a drovers' tavern, I think, where some of them would halt before taking their herds a thousand feet over Corrimoillie to Strath Bran, saving time and distance to the Muir of Ord. The hotel was already closed for the winter but a bar at the back was still open, a stone-flagged floor and wooden benches, the air blue with peat-smoke. There were shepherds at the bar-counter, dogs lazily beating the floor with their tails. Aware of faces made familiar by television, the landlord's wife brought an autograph book with our beer and

Winter-bare birch on the headland mask the white house of Spinningdale. There are no greylag on the shore, and no pointers in the grass above the stones.

sandwiches, taking all names lest one might be overlooked in ignorance. She returned in ten minutes to tell me that she had read only one of my books, but "Jeannie in the kitchen has got them all." Whatever conceit that gave me was deflated by the ribald mockery of my companions as we drove on into the dusk of Strath Conon, toward the night-train from Inverness.

Now that James is gone from Spinningdale, and from Tigh an Allt at Ardgay, I do not often travel over Struie to the Kyle of Sutherland, and when I reach Inverness I go down the Great Glen to Lochaber, to Morvern or Kintail. I rarely use the road from Edinburgh to Inverness, the old hated road by Drumochter to the valley of the Spey. Now improved and widened, with long dual-carriageways, it avoids Newtonmore and Kingussie where the best bridies in the Highlands were once sold and perhaps still are. Sometimes I take the overnight sleeper to Inverness, more in nostalgia than pleasure, for the Royal Highlander is not the train it once was, when a breakfast-car was attached at Aviemore, the platform noisy with hungry, quarrelling gulls. I do not remember the rain that must often have been awaiting me at Inverness, only pale sunlight falling on the station square and on the white eroded statue of a Highland soldier, less honoured now for his valour at Tel-el-Kebir than for his value as a right flank marker for a platoon of parked cars.

There has been a town or settlement at the mouth of the River Ness for two thousand years. It was already old when Columba the Irish missionary came to convert the nothern Picts, miraculously opening the locked gates of their stronghold with the Sign of the Cross. History is rich with ironic coincidences. That conversion at Inverness, real or expedient, ensured the eventual domination of Scotland by the incoming Irish. Twelve hundred years later, when David Lloyd George was staying in the Highlands, he summoned his Cabinet to Inverness and there discussed Eamonn de Valera's terms for a treaty and the recognition of Ireland as a sovereign state.*

Inverness was among the first of Scotland's Royal Burghs. There was a King's Highway between it and Aberdeen in the 13th century, but no good road from the south for another four hundred years, and no railway until 1858. It was a trading port and a military stronghold commanding the Great Glen and the approaches to the northern mountains. Its possession was disputed for centuries, by the Crown's contenders and by feuding clans, and within half an hour's drive from its centre there are the sites of a dozen massacres and battles. Macbeth the Mormaer of Moray had a timber castle on a prehistoric mound above the town, but if he killed Duncan in envious ambition it was not here. I would like to believe, however, that his castle did have a gate-porter with so perceptive an understanding of the relationship between lechery and strong drink. There were earlier fortresses on the green hill of Craig Phadrig across the river, and others later on the earthwork

* The ministers met in the Council Chamber of the Town House on September 7, 1921, the only time a British Cabinet has been convened outside London.

where the Anglo-Norman mercenaries of David I built a keep of stone. This survived in one form or another until George Wade repaired its walls and gave it useful employment as a garrison, but the Jacobites destroyed this in 1746. In the last century its remaining stones were replaced by a municipal castle of red sandstone, erected from plans which would also have served for the façade of a Victorian prison, a work-house, railway station or baronial hall.

Three hundred years ago, Commonwealth soldiers sent by the Protectorate built a Citadel on the quay, on a site now occupied by oil storage-tanks. It placed Cromwell's military boot and England's will upon the town and the Highlands, but Inverness had been an English-speaking if not an Anglo-Saxon enclave long before that. In many respects it is perversely English today. Not the harsh, arrogant, self-esteeming and self-destroying England of the late twentieth century, but the Anglo-Scottish world of the Victorian age, comfortable and almost complacent in the knowledge that it is "the hub of the Highlands", as it somewhat inaccurately describes itself. It is certainly still the centre of their industrial, agricultural, educational and professional life, but is less concerned than it should be with the fact that its increasing role as a tourist centre is suffocating much of its old character and spirit. Its domestic and commercial architecture is largely Victorian and Edwardian, sometimes monstrous and often beguiling, but this too is changing, and its principal streets are becoming indistinguishable from other drear thoroughfares in Britain.

The property speculation of twenty years ago began that unpleasant change, and one of the men involved in it was a friend of my schooldays. When I see what he brought to Inverness I sadly remember our early and fervent interest in Scotland's history. We gave ourselves Scottish names, writing them on house notice-boards, and we wore tartan ties instead of the obligatory black, blue and white. He had a talent for memorising verse and could declaim Scott and Aytoun at great length. One poem to which he was particularly attached began with the only line I now remember, nor do I recall its source. "*Mo chreach* ... my sorrow, at seven tomorrow I must be back in a garrison town." He was a Jew, and when an insensitive master told him that it was ridiculous for him to have such an attachment to the Gaelic people of Scotland he said it was because he *was* a Jew.

I visit Culloden when I am in Inverness, no matter how brief my stay. Much of the work done in the past to preserve the battlefield, and honour the men who fought there, was due to the scholarship and devotion of Iain Cameron Taylor of the National Trust, without whose guidance and friendship my book would have been less than it is. He understood that the battle was not just the end of the Jacobite cause, to which he was nonetheless attached, but the climax of the Highlanders' long struggle for survival and the beginning of their betrayal and dispersal. Each visit I make to the moor brings another small discovery, not factual but emotional, a deepening rapport with place and past. No battlefield, however sympathetically maintained, can present the sights and sounds of bloody conflict, and when this is attempted the result is often theatrical and absurd. Understanding must come from knowledge and a creative imagination, and the duty of the custodians is to supply one and inspire the other. Culloden does not look as it did in the sleet of that distant day, but now that some of its forestry trees have been felled it is again possible to look northward to the firth and the Black Isle and westward to the mountains, to see them as they were in that waiting hour before the armies began their killing. The great stones above the mass graves, erected less than a century ago, are starkly simple and painfully moving. Stripped naked by beggars, the Jacobite dead lay on the moor for two days before they were buried in great pits, by detachments of Cumberland's soldiers whose white gaiters were soon as red as their coats. Thus no one can say with certainty that the clan names on the headstones correctly identify the men beneath, nor does it matter perhaps.

My visits to Culloden are not always melancholy, and should not be. There was joking that day, I think, for laughter is the reassuring companion of desperate courage. I remember that Iain once stood by the great cairn with Lord Doune, a member of the Culloden Committee and descended from the bastard half-brother of Mary Queen of Scots. The day was cold with rain, and in the shelter of the cairn a Scots guide was talking to a small group of Americans, bright plastic hoods tied beneath their earnest faces. As he reached the end of his galloping history of the Stuarts and the Jacobite cause he pointed over their heads to Lord Doune. "And there," he said, raising his voice above the wind, "there but for the thickness of a blanket is the rightful King of Scotland!"

When I left Spinningdale at the end of one of my last visits my car was filled with daffodils. "For your friends in the south," I was told. I drove southward by Culloden and gave some of the flowers to Neil MacDonald, the gentle Islesman who was then warden of the site. Others I laid on the Field of the English and the newly-discovered graves of the Campbells. The rest I took to Iain. He is gone now, as James and Rory are gone, but their memory is with me whenever I go to the Highlands.

S ERGEANT DONALD MCLEOD WAS BORN ON June 20, 1688, at Ullinish on the west coast of Skye. If not the greatest of the many soldiers this island has produced he was perhaps the most astonishing, and for some years now I have thought of writing a picaresque novel based upon his *Memoirs*. They were published in 1791 when he was still alive, an outpensioner of the Royal Hospital, in tolerable health and happy with the last of his several wives. His eldest son was eighty-three, the youngest nine. "Of the sixteen sons that he knows of," said his biographer, "not a less number than twelve are in different stations in the army and navy."

In the prime of life he was five feet and seven inches in height. He is now inclined by age to five feet five inches. He has an interesting physiognomy, expressive of sincerity, sensibility, and manly courage, though his eyes have lost their lustre and become dim and languid. With regard to his mental qualities, that which is most impaired is the faculty of memory, and of discriminating lively conceptions and ideas from historical truths.

He was proud of his age but he had no explanation for it, and when asked for one he said "I eat when I am hungry, and drink when I am dry, and never go to bed but when I can't help it." If told after his evening glass that it was time for him to sleep, he replied, "My eyes are not shut yet," and prolonged that condition by keeping one open for several minutes after the other was closed. But in the morning, "the moment he awakes, up he springs, washes his face and hands, and goes somewhere or other, for he seems to have an aversion to rest, and is constantly in motion."

Although the fact of his existence is confirmed by one contemporary record only outside the *Memoirs*, and that brief and deflationary, his longevity, fecundity, amorous adventures and military prowess have been accepted without question by clan and regimental histories, the former in family pride, and the latter in gratitude no doubt for such astounding proof that old soldiers never die. According to his biographer, he was born the son of John MacLeod of Ullinish, "as appears from the parish register of Bracadale" which has not, however, survived. He was thus descended from the great chiefs of Dunvegan, but his father,

MEMOIRS

OF THE

LIFE AND GALLANT EXPLOITS

OF THE

OLD HIGHLANDER,

SERJEANT *DONALD MACLEOD,*

W H O,

HAVING RETURNED, WOUNDED, WITH THE

CORPSE OF GENERAL WOLFE,

FROM QUEBEC,

WAS ADMITTED AN OUT-PENSIONER OF CHELSEA
HOSPITAL, IN 1759 ;

AND IS NOW IN THE

CIII.d YEAR OF HIS AGE.

LONDON:

FROM PETERBOROUH-HOUSE PRESS,
BY D. AND D. STUART.

SOLD BY J. FORBES, COVENT-GARDEN ; J. DEBRETT,
PICCADILLY ; AND J. SEWELL, CORNHILL.
MDCCXCI.

Serjeant D. Macleod.

Born in the Isle of Skye Aged 102 Who has Served five
crown'd Heads. Is now in Good health: has 12 Sons in
his Majesty's Service. And one Son 9 years Old.

Pub.d as the Act directs 10 Jan.y 1791 by I.Forbes, Covent Garden.

Sergeant Donald MacLeod From Ullinish on Skye. In 1791 he claimed to be 102 and this, like his campaigning exploits, was perhaps exaggerated. But his spirited courage seems real enough, and so does his readiness to fight any man called Maclean.

whose runaway marriage at sixteen had angered his own parents, soon abandoned his wife and children "for a course of dissipation which terminated in a military life", a lieutenancy of Marines in the Chatham Division. Donald was no better treated by his grandfather who apprenticed him to an Inverness stone-mason at the age of nine. Four years later he ran away to Perth, where a captain of the Royal Scots, "recognising him to be the descendant of a gentleman, immediately enlisted him." Before his fourteenth birthday he was a recruiting-sergeant.

He served with the First of Foot in Marlborough's wars, fighting at Blenheim, Ramillies and Malplaquet, as well as "engaging in several private encounters", hot-blooded duels with any man who provoked him, and later any man called Maclean whom he could himself provoke. He was at Sheriffmuir during the Rebellion of 1715, he said, although the Royal Scots were not. There he cut down a French officer in the Pretender's service, but was wounded by a dragoon whom he also killed. The horseman's sword laid open his brain, but "he bound his head fast with a handkerchief, otherwise, as he says, he verily believes it would have fallen into pieces." He recovered slowly at Chelsea Hospital, returned to Scotland and joined the Black Watch, pursuing cattle-thieves and taking the daughter of one as his first wife. He fought with the Watch at Fontenoy where he was wounded in the leg by a musket-ball. "Yet he did not drop down, nor yet fall behind, but was among the first that entered the trenches." He slew a French colonel, and was pocketing the dead man's purse and watch when he was attacked by an Irish officer whom he was able to defeat "after an obstinate and skilful contest."

At the beginning of the Seven Years War in 1756 he was transferred from the Black Watch to Fraser's Highlanders, as a drill-sergeant. He was now almost seventy, but well-known for his exploits and much esteemed by James Wolfe. "The General finding that our Sergeant, to courage, honour and experience added a tolerable knowledge of both the French and German languages, employed him on sundry occasions." Charging with Fraser's regiment on the Plains of Abraham, MacLeod was twice wounded, in the arm and leg, but he nobly surrendered his plaid so that it could be wrapped about his dying general. "With General Wolfe's corpse, being now an invalid, he was sent home to Britain in November, 1759, in a frigate of war named the *Royal William*." A year later, MacLeod was serving in Germany with Keith's Highlanders and was again wounded, by one bullet in his shoulder and another in the groin, "on account of which he still wears a bandage." In his ninth decade he sailed to New York on a military transport and offered his services as a volunteer against the American rebels. Sir Henry Clinton, the commander-in-chief, gave the old man the munificent sum of half a guinea a day from his own pocket, but kept him away from battle and finally sent him home.* That was not the end of his adventures, of course. Travelling by sea from London to Aberdeen, he was ship-wrecked and washed ashore on the coast of Yorkshire, lashed to a plank.

For ten years he worked as a stone-mason in Inverness, apparently using the skills he had acquired during his broken apprenticeship eighty years before. In 1789 he walked to London with his third or fourth wife, Jane MacVean, in the hope of persuading a dilatory bureaucracy to pay his meagre grant as an out-pensioner of the Royal Hospital. Sympathetic officers secured him an audience with George III, and although the King was at this moment losing his mind for the first time he had enough sense left to give the old soldier eleven guineas and instruct the Governor of the Royal Hospital to pay him a shilling a day. The MacLeods went home to Inverness in great joy.

> But see again the crooks of one's lot, the labyrinths of life! Though Macleod's name was inserted in the King's List he was to wait for the actual receipt of a shilling a day until there was a vacancy, which has not yet happened. Behold, therefore, Serjeant Macleod and Mrs Macleod again in London, in September, 1790, after a journey performed on foot, from Inverness, upwards of five hundred miles, in the space of three or four weeks, accompanied by their youngest son, a lively little lad, about nine years old, as above-mentioned.

It was while MacLeod was waiting for an answer to his second petition that his literary ghost discovered him in a Chelsea tavern

* A Private Soldier's pay at this time was approximately tenpence a day, including deductions.

or lodging-house. William Thomson had been an assistant minister at Monzievaird in Perthshire until complaints about his behaviour, or his interpretation of the Scriptures, forced him to resign. He came to London and made a comfortable living as a miscellaneous writer. One of the books he may have ghosted was the entertaining *Travels* of John MacDonald, a Keppoch man who became a London footman. If Thomson did not write this book he plagiarised it, for some of its anecdotes are repeated in MacLeod's *Memoirs*, published a year later. In his defence it might be said that he was sometimes disappointed by his subject. "I have noticed the proneness of the old Serjeant, in the present debilitated state of his mind, to confound mere imagination with realities."

I do not know if the Sergeant received his shilling a day from the Royal Hospital, or a share of the money earned by the *Memoirs*. I have been unable to find his portrait which Thomson said was engraved at this time, and I have discovered no record of his death or burial in the parish records of Chelsea. Perhaps he returned to Inverness, dying there or upon his long journey home. It was to establish a physical contact with him that I first went to Ullinish some years ago, a strange and unreal visit. I drove from Kyleakin to Loch Sligachan, by the perfect conical hill of Glamaig to the dark cathedral ruin of Sgurr nan Gillean at the loch-head. The day was warm and sunlit on the eastern coast of the island, but as I drove westward through the narrow defile of Glen Drynoch to Loch Harport the weather changed. There was shapeless cloud on the black ramparts of the Cuillins, and before I reached the mouth of the loch a golden gauze thickened to mist, damp and grey. At Struanmore I took a side-road to the little peninsula of Ullinish, and now visibility was only a hundred yards and decreasing. I did not know what I expected to find. Not a township, that was long gone with the Clearances, and not the "very good farm-house of two stories" where Boswell and Johnson were guests of the Laird of Ullinish, and where the Old Sergeant was perhaps born. I wanted to see the shore, the rocks and caves where MacLeod once played and was taught his murderous skill with the broadsword, the hill-road he walked to the parish school at Bracadale, carrying his young brother on his back. I saw nothing but mist and the warning fronds of barbed-wire on a dry-stone wall at the roadside, until suddenly there was a building ahead of me, dark and silent, like a ship becalmed in fog. It was an empty hotel, not abandoned but oddly deserted. Its door was open, tables were laid in the dining-room, the linen fresh and white, and there was a warm smell of cooking. But there was no one in any of its rooms, no one to answer my call.

I have since been to Ullinish on clear, blue-bright days and found the hotel busy with noise. I have seen a westering sun turning the water of Loch Bracadale to polished copper, and drawing long shadows from the stooked sheaves on the sloping fields. I have watched a fall of snow quickly approaching from the Cuillins, like a sheet expertly flung. I have seen a black-faced and white-lipped tide coming in from the horizon rim of the Uists, and

thought of the "melancholy sight" which disturbed Boswell's morning walk along this shore, an emigrant ship under way for America. I would like to believe that Donald MacLeod was indeed a child here three centuries ago, and that the brother he carried on his back grew to be the Laird of Ullinish, that "plain honest gentleman" who was greatly impressed by Johnson's knowledge of tanning and the manufacture of whey. "He is a great orator, sir," he said to Boswell, "it is music to hear the man speak."*

There are not only memories of Donald MacLeod on the shore of Loch Bracadale. Fifty years after his birth, the Irish ship *William* put in to the bay, ostensibly to unload brandy for the gentry of Skye but also to take aboard one hundred tenants of the lairds of Dunvegan and Sleat, sixty of them women and children. They were forcibly taken by the ship's crew, to be sold as indentured servants in America. Both Norman MacLeod of Dunvegan and Sir Alexander Macdonald of Sleat were party to the kidnapping, although they protested that their intention had been to rid their estates of "thieves and undesirables." Nothing might

Marsco, the green peak at the head of Glen Sligachan, between the Red Hills and the Cuillins. This is wild and lonely ground. Alexander Smith, the young Victorian who wrote *A Summer in Skye*, said that compared with Sligachan "Glencoe is Arcady."

* Alexander MacLeod of Ullinish, sheriff-substitute of Skye also lived to a great age. He was already a centenarian in 1791 when the Sergeant's *Memoirs* were published. Thomson refers to him as Donald MacLeod's uncle, but earlier writes of a brother Alexander born in 1690. Why the Sergeant, as the first son, was not recognised as the laird when his father was killed at Belle Isle in 1761, I do not know. He may have been born before his parents' marriage. His illegitimacy would perhaps explain his grandfather's cruel indifference in sending him away to Inverness.

To include the Cuillins, Moses Griffith moved them through 90 degrees to put them in his "View from Beinn na Caillich." This scalloped hill above Broadford was named for the Old Woman who was said to have laid a chain between Kyleakin and the mainland, levying a toll on shipping.

have been remembered of this sad incident had not the *William* called at its home port of Donaghadee in Ireland, where some of the prisoners escaped and a magistrate ordered the shipmaster to release the rest. In historical hindsight it was a warning of greater suffering to come, when the profit to be got from sheep would be a stronger temptation than a few guineas from the sale of helpless tenants. And it would be a bard to the Macdonalds of Sleat, Iain MacCodrum, who would make an angry and bitter protest against such inhumanity.

> Look around you and see the gentry
> with no pity for the poor creatures
> with no kindness to their kin.
> They do not think you belong to the land,
> and although they leave you destitute
> they do not see it as a loss.

To an English ear, the island is happily-named. The sky is its broad ceiling, supported by the ancient columns of its hills. Its moorland pools are windows through which another sky can be seen, the untroubled heaven of *Tir nan Og*, the land of the always-young, stretching beyond the Hebrides. There is no agreement on the meaning of its name. To some it is Norse for a clouded isle, to others a shield or a dirk, but the derivation I prefer is from the Gaelic *sgiath* a wing, for that is how it appears on a map, an eagle's wing with feathers extended in upward flight.

The island was created sixty million years ago by the terrible

Duntulm, the fort on a meadow by the sea, looking westward to the Outer Hebrides. It was the home of the chiefs of Clan Donald until they moved to softer quarters at Armadale, Edinburgh and London. MacDonald women made a garden here, with earth brought from seven kingdoms.

volcanoes which burst through a crust of sandstone three times as old, spewing out the black lava and igneous rock which form the red wall of Beinn Dearg, the hostile escarpment of the Cuillins, great terraces and high cliffs like the impregnable strongholds of warring gods. Ice and sea carved the chaos of volcanic fury into a majestic beauty, the Red Hills above Broadford Bay, the sleeping giant of Blaven with a shawl of scree and heather drawn up to its scarred face, the basalt plateaux of MacLeod's Tables where a braggart chief once dined with a southern guest, fifteen hundred feet above the sea and in the light of torches held by a hundred clansmen. The green and storm-grey sea-lochs create the feathers of the island wing, and as the eye turns inland from them it is drawn to the southern mass of the Cuillins, twenty-four mounting peaks with names like the clash of steel upon a shield. The young Irish warrior Cuchulainn built a fortress in their shadow, across Loch Eishort at Dunscaith and above a pit where he had killed its guardian snakes, dragons and monstrous toads. The mythology which claims that his name was given to the Cuillins is persuasive, but there is another explanation. When they appear paper-thin against a pearl-grey dawn their thorned outline resembles a leaf of *cuilionn-mara*, the blue-flowered sea holly that grows on the saline shore of the lochs. No one writing of the Cuillins has used adjectives of affection. The ice which carved their soaring crags and plunging falls of stone still chills the emotions. When Boswell saw them from Ullinish he could only describe them as "prodigious", and add that they reminded him of the mountains in Corsica "of

Frozen waves of lava make the strange formation of the Quirang on the northern tip of Skye. Cattle were once hidden from raiders in its higher folds, and eager Victorians came in great parties to climb its bleak walls.

which there is a very good print." Johnson said nothing that Boswell thought worthy of record, and wrote nothing in his *Tour*.

Except for the green littoral on the Sound of Sleat, the island is largely treeless, wastes of sepia moorland, harsh rock, indigo and terracotta cliffs dwarfing the white cottages at their feet. Nowhere in the Highlands is there a deeper loneliness than on the peninsula of Trotternish, the index feather of the eagle's wing, where the pleated folds of Kilt Rock glisten with climbing spray, and the Old Man at the postern-gate of Storr looks across the sea to Raasay. On the shore at his feet, a century ago, a Viking treasure was found, including coins from the western foothills of the Himalayas. Trotternish, the bear's cape of the Norsemen, was later Clan Donald ground, and the Lords of the Isles held a fortress on its northern tip, at Duntuilm above a beach of olivine stones. It is now a desolate ruin, heather and yellow grass cover the garden made with earth brought from seven kingdoms, and there is only the

stump of a tower where fifty unmarried girls danced at a great ball given by Donald of the Wars. Upon Staffin Bay, eighteen miles northward from Portree, the strange formation of the Quirang was created by a great landslip at the end of the Ice Age, wher a floor of lava one thousand feet deep first cracked, then broke and moved toward the sea. The Norse called it The Crooked Enclosure, recognising its great pillars, buttresses, and pinnacles of stone as a massive stock-pen, and within its walls three thousand cattle could be hidden from sea-borne raiders. It is said that the land on this part of the coast is still sliding into the sea, and in time will take with it the house where Flora MacDonald lived for twenty-two years after her marriage, and where she bore five of her seven children. It is sometimes difficult to see that young woman of the speeding, bonny boat as the abundant matron she became.

In the 18th century the chiefs of Clan Donald moved from Duntulm to softer living at Armadale on the Sound of Sleat.

A ruined castle on tranquil water, but the camera has its back to the wide stone jetty at Kyleakin where great car-ferries bring two million visitors to Skye, and there is no black nuclear submarine to be seen in Loch Alsh.

"At Dunvegan I had tasted lotus," said Johnson, explaining his reluctance to leave. This is how he saw the castle, "partly old and partly modern." Later MacLeod chiefs improved it with turrets and battlements, to the approval of Scott if not everyone since.

Johnson and Boswell stayed there as the guests of Sir Alexander Macdonald ninth baronet and eventually first Baron Macdonald of Macdonald and Sleat, heir-male of *Clann Uisdein*, descendant of Iain the first Lord of the Isles. He was hawk-nosed and chinless, an anglicised chieftain with an English wife and a preference for life in London or Edinburgh, tastes which most of his descendants would inherit. Johnson had a great contempt for chiefs whom he believed to have degenerated from patriarchal rulers into rapacious landlords, and most particularly did he despise Sir Alexander Macdonald of Macdonald. "He has no more the soul of a chief than an attorney who has twenty houses in a street and considers how much he can make by them."

The Doctor was much happier as a guest at the MacLeods' faery castle on Loch Dunvegan. He admired the dowager Lady of Dunvegan and talked with her until a late hour after supper, giving her his opinions on literature, gout as an hereditary ailment, polygamy in Formosa, and the publication of truth. His reflections on the last may have confused her – "There is something noble in publishing truth, though it condemns one's self" – but he was more understandable when he spoke of good humour which, he said, increased as a man grew older. His own benign agreeability was largely the result of the hospitality lavished upon him. "At Dunvegan," he wrote, "I had tasted lotus, and was in danger of forgetting that I was ever to depart, till Mr Boswell sagely reproached me with my sluggishness and softness." He would not recognise the castle today. It is said to be the oldest inhabited castle in Britain, but it might have been more pleasing to the eye had it become an abandoned ruin. At the beginning of the last century, when Macdonald of Sleat was turning Armadale into an imitation of Breadalbane's Gothic horror, the twenty-fourth and twenty-fifth Chiefs of MacLeod equipped Dunvegan with a defensive mound, mock battlements, towers, turrets and drawbridge. Later in the century the remaining visible stones of the original building were covered with a drear coat of stucco, creating a passable

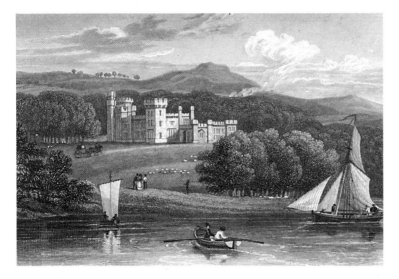

The second Lord Macdonald built this Gothic castle in 1815, at Armadale. It replaced a more modest house where his father had aroused Johnson's contempt. Subsequent chiefs continued the improvements, paying their increasing debts with eviction and land-sale. The down-at-heel castle is now owned by the Clan Donald Society and used as a museum, in which there may be some historic irony.

likeness to the castles which once appeared in advertisements for dentifrice.

Walter Scott visited Dunvegan when the improvements begun by the twenty-fourth chief were well under way, and MacLeod was no doubt pleased with his guest's approval. Towers and draw-bridge, said Scott, "if well executed, cannot fail to have a good and characteristic effect." He was cruising about the coast of the island in a lighthouse yacht, sending his card ashore to its gentry and accepting their hospitality. His imagination was romantically excited, his mind filled with scenes and impressions that would inspire much of *The Lord of the Isles*, "rocks at random thrown, black waves, bare crags, and banks of stone." He had not yet understood the darker side to such grandeur, the tragedy and despair which had already begun before his visit, and would increase in the years following. Emigration and eviction came early to Skye, although they would not reach full spate until the middle of the 19th century. When Boswell and Johnson were the guests of John Mackinnon of Corriechatachan, the diarist took part in a dance

> ... which I suppose the emigration from Skye has occasioned. They call it *America*. Each of the couples, after the common involutions and revolutions, successively whirls round in a circle, till all are in motion; and the dance seems intended to shew how emigration catches, till a whole neighbourhood is set afloat.

But if he thought this was a demonstration of the people's joy, their eagerness to emigrate, he was soon disenchanted. Mrs Mackinnon told him that when a ship had sailed from Portree a year before, the relatives of the departing lay down on the earth in grief, tearing at the grass with their teeth. "This year there was not a tear shed. The people on shore seemed to think that they would soon follow. This indifference is a mortal sign for the country."

Fifty years later the flow of emigration was irreversible. The kelp industry, by which the lairds of the Isles had enjoyed a brief prosperity, was now in decline. There were too many people, and rents were too low. When Robert Southey came to Skye with Telford, who wished to enlist labourers for work on the Caledonian Canal, they discovered that "a villainous adventurer by name Brown" was advising the proprietors. This was probably Robert Brown, once a detested factor of the Clanranald estates who was now suggesting that all rents should be doubled, trebled or quadrupled "according to the supposed capability of the tenant." While the kelp industry flourished his advice was followed with profit, but eventually, said Southey

> Cattle and kelp fell to their former price; the tenants were unable to pay; and some of the Lairds were at once unthinking and unfeeling enough to go thro' with the extortionate system, and seize their goods by distress ... These grasping and griping Landlords have gone far toward ruining themselves.

Ruin came to most before the Great Cheviot saved the remainder. There are few sheep on the braes of Skye now, but at one time, it was said, the hills were covered with summer snow, and the people they dispossessed were caught by the dancing involutions and revolutions of *America*. Destitution, eviction and dispersal inspired the formation of the Skye Emigration Society, which would later embrace all the Highlands and Islands. Although the directing members of its board were sympathetic to the Policy of Improvement, their consciences were disturbed by its effect upon the people.

> The great mass is reduced to such a state of wretchedness as could not fail, in almost any other country to produce acts of lawless violence. Yet these poor people remain quiet and peaceable, wishing and praying for, rather than expecting better times.

The better times did not come, and with sorrowing hearts the people surrendered to the Society's appeal. "*We will do what we can to assist you, and we will endeavour to procure assistance for you from others* ..." The proprietors also responded, some with donations but all grateful for a Society ready to send ships and guarantee passage for the tenants they were evicting. By the middle of the last century all the Hebrides were in movement, their sea-lochs and their bays filled with emigrant ships, their white beaches loud with the barking of dogs, the cries of women, the angry shouting of sheriff-officers as the people were driven to the boats, often bound or manacled. "Oh the turns of the hard world," recalled one of them many years later, "oh the suffering of the poor folk and the terrible time that was!"

The first great wave of evictions was on the valley floor of Strathaird in 1851, where the green braes look westward across Loch Scavaig to the Cuillins. It is a lonely drive to Strathaird now, beautiful and lonely, the sun yellow on the hills, and the loch-water bright with sequins. Five hundred people were driven from the land by their new laird, Alexander MacAlister, who styled himself

This illustration first appeared in Donald Ross's account of the Clearances, published in 1854. It is closer to the harsh truth than the sentimental canvases of more fashionable artists who painted no smoking cottages, no factors with writs in their hands.

of Torrisdale Castle in Argyll. He was generally thought to be an amiable fellow, which meant, said Thomas Mulock, that he was "a man who does all his harsh deed by deputy." The people owed him £450 in unpaid rents, but he told them he was ready to waive this, and advance them £12,000, if they went to Canada or New South Wales, and he was surprised when they refused. "Ah, Mr MacAlister of·some Argyll ilk," said Mulock, "how would you like to be transported against your Scottish will from Torrisdale to Toronto?" Before he could persuade the people to go, Mac-Alister was obliged to enlist the help of the Sheriff, sheriff-officers, members of the Destitution Board, and the threat of deploying two companies of the 13th Regiment, Prince Albert's Own.

While the eight townships of the Strathaird estate were being cleared, the Trustees of Lord Macdonald's land were evicting the people of Suishnish and Boreraig on the eastern shore of Loch Slapin. It was two years before all were gone. Two men who resisted the evictions were arrested and tried at Inverness, but the jury refused to find them guilty after their counsel had asked it to consider "how far the pound of flesh allowed by the Law is to be extracted from the bodies of Highlanders." Their acquittal changed nothing. Five days after Christmas in 1853, the factors and the officers came again to Suishnish and Boreraig and drove out the remaining people. Among the last to go was a child of seven who cried out to the men who were dismantling the cottage in which he was born, "If my father were here today, who would do this to us?" Lord Macdonald's Trustees defended him against a public outcry by saying that he had been over-indulgent to the people and had allowed them to waste good land, therefore their removal was in their own good interest. Developing this exculpatory argument his Commissioner, Patrick Cooper, who had recently cleared Macdonald's estate on North Uist, explained that his lordship had been prompted to remove the people "by motives of benevolence, piety and humanity, because they were too far from the church." It was some months before a buyer could be found for the estates. The market for wool and mutton was unsteady, due to the war in the Crimea, but the *Wool Market Circular* reported that prices for ewes and wedders were still high, and there could be confidence in an early return to stability.

His pious and benevolent lordship is long gone, his descendant owns no wide lands on the Isle of Skye, and the gothic castle at Armadale, built and maintained by some of the profit got from the dispersal of Clan Donald, is now a museum to their memory. To the north in Minginish, at the mouth of a narrow glen from Loch Harport to Talisker Bay, there is a distillery producing Skye's only malt. Stevenson called it "a king of whiskies", and Neil Gunn, who wrote the finest book on the subject said "Talisker at its best can be superb, but I have known it adopt the uncertain manners of Skye weather." It is a talking-whisky, almost as fine as Lagavulin when there is frost in the evening air and a night of good conversation ahead. The little glen from which it comes is narrow and dark, a cleft of waterfalls and steep rocks between the sea-loch and the sea. Johnson stayed here as the guest of its MacLeod laird and thought it a depressing place "from which the gay and the jovial seem utterly excluded, and where the hermit might expect to grow old in meditation, without possibility of disturbance or interruption." But before the building of the distillery, sixteen families were removed from this glen, and when I drink Talisker I remember them.

Skye's agony did not end with the clearances in Strathaird, Boreraig and Suishnish. In 1882 the people began to fight back. At Glendale in Duirinish, below the lava plateaux of MacLeod's Tables, they had suffered bitterly from increasing eviction, and from a harsh factor who forbade them to keep dogs or gather driftwood from the shore. At the beginning of February the most resolute of them met in the church and decided to take a stand against further evictions, to demand the reinstatement of those who had already been removed. Authority's response was to send the gunboat *Jackal*. When it anchored in Loch Pooltiel and landed an officer he was met by the sound of horns and by a crowd of six hundred orderly but determined people. Three men of the townships voluntarily surrendered to arrest, willing to plead their case before the Court of Sessions, but because they would not have it said "that Glendale men had to be taken away from their homes in a man-of-war" another ship was sent. They went aboard the *Dunara Castle* after a weeping farewell and the reassurance that "We go to uphold a good cause, to defend the widow and fatherless, and the comfort and needs of our hearths and homes." They were taken to Calton Prison in Edinburgh but the governor refused to admit them, sending them under a Messenger-at-arms to the Ship Hotel where they became the astonished centre of public sympathy and admiration.

In April that same year, Lord Macdonald's factor was faced with the angry defiance of his tenants on The Braes, a coastal strip between Loch Sligachan and Tianavaig Bay. The immediate cause was their refusal to pay their rents until it was acknowledged that they had an ancient right to graze their stock on the lower slopes of Ben Lee, but there were other grievances and older fears. When writs of eviction were brought, the papers were burnt and pails of water were thrown over the sheriff-officer. Fifty Glasgow policemen were then sent to enforce the writs, and as their approach from Portree was signalled by braying horns "men, women and children rushed forward in all stages of attire, most of the females with their hair down and streaming lovely in the breeze. Every soul carried a weapon of some kind." They fought with sticks and stones and clawing hands. When the police retreated, with five prisoners they had taken, they were ambushed by another party, hurling large stones from above the road. The discontent, the brooding threat of further violence lasted for another year, until warships arrived from Rosyth and an armed party of Marines was landed at Uig.

The Crofters' War, which spread to other islands and the mainland, is still remembered with pride and sadness. Its most positive achievement was to persuade Gladstone to establish a Commission of Enquiry. The august members of this Board came to the Highlands by sea, patiently interviewing hundreds of witnesses: factors, tenants, sub-tenants and cottars, men and women, old and young. They heard the story of clearance and emigration over the past seventy years, during which, on Skye alone, more than thirty-five thousand people had been evicted. Many of the witnesses spoke in Gaelic, the only tongue they knew. Their evidence was translated literally by interpreters, recorded and subsequently printed. It retained the rhythm and poetry of the original language, and those who have the time and patience to read the Report and Evidence of the Commission will hear moving voices from the past, the sound of weeping and the laughter it replaced.

Much was won by the Crofters' War, by the Commission's diligent Enquiry and the reforming Act which followed. The violence of protest in Lewis and Assynt, in Skye and the Outer Isles aroused the sympathy and generosity of Scottish exiles throughout the world, and it inspired a political initiative in the Lowlands which eventually led to the development of the Scottish Labour movement, without whose energy English Socialists might have remained a minority party. But in the Highlands the changes in Law and political consciousness came too late, perhaps, nor did they stop depopulation or alter the basic nature of land ownership. Much of Skye still belongs to anonymous consortiums, to foreign speculators who play cynical games of chance with the land. The old Highland belief that the fish in the burn, the bird on the wing, and the stag on the brae were put there for all men to take was never much of a truth, I think, and the Law still protects all three on behalf of the proprietor. The bitter years of the Crofters' War have left a lingering anger in the Western Highlands and the Isles, but also pride, and both are occasionally voiced in the pages of the *West Highland Free Press*, published from an old school-house at Breakish. When this bold newspaper first appeared ten years ago its young writers alarmed an establishment accustomed to a subservient press. It insistently questioned the rights of property, entrenched privilege and autocratic central government, and it honoured the example set by polemical Highland journalists a century ago. Time has mellowed it, but it still has the ability to make authority pause and sometimes withdraw, and I hope it will not think it presumptuous of me to suggest that it should exercise that power as often as it once did.

It is perhaps irrelevant to return to the Old Sergeant, but I have not finished his story and it requires a final comment. When I first thought of using his *Memoirs* as the inspirational basis of a novel, I looked for some confirmation of them in the records of out-pensioners at the Royal Hospital. These are brief but informative, and against each man's name is an account of his age, his wounds and disabilities. The man I found and believe to be Sergeant Donald MacLeod was certainly very old, but some years younger than he or Thomson claimed. There is no reference to those terrible wounds received at Sheriffmuir, Fontenoy and the Plains of Abraham, only this laconic entry: *Suffering from fits*.

THERE WAS A POST-VAN AHEAD OF ME WHEN I reached the eastern end of Loch Naver, where the river curls in hesitant bends before flowing northward to the sea. The van was stationary, pulled to one side and leaning into the soft earth, and although there was room to pass I stopped to watch the postman. With his bag tied about his body like a guerrilla's blanket, he moved over the emerald green of the rough pasture to a swinging foot-bridge, crossed the water and went up the brae to the white-walled farm at Achness, three-quarters of a mile from the road. He did not return within the time I stayed there, and I saw no one else in this part of Strath Naver that morning. The spring sun was low in the sky, and the dark silhouette of Ben Klibreck across the loch was a sleeping woman, a shawl of white smoke across her hips. The silence and the stillness were unnatural, as if they were a pause only, and before long the people would return, apologetic for their absence and filling the glen with noise.

Achadh an Eas, the cornfield by the waterfall, was once a township. A dozen families lived in its dry-stone and sod-roofed cottages beneath the three cones of Rhimsdale, and amongst the heather and deer-grass of the braesides there are a hundred cairns and hut-circles of earlier inhabitants. The strath was also the most fertile in northern Sutherland, a green fold in the brown mountains, a gentle glen down which the black water of its river moves to the white sand of Torrisdale Bay, to the cold sea and the Arctic Circle. Until Loch's Policy of Improvement, Telford's energy and a rich lord's money built a carriage-road from Bonar Bridge, this northern land was almost inaccessible except by ship. It had few visitors, and those who did come usually recoiled from it in horror, deciding that it was either a gateway to Hell or the edge of the world. It is still a wild country, the waste-heap of a glacial age, open to the wind and at war with the sea. Yet its wildness is beautiful, and it was loved by its people. Knowing both it and the bleak, short-grass country of the Canadian prairies, I think I understand the anguish of the men and women who were forced to exchange one for the other.

The people who lived in Strath Naver at the beginning of the last century were mostly Mackays by name or clan allegiance, although the Countess Elizabeth of Sutherland was their Great Lady, and the Marquess of Stafford her husband was their landlord. They lived in what she and the Marquess considered to be poverty, squalor and slothful indolence, and thus their eviction and their enforced employment in fruitful industry elsewhere should be the Christian duty of their superiors. The first great clearance of Strath Naver by Patrick Sellar was in 1814, *Bliadhna an Losgaidh*, the Year of the Burnings. If the land from which they were driven was not the paradise some of the people remembered, the thought of it gave them pain until the end of their lives. More than sixty-five years after the first clearance, there was perhaps exaggeration in what Angus Mackay told the Crofters' Commission, but his love and longing for the past are unmistakable.

> I remember you would see a mile or half a mile between every town if you were going up the strath. There were four or five families in each of these towns, and hill pastures for miles, as far as they could wish to go. The people had plenty of flocks of goats, sheep, horses and cattle, and they were living happy, with flesh and fish and butter, and cheese and fowl and potatoes, and kail and milk too. There was no want of anything with them, and they had the Gospel preached to them at both ends of the strath.

The last preacher of the Gospel at Achness was Donald Sage. He had been born thirty years before in his father's manse at Kildonan on the Helmsdale river, south-eastward from Loch Naver over the high ground of Borrobol. He came to Achness in 1818 and with profound disquiet at the changes taking place on the Sutherland estate, but he was proud of his family's resistance to the clearance of their own parish in 1813. Patrick Sellar, he said, had "laboured hard to involve my father and mother in the criminality of these proceedings, but he utterly failed." He had not been at his ministry many months when he heard that there was to be a final clearance of Strath Naver, by which all his congregation would be evicted. "I can yet recall," he wrote long afterwards, "the deep and thrilling sensation which I experienced as I sat at the fireside in my rude little parlour when the tidings of the meditated removal of my poor flock reached me." Many of his congregation refused to believe this was possible, although they could see the smoke-blackened stones of the houses Sellar had emptied in the Year of the Burnings. But the remaining townships were now to be levelled, and sixteen hundred people removed. The writs of eviction, said Sage

> ... were distributed with the utmost preciseness. They were handed in at every house and hovel alike, be the occupiers of them who or what they might be, minister, catechist, or elder, tenant or sub-tenant, out-servant or cotter, all were made to feel the irresponsible power of the proprietor.

On a May morning in 1819, he stood at the door of his little house and watched the burning of two hundred buildings, along the lochside at Grummore and Grumbeg, and northward up the strath by Syre, Langdale and Skailburn. His church and home were

also destroyed with the cottages of Achness, some of their stones taken to make the road from Lairg to Tongue, and their timber for the building of an inn at Altnaharra, seven miles to the west at the head of the loch. My car has often passed over the stones, and I have sometimes taken a dram at the hotel, looking up to its ceiling and thinking of the beams beyond the white plaster. On the Sunday before the evictions Sage preached his last sermon in the open. "I selected a text which had pointed reference to the peculiarity of our circumstances, but my difficulty was now to restrain my feelings ... I preached and the people listened, but every sentence uttered and heard was in opposition to the tide of our natural feelings." He could not finish the sermon, for both he and his congregations were soon weeping. A year later, a woman who had returned briefly to the strath was asked what she had seen. "Oh, sorrow!" she said, "I have seen the timbers of our church covering the inn. I have seen the kirk-yard filled with tarry sheep, and Mr Sage's study turned into a kennel for Robert Gunn's dogs, and I have seen a crow's nest in James Gordon's chimney-head. Oh, sorrow!"

Patrick Sellar had retired from Stafford's service before the second evictions in Strath Naver, although he must have been involved in their planning. He had taken a lease on the ground he had cleared to the east of the river, almost a hundred square miles, and the people on the west bank could see his great flocks on Rhimsdale and as far as the lower braes of Ben Griam. He was now one of the most prosperous sheep-farmers in the north, and his

Daniell's aquatint of the mouth of Strath Naver which he visited in 1815. The scene is little changed today, although no one lives in the buildings and it would be strange to see so many boats.

brutal conduct during the Year of the Burnings had been dramatically vindicated. In April, 1816, he had been brought to trial by the Sheriff-Substitute of the county, Robert MacKid, to whose children Donald Sage was once tutor. There was undoubtedly more to MacKid's motives than compassion and a desire for justice, perhaps jealousy, perhaps social and political ambition, but the charges he laid were serious and put Sellar's life at risk. The factor was accused of "culpable homicide, as also oppression and real injury". And more, so much more that the Advocate-Depute spent two hours reading the charge before an Inverness court. The deaths for which Sellar was held responsible were those of Margaret Mackay and Donald MacBeth. The former had died after she was carried from her burning cottage, crying "God receive my soul! What fire is this about me?" MacBeth was an old man, suffering from cancer of the face, and he lay in the open for nearly a week after his eviction, bringing death upon him earlier than it might have called, it was said. Sellar was acquitted of all charges and returned to his employment with his good name restored. Sensing that public opinion was now against him – that is to say, the opinion of men of property and influence – MacKid sent a grovelling apology to Sellar, hoping the factor would withdraw a suit for damages against him. Sellar did so, more in disgust than pity, insisting only that MacKid pay his expenses and £200 besides.

Some of the Strath Naver people, the young and the robust, left the country, said Donald Sage. "But the aged, the females and children, were obliged to stay and accept the wretched allotments allowed them on the seashore and endeavour to learn fishing." Among these was an old woman who was thrown into a fit by the approach of any stranger, rolling her eyes, hugging her body and crying *"Oh! Shin Sellar!* There's Sellar!"

I had read these accounts, and many others, before I first went to that distant strath, and the thought of them was in my mind and heart as I watched the postman climbing the lonely brae to Achness. It is not difficult to find the sites of some of the old townships, although one must learn to distinguish their scattered stones from natural outcrops, if only by the surrounding patches of green earth, enriched by half a millennium of diligent manuring. The clearances of Strath Naver are the most bitterly remembered of all in the Highlands. The people now remaining, and living for the most part on the northern coast to which their ancestors were sent, have kept the past alive. Eight years ago a museum of the Clearances was established at Bettyhill, in a white church above Torrisdale Bay, containing relics of the removals and of the life of the people before they were dispersed. It is a matter of pride to me that the manuscript of my book was accepted by its keepers, an acknowledgement far exceeding all critical approval.

Dispute about the Sutherland Clearances also continues until this day. In 1976, when Golspie was chosen as the next location of the annual Gaelic Festival of The Mod, the Countess of Sutherland was invited to be its honorary president. There was some logic in this, albeit a want of tact, for the town and the nearby castle of Dunrobin had been the centre of her family's history and power. Protest and argument were immediate and acrimonious, and she discreetly withdrew her acceptance of the invitation.* The impassioned wrangle continued, however, and soured much of the euphoria of the International Clan Gathering in Edinburgh, during which I made that intemperate interruption. In the spirited defence of the House of Sutherland at this time there was a curious echo of past debate, and occasional references – as if citing Holy Writ – to James Loch's apologia of his Policy and of his noble master. *An Account of the Improvements on the Estate of Sutherland.* In this he declared that the object of the improvers had been

> to emancipate the lower orders from slavery ... to render this mountainous district contributory as far as it was possible to the general wealth and industry of the country, and in the manner most suitable to its situation and peculiar circumstances. To convert the former population of these districts to industries and regular habits ... (It was) a wise and generous policy and well calculated to increase the happiness of the individuals who were the object of this change, and to benefit those to whom these extensive domains belonged.

Its proposals were high-minded and autocratic, and Loch's account of their execution used the language of established power and of a class which had no doubt that it alone knew what was best for the majority. But against its impressive figures of acres cleared, roads built, rivers crossed, wool baled and fish barrelled, may be set the voice of William Morrison whose home was one of twenty cottages destroyed at Rossal, and who spoke of that day to the Crofters' Commission, "For people to say that there was no cruelty or harshness shown the people when they were burnt off Strathnaver is a glaring lie, which no amount of flowery language can hide." Or the words of Angus Mackay who told the Commissioners he was eleven in the Year of the Burnings, and that he ran naked from the evictors, carrying his brother across the river.

> It would be a very hard heart but would mourn to see the circumstances of the people that day. He would be a very cruel man who would not mourn for the people ... You would have pitied them, tumbling on the ground and greeting and tearing the ground with their hands. Any soft-minded person would have pitied them.

I was granted no access to the Sutherland archives at Dunrobin when I was writing my book. I wrote twice to the 5th Duke asking for this, and having twice received no answer I did not try again. When I heard that an academic historian of St Andrews was studying these papers I wrote to him, explaining my purpose and hoping he would tell me how I might also have an opportunity

* The 5th Duke and 23rd Earl of Sutherland died without issue. The earldom went to his niece, Mrs Elizabeth Janson, by right of primogeniture and inheritance through the female line. The dukedom, which had no such recognition of women's rights, passed to a collateral male descendant of the first duke. Thus, for the first time in two centuries, there was once more a Countess of Sutherland in her own right.

to see them. He replied courteously, but briefly. Since he was himself writing a book upon this same period, he said, I would of course understand that he could give me no help with mine. I understood that less, I think, than I did the Duke's indifference to my application. Some years before this, the newspaper for which I was then working had sent me to interview him at his London home, upon what subject I cannot now remember. I recall the noble aloofness of his face, sculpted in marble from a descriptive passage by Ouida, but most of all I remember his butler. When called to show me out at the end of the interview, he sensed the Duke's unspoken thoughts and took me through the kitchen to the servants' door. In his autobiography, Sutherland included an account of his family's rise to great wealth and influence at the end of the 18th century, the improving zeal of the first Duke, and the criticism it provoked. He softened the word *evictions* with inverted commas, combining distaste for its vulgar meaning with contempt for those who used it, and in his final sentence he put the bitter suffering of the Clearances into what he thought was its proper perspective. "As in most disputes, there were probably faults on both sides, and a great deal of misunderstanding."*

Sutherland is still the wildest and most lonely part of the Highlands. It is traversed by one principal road only, moving northward by Lairg to Tongue like the flight of an arrow from the sprung bow of the kyle. The cost of this highway, with the coastal road from Bonar Bridge to Wick, was £16,500, and when they were finished in 1819 it was proudly said that a mail-coach leaving Inverness at six in the morning could reach Thurso by noon on the following day, provided there were no delays caused by "snowstorms and sudden thaws . . . the inexperience and want of accurate habits in the persons engaged in such an undertaking." The four hundred and fifty miles of these roads, with the thirty-four bridges they crossed, are the lasting achievement of James Loch and his master. Before they were completed, the great clearances on the Sutherland estate were over, in the parishes of Farr and Lairg, Dornoch, Rogart, Loth, Clyne and Golspie, Kildonan and Strath Naver. The flocks of True Mountain Sheep already upon the braes would shortly increase to 200,000 with the promise of 415,000 pounds of wool annually. Loch's *Account* said that 600 families were removed between 1810 and 1820, and in addition there were 408 more who, in his opinion, had no right or title to be in the county and were justly driven from it. Assuming an average of five to a family, this makes a conservative estimate of five thousand men, women and children, a third of the total population of the Sutherland estates. Loch's figures do not include the removals carried out by Sellar before 1810, and they do not include the cotters and out-servants whom I have not counted as members of a family.

The majority of the evicted were removed to the coasts of the county, there to become part of Loch's great plan to develop a

* *Looking Back, the Autobiography of the Duke of Sutherland*, London, 1957.

fishing industry. Factories and cottages were built, and the people from the glens were drilled into a new economy and a new discipline under which their sons and daughters had first to ask the permission of Mr Loch, or his agents, before they married. The town of Helmsdale at the mouth of the strath was the Commissioner's greatest experiment, and for a time it prospered as a fishing-port. Little is left of its ambitious beginning. When I first visited it the grey shells of the fishery sheds remained, and on the high ground beyond the bay were roofless buildings which might have been mute evidence of clearance and eviction, but were once barrack cottages, now empty monuments to Mr Loch's great dream. Along the strath, northward to the deer forests of Borrobol, Baddanloch and Achentoul, there are sporting estates where the Kildonan parishioners of Alexander Sage once lived, and from which they marched to Dunrobin in 1813, believing the Countess Elizabeth would save them from eviction. She was in London, but she recorded their protest in a letter. "I am uneasy about a sort of mutiny that has broken out in one part of Sutherland, in consequence of our new plans having made it necessary to transplant some of the inhabitants to the sea-coast." She attributed their discontent to their preference for distilling whisky, and their unwillingness "to quit that occupation for a life of industry of a different sort which was proposed to them." That reluctance was answered by the arrival of a detachment of Royal Scots Fusiliers, some artillery and wagons loaded with powder and ball, and those people of Kildonan who did not leave for Lord Selkirk's colony on the Red River went instead to the fisheries on the coast. The parish now is not what the young men and women remembered in their Canadian exile, and it is not what the Duke of Sutherland and James Loch confidently expected it to become. A man from Kildonan, who was himself evicted from the strath in 1959, and who treasures the red-stocked flintlock with which his ancestor defied the incoming sheepmen, replied sadly to a letter from me.

What is the position in Kildonan today? Six alien proprietors owning land and water where once hundreds of good, happy people lived, a red Post Office van, a score of gamekeepers and shepherds. In addition to deer, grouse and salmon, the proprietors do quite a side-line in sheep and cattle. They sometimes open baby shows and strut at Highland games, and the people think it fine.

Not all of them perhaps. There are some who detest the red sandstone figure of the first Duke of Sutherland, in a red sandstone toga, thirty feet from his bare head to his square-toed shoes, standing on a column seventy feet high at the top of Ben Bhraggie, which is itself thirteen hundred feet above the green water of the Dornoch Firth. It cost almost £15,000, which was approximately the rental of the Sutherland estate when that became his by marriage. Much of the money was raised by contributions from the tenantry, and allowing for his understandable hatred of the Duke I am inclined to believe Donald MacLeod, the stone-mason from Strath Naver who said, "All who could raise a shilling gave it, and

The long ridge of Ben Loyal. This is the eastern wall of Lord Reay's country, six hundred square miles and the land of the Mackays. In 1830 Eric Mackay, 7th Baron Reay, sold it and his people to the Marquess of Stafford, and Mr Loch began his Improvements. In no other part of the Highlands is the memory of the Clearances so intense as it is along this northern coast of Sutherland.

those who could not awaited in terror for the consequence of their default." The statue has its back to the glens the Duke emptied, and it faces the sea to which he committed their people. It is a grotesque example of the 19th century's taste for monstrous monuments, and the most cruelly ironic in Scotland.

I saw much and revisited much of Sutherland with James during the years of our friendship. Westward from Telford's road the land is dominated by lonely mountains, rising from the desolate moors like dark tents of stone, or great hangars for the airship clouds above them. By the Kyle of Tongue and to the north of Altnaharra, the long ridge of Ben Loyal is a frozen wave, triple-peaked and white-capped until early summer. It can change colour at each turn of the road, sometimes mist-blue and sometimes indigo, and one evening when it was lit by an angry sunset I saw it glow like an embered fire. Its sentinel friends to the west are Ben Hope and Ben Spionnaidh, watchers of the sea-lochs and gatemen to Lord Reay's Country, the land of the Mackays from which came those 17th-century soldiers whose names I found carved on the timbers of a Dutch mill in the winter of 1944. This northern coast, from Torrisdale Bay by sea-skirted peaks to Cape Wrath, was truly *Sudrland*, a southerly land to the Vikings who came down from the great shield-rim of Norway, settling on the shores of its sea-lochs, moving inland by its narrow straths, leaving their imprint in the names of its waters and stones, and their blood in the veins of its Pictish inhabitants. Seven hundred years ago, King Haakon of Norway anchored his great fleet in the shelter of Loch Eribol, on his way to chastise the young King of Scotland and re-affirm

his lordship of the Hebrides. That day he watched an eclipse of the sun above the high wall of Foinaven, and his heart was darkened by strange premonitions. But he sailed on by the coast of Wester Ross and between Skye and the mainland, where the strait of Kyleakin remembers his name. On the Ayrshire coast at Largs his army was defeated in "a dangerous and cruel battle." It was said that sixteen thousand Norsemen and five thousand Scots were slain, and all but four of Haakon's ships destroyed. The figures are fantasy, of course, and the brief charge and counter-charge of the confused battle were not the epic conflict remembered by chronicle and legend. But it was decisive, and the Norse threat to the Crown of Scotland was at last ended.

The sea beyond the northern coast of Sutherland was once a safe highway for Scottish shipping, a north-about route from the Firth of Forth to Europe and the New World, free from English molestation. At the end of July in 1698, and ten days out from Leith, the first fleet of five ships which the Company of Scotland sent to Darien was scattered by gales in the Pentland Firth, and those vessels which at last sighted each other were then separated by mist and fog to the west of Cape Wrath. They kept together by firing signal guns, and by answering each muffled hail of *"Success!"* with the cry *"God grant!"* They were neither successful nor favoured by Providence, for none of the ships returned from the wretched, fever-rotted Colony of Caledonia. The waters of Tongue Bay, Loch Eribol and Loch Durness were safe harbouring for French and Baltic merchantmen, for the transports which came to embark Lord Reay's volunteers for the Dutch Wars. In March, 1746, the

The Chiefs of the Mackays traditionally had their home here, above the white sand of the Kyle of Tongue. It has been said that but for the capture of a French ship in this bay, and the coin it carried, Charles Stuart would not have made his calamitous decision to fight at Culloden.

The Victorians, for whom this picture of Ardvreck Castle was taken, were excited by the barren wilderness of Assynt, its history of flight and betrayal. But there were once people and industry enough to support an 18th-century Mackenzie laird, whose fine house is now the ruin in the foreground.

French ship *Prince Charles* put two hundred soldiers ashore at Tongue with a chest of silver coins for the Young Pretender, then retreating to Inverness. The soldiers were routed and the money captured by a small detachment of Loudon's Highlanders under a young lieutenant, John Reid of Straloch. It was a small skirmish and almost forgotten, but the loss of the money is said to have forced the Jacobites to fight at Culloden.

What endears that story to me, as it did to James when I spoke of it one day on the road to Lochinver, is its lingering and pleasant echo. John Reid died in 1807, a general and a man made wealthy by a fortunate marriage. His will endowed the University of Edinburgh with a chair of music, with the simple condition that every year on or about the February day of his birth a concert should be given, and that among the pieces played should be a march or a minuet of his own composition. The condition is still kept, perpetuating the memory of an amiable man to whom, it was said, the Highland soldiers of his command "were much attached for his poetry, his music, and his bravery."

James and I often drove to the west, leaving Telford's road at Invershin and going by Strath Oykel across that central plateau of crumpled rock and moor to the buckler of mountains on the Atlantic coast. The road took us by Loch Assynt, silent water in a leather-brown valley of treeless hills, and to the ruined stones of Ardvreck Castle, below which there are said to be cannon, still primed and loaded. Once we sat in its shadow for half an hour, talking briefly of Montrose's surrender and betrayal here, and then we were silent, watching red-throated divers on the loch, admiring their pearl-grey heads and sad, orange eyes. When we spoke again it was of Inchnadamph at the loch-head, and the caves nearby where geologists had found evidence of communities eleven thousand years old, the scars of their fires, the discarded bones of deer, ptarmigan, brown bear and lynx. On the winding road to Lochinver, where we went to meet the prawn-boats, we sometimes paused to stare at the great heads of Suilven and Canisp, upthrust from the wide earth in frozen astonishment.

When this photograph of Lochinver Hotel was taken a century ago the only comfortable approach to it was by steamer from Glasgow, although a mail-gig left three days a week for Lairg over a rocky, twisting road. The hotel took the overflow from the Duke of Sutherland's shooting-lodge, some miles inland beyond the sugar-loaf of Suilven.

Northward at noon on the road to Kylesku a year or so ago I wondered why we had agreed that Glasven was like a sprawling grey seal on the tidal bank before Spinningdale, for now, in a storm of bitter rain, it was monstrous and ugly.

For our mutual pleasure and information we peopled the emptiness of the land, the wide debris of bog, rock and heather, rolling toward the grey cone of Ben Stack or the wave-curl of Foinaven. As we passed a quiet mountain loch, and saw the first island with its sentinel pines, he would tell me or I would tell him – it mattered not, so long as the story was told – that the trees had been planted

Ben Stack is a venerable, isolated hill on the western seaboard of Lord Reay's Country. The glen below it was once an assembly point for drovers taking their herds south to a tryst. Before the coming of sheep, 6000 head of cattle were raised in this part of Sutherland, and cattle-thieving was accordingly endemic.

by home-coming soldiers, in memory of companions who would never return. It is a myth, I think, but more pleasing to the mind and the heart than the probable truth, that the islands were too small for sheep-grazing and thus the trees had grown unhindered.

We sometimes listened to a lark in the hot sky above Loch Shin at Overscaig, and were once blessed with the rare sight of a fulmar, snow-headed and stiff-winged on its seaward flight from the rock shore by Drumbeg. We counted goldcrests, finches and warblers in the garden at Spinningdale, collected gulls' eggs from the sand on Dornoch links, drove to Croick church, and once walked by the dried bed of Loch Migdale in a summer of drought, wondering when it would again fill the burn that gave Spinningdale its light and power. We were alone in the house at that time, and for almost a week we ate cold meals of grouse in aspic, and talked without lights at night. It may have been then that we spoke of the great mound which Telford built across the tidal water of Loch Fleet, reclaiming four hundred acres for the Marquess of Stafford. There is now a wide muskeg of saplings and green water on the inland side, and James believed that it would be possible to introduce the beaver there. How that should be done, by stealth or not, we never decided, and we differed on the choice of the animal. He believed it should be the European beaver, and when I said that the Canadian species would be more proper, remembering the people who had gone to that country, he agreed with the thought but said the animal would not flourish in Sutherland, and I have no doubt he was right.

Fresh thoughts on this fanciful proposal, and others like the possibility of finding a hoard of Spanish silver on Migdale, were always exchanged in the first hours of my arrival, as if it were necessary to knit up the threads of old conversations before new subjects were begun. This became a ritual, as much to be honoured as lifting a hand in salute when we drove by the Norse standing-stone at Ospidale. We talked often of the Clearances, for these had encouraged him to write to me in the beginning, with the hope that I would join him and Compton Mackenzie and Eric Linklater in the making of a film about them. It was never written, nor could be, perhaps, but we came back to the subject again and again. Sometimes when we sat together at dusk in that still hour of the tide's turn. Sometimes in a Land Rover on the hill, too old, we said, to follow the hawks on foot, but watching them on the high brae, hearing the gentle sound of their bells and the echoing voice of Stephen the falconer, calling in the pointers.

As I come by the top of Struie now, and see the white brush-stroke of the house across the water, there is always sadness, of course, but also the warmth of memory. I hear his voice shouting a greeting in Gaelic above the barking of the dogs. And I hear his valediction when time took me away, "Haste ye back!" And so I do, and always shall to the Highlands, but nevermore to Spinningdale.

ACKNOWLEDGEMENTS

Black and White Illustrations

Crest	Photograph: Bernt Federau
p. 3	Author's collection
p. 4	Mary Evans Picture Library
p. 5	Mary Evans Picture Library
pp. 6 & 7	Scottish Records Office
p. 9	The National Trust for Scotland
p. 12	*Abbotsford* by T. H. Shepherd, courtesy of the British Museum
p. 13	Robert Harding Picture Library
p. 15	Borders Regional Council
p. 16	Author's collection
p. 17	Photograph: Alex Gillespie
p. 18	Photograph: Bernt Federau
p. 19	Photograph: Bernt Federau
p. 20	National Galleries of Scotland
p. 21	Royal Commission on Ancient and Historical Monuments of Scotland
p. 23	City of Aberdeen Library and Museums
p. 24 (top and bottom)	National Portrait Gallery, London
p. 25	National Portrait Gallery, London
p. 28	Mary Evans Picture Library
p. 29	Aberdeen University Library
p. 30	Mary Evans Picture Library
p. 31	Mary Evans Picture Library
p. 33	Aberdeen University Library
p. 34	Author's collection
p. 35	British Museum
p. 37	From "Johnsoniana" by John Murray lent by Margaret Lane
p. 38	National Galleries of Scotland
p. 39	National Galleries of Scotland
p. 40	Mary Evans Picture Library
p. 41	Aberdeen University Library
p. 42	Glasgow Art Gallery
p. 43	Aberdeen University Library
p. 44	Aberdeen University Library
p. 45 (top and bottom)	Aberdeen University Library
p. 46	Mary Evans Picture Library
p. 47	Aberdeen University Library
p. 48	Author's collection
p. 50	The Photo Source-CLI
p. 51	James Weir – Woodmansterne
p. 53	Spectrum Colour Library
p. 55	Spectrum Colour Library
p. 56 (top)	Mary Evans Picture Library
p. 56 (bottom)	RCoAHMS
p. 57	Author's collection

INDEX